# WITHDRAWN
## UTSA LIBRARIES

**DATE DUE**

| | | | |
|---|---|---|---|
| | | | |
| | | | |
| | | | |
| | | | |
| | | | |
| | | | |
| | | | |
| | | | |
| | | | |
| | | | |
| | | | |
| | | | |
| | | | |
| | | | |
| | | | |
| | | | |
| | | | |
| | | | |
| | | | |

# The International Migration of Health Workers

# Routledge Research in Population & Migration

**SERIES EDITOR: PAUL BOYLE,** *University of St. Andrews*

# The International Migration of Health Workers

### Edited by
### John Connell

Routledge
Taylor & Francis Group
New York   London

First published 2008
by Routledge
270 Madison Ave, New York, NY 10016

Simultaneously published in the United Kingdom
by Routledge
2 Park Square, Milton Park, Abingdon, Oxon OX14 4RN

*Routledge is an imprint of the Taylor & Francis Group, an informa business*

© 2008 Taylor & Francis

Typeset in 10 pt. Sabon Roman by IBT Global.
Printed and bound in the United States of America on acid-free paper by IBT Global.

*Library of Congress Cataloging in Publication Data*
The international migration of health workers / edited by John Connell.
p. cm. — (Routledge research in population and migration ; v.10)
ISBN 978-0-415-95623-9
1. Medical personnel—Employment—Foreign countries. 2. Medical personnel—Supply and demand—Foreign countries. I. Connell, John, 1946–

RA410.6.I578 2008
362.1072'3—dc22                                                                 2007048350

ISBN10: 0-415-95623-4 (hbk)
ISBN10: 0-203-93245-5 (ebk)

ISBN13: 978-0-415-95623-9 (hbk)
ISBN13: 978-0-203-93245-2 (ebk)

# Contents

# List of Figures

# List of Tables

# Contributors

**Isabella Aboderin,** Institute of Aging, University of Oxford.

**Rochelle Ball,** School of Geography and Oceanography, University of New South Wales, Australian Defence Force Academy, Canberra.

**James Buchan,** Faculty of Health and Social Sciences, Queen Margaret University, Edinburgh.

**Abel Chikanda,** Department of Geography, University of Western Ontario.

**John Connell,** School of Geosciences, University of Sydney, Sydney.

**Jonathan Crush,** Southern African Migration Project, Queen's University, Kingston, Ontario.

**Silvia D'Addario,** Department of Geography, York University, Toronto.

**Sarah Harper,** Institute of Ageing, University of Oxford.

**Christina Ho,** Faculty of Humanities and Social Sciences, University of Technology, Sydney.

**Philip Kelly,** Department of Geography, York University, Toronto.

**Colleen McNeil-Walsh,** School of Business, University of Birmingham.

**Parvati Raghuram,** Department of Geography, The Open University, Milton Keynes.

**Avelina Rokoduru,** School of Sociology, University of the South Pacific, Suva, Fiji.

**Christian Rogerson,** Department of Geography, Archaeology and Environmental Studies, University of Witwatersrand, Johannesburg.

**Iva Ruchieva,** Institute of Ageing, University of Oxford.

**Philomina Thomas,** All India Institute of Medical Sciences, New Delhi.

**Nicola Yeates,** Department of Social Policy, The Open University, Milton Keynes.

# Preface

Amidst the rapid rise of international flows of people, technology and capital, captured in the parallel rise of such words as transnationalism, globalisation and diaspora, few themes have created such international interest and concern as the migration of skilled health workers, yet few flows have been so poorly documented. This book seeks to go some way toward filling this gap. Its companion (*The Global Health Care Chain: From the Pacific to the World*), seeks to approach this from the perspective of nine South Pacific island states and focuses rather more on policy issues, and the subtleties of decision making and management.

Sober academic accounts have sought to analyse trends and impacts, and newspapers have popularised the more dramatic of their conclusions, using words such as "poaching" to describe the inherent inequalities in skilled migration. At the same time the migration of health workers had caused even more drama in certain places. In Libya, in 2007, where migrant health workers are as common as in many other Middle Eastern states, five migrant Bulgarian nurses and one Palestinian doctor were sentenced to death for allegedly infecting more than 400 children with HIV. On the other side of the world in Australia long-drawn out legal cases considered the role of a doctor of Indian ethnicity, dubbed "Dr. Death," who had fled to the United States, and whose inadequacies while working in one of Queensland's small towns, had led to the death of several patients. Some months later it was reported that in another Queensland town immigrant doctors were being given a ten-week course of speech lessons to improve communication with Australian patients and colleagues and avoid medical mishaps. Literally four days later an acute shortage of doctors had led to the regional surgery in the tiny inland town of Temora offering any GP willing to work there for five years a signing on fee of A$500,000 (US$420,000) which eventually proved inadequate (*The Australian*, 14 June 2007). In quite different ways these cases raised critical issues concerning the ethics of international (and national) migration, cultural competencies, etc., but above all the crucial and very personal nature of adequate medical care.

Despite the significance of this migration, in numbers, impacts (medical, economic, social and political) and its seemingly inexorable growth, at least until quite recently, there have been no books that examine the overall situation in any detail, despite recent work on the migration of nurses by Mireille Kingma and Andrea Winkelmann-Gleed. A number of studies have examined the migration of skilled workers from the perspective of human resources but relatively few have examined migration from the migrants' perspectives. While the human resource context remains central to each of the chapters, since this underlies the migration process (and its outcome), rather more attention is given to the migrants themselves and their aspirations. Thus the book focuses on who migrates, why them, the outcomes for them and their extended families, their experience in the workforce, and ultimately the extent to which this expanding migration flow has some relationship to development issues. It therefore provides new, interdisciplinary reflections on such core issues as the brain drain, gender roles, remittances and sustainable human resource development at a time when there has never been greater public and political interest in the migration of health workers.

As the book was nearing its end I was hospitalised overnight in one of Sydney's major hospitals, an experience which, fortunately briefly, transformed a more academic perception of migration into a more personal one. I had just returned from the Pacific island state of Vanuatu where a migrant Bulgarian doctor in the main Vila Central Hospital had referred me home to Sydney. There, at late afternoon triage, I was examined by a Caucasian nurse with an Australian accent, before being admitted by a Filipina doctor, who transferred me to the emergency ward where I was welcomed by a Spanish male nurse. Half an hour later a vegan sandwich "dinner" was delivered by an orderly with an east European accent (who advised me "don't try the hot food, you wouldn't like it"). During the night, tea, injections, and some degree of sympathy came from a series of nurses from China (perhaps Hong Kong), Vietnam, Ireland, the Philippines and England. Cleaners, lifters and security staff had a variety of continental European accents. After triage not one seemed to have an Australian accent. I was discharged in mid-morning by a nurse who originally came from the same northern English city as me. The Asian nurses and orderlies spoke to each other in a version of English, which might even have represented a new sociolect, and all were unfailing helpful. I simultaneously mused on the personal advantages of migrant health care, but also pondered on the situation in their home countries, mostly much poorer than Australia.

I am indebted to many people without whom this book would never have been completed, not least to the contributors most of whom (you know who you are) managed to submit their chapters more or less on time! The WHO first drew me in to the health worker scene at the start of this century when I initiated a study of migration in several Pacific island states, the subject of the "other" book. In 2005 the WHO invited me to spend part of my study leave at WHO headquarters in Geneva. I am grateful to the Australian Department of Health and Aging for subsidising this. As the seasons went from winter to summer, and an endless variety of wines and cheeses sustained me, as I commuted from just across the French border, I was able to play a part in producing a global overview of the migration of health workers for the World Health Assembly. My colleagues, especially Barbara Stilwell and Pascal Zurn, were founts of experience and wisdom, and undoubtedly some of their ideas have found their way into the first chapter, and that can only be good.

This is now the sixth book I have worked on with Routledge and that repetition is testimony that it has always been a pleasurable experience. In this case I am particularly indebted to Ben Holtzman for his support and encouragement and, yet again, to Anna Warr who managed to skilfully do the formatting that my luddite tendencies were quite incapable of.

John Connell
School of Geosciences, University of Sydney
June 2007

# 1 Toward a Global Health Care System?

*John Connell*

This book is the first to draw together work on the migration of health workers in a range of international contexts, hence this introduction provides an overview of the growing phenomenon of the international migration of skilled health workers (nurses, doctors and a range of more specialised workers, such as pharmacists, radiologists and lab technicians). For more than a quarter of a century there has been significant international migration of skilled health workers (SHWs), particularly from countries like the Philippines, which is prominent here. In the past decade, migration has become more complex, more global and of growing concern to countries that lose workers from fragile health systems. As health care has become more commercialised so too has migration. With critical changes in both sending and receiving countries, few parts of the world are now unaffected by the consequences of the migration of health workers, either as sources, destinations or both. China and eastern European countries have recently become sources and Japan a destination. Most migration is to developed OECD countries while those most affected by emigration are relatively poorly performing economies in sub-Saharan Africa alongside some small island states in the Caribbean and Pacific (though numbers have been greatest from such Asian countries as India and the Philippines). Developing and developed countries are increasingly linked through migration in a now global health care chain.

The international migration of SHWs parallels somewhat similar migrations of other professionals, notably IT workers (Xiang 2007, Millar and Salt 2007) but also sportsmen (Lanfranchi and Taylor 2001), engineers, teachers, and others, most of whom are men. This reflects the growth and accelerated internationalisation of the service sector in the last two decades (e.g., Iredale 2001, Findlay and Stewart 2002, Lowell and Findlay 2002), rising demand for skilled workers in developed countries (where training is increasingly costly) and their supply in countries where once they were absent: a growing globalisation of flows of goods and services, of people, information and capital. Increasingly global migration is linked to skill status. Skilled professionals constitute a growing proportion of migrants, as new technologies enable and promote a global labour market, and production of skilled workers is inadequate in many developed countries that therefore seek to hire, regulate and recruit skilled migrants. Many countries have eased their legislation on the entry of highly skilled workers (OECD 2005) and introduced points systems where skills facilitate entry. Such professional services as health care are part of the new internationalisation of labour, and migration has largely been demand driven (or at least facilitated), with the growing global integration of health care markets. Thirty years ago doctors—mostly men—were the main migrant group, but nurses—mostly women—have become more numerous, and migration has taken on a new gendered structure. There are both new pressures and opportunities for women to work. Demographic, economic, political, social and, of course, health transformations have had significant impacts on global, and also local, migration flows.

Significantly the health sector is rather different from other skilled sectors since most employment remains in the public sector, but conditions have tended to worsen (relatively and sometimes absolutely) with restructuring, and there has been movement into the private sector. Moreover, and more dramatically, migration literally involves matters of life and death. The migration of less visible health workers, who are not on the "front line," such as pharmacists and radiologists, whose migration may be equally critical, has largely been ignored (cf. Wuliji 2006). Technology cannot easily replace workers, despite telemedicine, the emerging role of "nursebots" and other Japanese endeavours (Folbre 2006, Bower and McCullough 2004), while the rise of HIV/AIDS and the aging of populations have put new demands on health workforces. At the same time there is now a greater range of jobs for women, other than in a sector that is seen by some as dirty and dangerous (and unrewarding), sometimes difficult and demanding, and perhaps degrading, again as HIV/AIDS become significant. Restructuring, often externally imposed, has similarly affected health systems of developing countries, contributing to concerns over wages, working conditions, training and other issues, all of which have stimulated migration.

Migrants move primarily for economic reasons, and increasingly choose health careers because they offer migration prospects. Migration has been at some economic cost; it has depleted workforces, diminished the effectiveness of health care delivery and reduced the morale of the remaining workforce. Countries have sought to implement national policies on wage rates, incentives and working conditions, but these have usually been cancelled out by global uneven development and national economic development problems. Recipient countries have been reluctant to establish effective ethical codes of recruitment practice, or other forms of compensation or technology transfer, hence migration may increase further in future, diminishing the possibility of achieving Millennium Development Goals, challenging work forces to manage HIV/AIDS and exacerbating existing global and national inequalities in access to adequate health care.

Accelerated recruitment from developed countries, where populations are aging, expectations of health care increasing, recruitment of health workers (especially nurses) is poor and attrition considerable, has intensified this crisis, raising complex ethical, financial and health questions. In a context of widespread existing health staff shortages in Africa, migration has further weakened fragile health systems. Moreover, the costs of training health care workers in developing countries are considerable, hence migration has been perceived as a subsidy from the poor to the rich (Save the Children 2005). Migration issues are not only linked to financial issues, serious though these are, but are critical for the delivery of health care. In these circumstances, where needs are greater in source countries and where recruitment has been significant in the first five years of this century (Connell and Stilwell 2006; Rogerson and Crush, this book) words such as "poaching," "looting," "stealing," and even the "new slave trade," let alone more familiar concepts of brain and skill drain (e.g., Garrett 2007), have become more common as newspaper articles became more polemical. In May 2005 the English newspaper *The Independent* splashed across its front page, above the photo of a sick child, the banner headline "An African Child Four Weeks Old Disabled by Britain," which was attributed to Britain's "voracious demand for Third World doctors nurses and midwives" so that too few remained in Ghana (27 May 2005). Two months earlier *The Times* had a headline "NHS strips Africa of its doctors" (22 February 2005). More sober academic accounts have referred to "fatal flows" (Chen and Boufford 2005).


## THE GEOGRAPHY OF NEED

Human resources are central to health care systems, and have long been unevenly distributed. The need for health care is at least as uneven. Though definition and measurement of needs and shortages is complex (Vujicic and Zurn 2006), and the competence and effectiveness of workers is hard to assess, demand for health care is greatest in the least developed countries and regions, most of which are tropical, and, in a perfect example of the "inverse health care law," these needs are less well served than those in developed countries.

The disease burden is especially great in sub-Saharan Africa. North and South America contain only 10% of the global burden of disease yet almost 37% of the world's health workers live in this region, whereas Africa has 24% of the global burden of diseases but just 3% of the health workforce and less than 1% of global financial resources (WHO 2006:8). The rise of HIV/AIDS has increased demands for health workers, especially in sub-Saharan Africa. The link between "health workforce density" and health outcomes has been clearly demonstrated: lack of health workers contributes to poor health status, and provision of such basic functions as adequate coverage of immunization or attendance at births. (Anand and Barninghausen 2004, Zurn et al. 2004). Consequently the world may be seen in terms of health clusters (Figure 1.1) where there are clear relationships between mortality rates and availability of health workers.

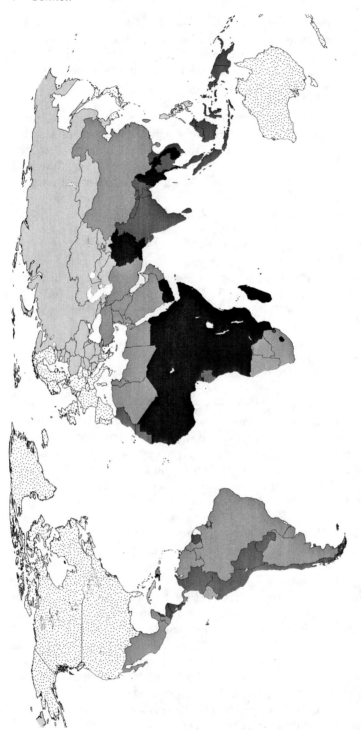

*Figure 1.1* Human resources and health clusters.

*Note:* See appendix 2.    *Source:* Joint Learning Initiative 2004: 30.

■ Low-density-high-mortality    ■ Low-density    ▨ Moderate-density    ▨ High-density    ▨ High-density-low-mortality

Some 57 countries have critical shortages of SHWs, equal to a global deficit of 2.4 million doctors nurses and midwives (WHO 2006:26–27), let alone pharmacists, dentists and others. Some 36 of 47 sub-Saharan African countries fall short of the minimum WHO standard of 20 doctors and 500 nurses per 100,000 people (Figure 1.2). Several have less than 50 nurses and 5 doctors per 100,000. Most SHWs are concentrated in urban areas and usually in the often primate city, as rural and regional areas are neglected, while such gross inequality may also be exacerbated by socioeconomic status and gender biases (Adkoli 2006, Bhutta et al. 2004, WHO 2006). Uganda and Niger have 6 or 7 nurses for 100,000 people while the United States has 773, yet migratory flows—a perverse flow—are invariably from the former to the latter.

## THE SCOPE OF MIGRATION

The first studies of the migration of health workers began to appear in the 1960s, mainly concerned with movement between developed countries, but a skill drain from less developed countries was already evident (e.g., Gish 1969a, 1969b). Britain, Australia and Canada were experiencing both the immigration of doctors, mainly from the Philippines, India, Pakistan, Iran and Colombia, and their emigration, usually to the United States. The Philippines had already contributed the largest number of overseas doctors in the United States, with training already oriented to overseas needs. Doctors and nurses from south Asia and elsewhere in the Middle East were beginning to go to the Gulf. The single most important international flow was probably from Ireland; some 71% of all graduates from Eire's medical schools between 1950 and 1966 had emigrated and as many Irish doctors were practising in Britain as in Eire (Gish 1971:20). By then the ethnic distinctiveness of this skilled migration into Britain was evident, and a geographical pattern had emerged that scarcely changed in later years. Two thirds of the overseas born doctors came from less developed countries, with those from India, Pakistan and Sri Lanka making up 70%, and the remainder coming mainly from the West Indies and the Middle East (Gish 1971:32–33). Over time what were then relatively simple migration flows, reflecting linguistic, colonial and post-colonial ties, became steadily more complex.

Such early flows were also characterised by active recruitment (notably in the Caribbean), and the employment of the migrants in the lower echelons of the health service; as Gish observed "it is no secret that professional chauvinism is likely to exclude outsiders trying to break into the 'club'" (1971:25). As early as 1961, in a British House of Lords debate on migrant health workers, it was simply pointed out that "They are here to provide pairs of hands in the rottenest, worst hospitals in the country, because there is nobody else to do it" (quoted in Gish 1971:52). By then less developed countries were experiencing the greatest costs from emigration, because of

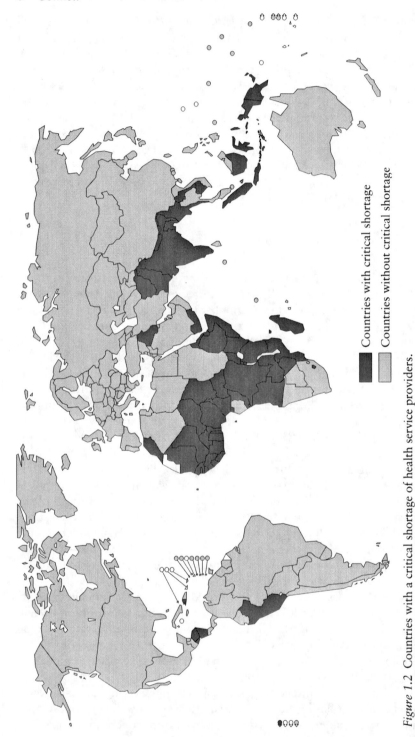

*Figure 1.2* Countries with a critical shortage of health service providers.

*Data source:* World Health Organization. *Global Atlas of the Health Workforce* (http://www.who.int/globalatlas/default.asp).

the disparity in the number of medical workers per capita and the heavier burden of disease (Gish 1971:63–64), hence, in the 1970s, a path-breaking study of some 40 countries responded to widespread concerns of uneven flows, "and had its roots in the international disquiet over the 'brain drain' of professional manpower [sic]" (Mejia et al. 1979:4). Then as now the migration of SHWs was of greater concern than other skilled international migration flows, and the idea of a brain drain largely emerged from analysis of migratory health workers. The movement from Britain to the United States of scientists, doctors and other highly qualified people was the first such migration to be called a brain drain (Gish 1971 cf. Gish and Godfrey 1979) and parallels were quickly recognised in other health contexts (e.g., Horn 1977, Joyce and Hunt 1982, Engels and Connell 1983). In the wake of Mejia's study, which emphasised emerging problems, the oil boom in the Gulf brought the construction of new hospitals and massive new migration flows.

After a period of quiescence demand for SHWs in developed countries increased in the 1990s, resulting from aging populations, growing demand and ability to pay, inadequate training programmes, high attrition rates (for reasons ranging from patient violence to discontent with working conditions, etc.), as jobs in the health sector were seen in many developed countries as too demanding, poorly paid and lowly regarded (in line with reduced public sector funding, and disregard for the public sector). Reduced recruitment of health workers also followed declining birth rates in developed countries: There were fewer young people and more diverse employment opportunities for women, many with superior wages and working conditions, and greater prestige and respect. Significantly these influences are similar to the reasons for attrition and migration in source countries.

Contemporary international recruitment of health workers is increasingly global. Where a quarter of a century ago it was mainly a movement from a few developing countries to a small number of developed countries, typified by the recruitment of nurses from the Philippines for the Gulf (Mejia et al. 1979), it has now extended, become more complex, increasingly involving governments and recruiting agencies (Bach 2004) and more dominated by women. New movements of nurses occur between relatively developed countries, for example from Finland to the United Kingdom. Ireland, once an exporter of skilled health workers, has become an active recruiter (Buchan, Parkin and Sochalski 2004; Yeates, this book). The new complexity of international migration is evident in Poland, as much a sending country as a recipient, where its source countries are eastern European countries (Ukraine, Belarus, Russia, Lithuania) and the Middle East (Syria, Yemen, Iraq) while Polish nurses head westwards. China has entered the market as a supplier of nurses (Xu 2003), and its considerable interest in becoming more involved has the potential to profoundly influence the future system.

Over the past 30 years the key receiving countries have remained remarkably similar, dominated by the United Kingdon and the United States. While demand in the Gulf has stabilised, other European and global destinations (including Canada and Australasia) have grown in importance (Connell et al. 2007). Despite policies of localisation, the Gulf states still employ 20,000 migrant doctors, and many more nurses, mostly from south Asia (Adkoli 2006) but also from neighbouring and poorer Middle Eastern states such as Egypt and Palestine. However in the United States, the number of foreign trained doctors rose from 70,646 in 1973 to 209,000 in 2003 (Mejia et al. 1979, Mullan 2005). Similar trends occurred in major recipient countries such as the United Kingdom, Canada, Australia and New Zealand. In the United Kingdom, the total number of foreign trained doctors increased from 20,923 in 1970 to 69,813 in 2003 (Connell et al. 2007; Raghuram, this book). The proportion of foreign trained medical workers in the health workforce has usually also risen. For example, in the United States and the United Kingdom foreign doctors now represent approximately 27% and 33% respectively of their medical workforces; similar percentages occur in Australia and New Zealand while comparable estimates are around 7% for Germany and France (Connell et al. 2007). Other OECD countries have become significant recipients. Hitherto Japan, virtually alone of countries that have experienced substantial post-war economic growth and aging populations, has largely managed its health services without resorting to overseas workers, but has recently entered into agreements with the Philippines.

Throughout this time the Philippines has remained the main global source of SHWs for almost every part of the world, as it has in other migratory contexts (Ball, Buchan, Yeates, Kelly and D'Addorio, this book), alongside India (Thomas, this book). Africa has emerged as a major supplier, and a major source of concern. Relatively recently other Asian states have become sources of SHWs (Ho, this book) while the some small Pacific states have become sources, following the same kind of pattern established in the Caribbean a couple of decades earlier (Connell 2008, 2007). Eastern Europe supplies western Europe, evident in Bulgarian migration to Greece (Harper et al., this book) while Latin America has tended to experience proportionately less emigration, though Latin America nurses move north to the United States and Europe, especially Spain (Malvarez and Castrillon Agudelo 2005).

Patterns of health worker migration from sources of supply such as sub-Saharan Africa have also changed. In the 1970s SHWs were from a relatively small number of African countries (the larger states of South Africa, Nigeria and Ghana) and predominantly went to a few developed countries outside Africa (Mejia et al. 1979). Since then migration has become much more complex, involving almost all sub-Saharan countries, including intra-regional and stepwise movement (for example from the Democratic Republic of Congo to Kenya, and from Kenya to South Africa, Namibia and Botswana), because of targeted recruitment, by both agencies and governments, as much as individual volition (Dumont and Meyer 2004). Emigration rates have often been high. Thus in 1966 there were 215 Nigerian doctors in the United Kingdom, representing 1.5% of all foreign doctors, while that figure had grown to 1,922 in 2003, representing 3% of foreign doctors (Connell et al. 2007). Roughly 40% of all graduates from one medical school in Nigeria had migrated overseas (mainly to USA, UK and Ireland) within 10 years of graduation (Ihekweazu et al. 2005), more than half of all Ethiopian doctors have left (Getahun 2006), and such figures seem typical of other parts of sub-Saharan Africa (Hagopian et al. 2004, 2005; Connell et al. 2007; Clemens 2007; Clemens and Pettersson 2007). The 20 countries with the greatest emigration factors (the ratio of emigrant to resident doctors) include six in Africa (Ghana, South Africa, Ethiopia, Uganda, Nigeria and Sudan), three in the Caribbean (Jamaica, Haiti and the Dominican Republic), the Philippines, India and Pakistan, a cluster of countries perhaps best characterised by crisis (Sri Lanka, Myanmar, Lebanon, Iraq and Syria) but also New Zealand, Ireland, Malta and Canada (Mullan 2005). Migration is now shaped by both market forces and cultural ties, and deeply embedded in uneven global development.

The greater complexity of migration is evident in the interlocking chains of recruitment and supply, though some were in place 30 years ago (Mejia et al. 1979). Canada recruits from South Africa (which recruits from Cuba), as it supplies the United States. Kenyan nurses first went to southern African countries such as Botswana, Zimbabwe and South Africa, and then moved on as "step migration" to Britain. In the Caribbean and the Pacific similar complex systems exist within and beyond the region (Connell 2008, Rokoduru, this book). Something of a hierarchy of global migration—the global care chain—links the poorest sub-Saharan, Asian and island micro-states, to the developed world, culminating in the United States. New transport technology and reduced costs have produced variants of "commuter migration" with Jamaican nurses flying to Florida for five- to ten-day shifts and returning home, Botswanan nurses spending periods of "sick leave" in South Africa and German doctors working long weekends in the United Kingdom.

Migrants themselves frequently choose different destinations, and migration is constantly in flux depending on labour markets, domestic pressures, evolving global legislation and codes of practice, and individual perceptions of amenable destinations. Migration links languages, training institutions, educational regimes, often in the context of other migration flows, sometimes characterised as chain migration in the context of a "transnational corporation of kin" (Connell 2008). Language proficiency is more crucial in the health sector that in any other arena of migration, skilled or unskilled. While recruitment has crossed new borders, and the Internet has become available, potential migrants are also more likely to be informed about global job opportunities and be in some position to choose more widely than hitherto. Migration ranges from fixed term contract migration (typified by that from the Philippines to the Middle East), usually negotiated between governments, and more personal, individual migration that may last a lifetime.

## The Migration

Migration of SHWs occurs for many reasons, despite remarkable uniformity across quite different regions and contexts, including incomes, job satisfaction, career opportunity and management alongside social, political and family reasons. Indeed the last of these factors, though often neglected, is particularly important since few migrants make decisions as individuals but are linked into extended families and wider kinship groups. The migration of SHWs is often not at all unique but exists within the context of wider migration flows. This is evidently so in India, the Philippines and most small island states, like those of the Caribbean and Pacific, where there have been steady and diverse migration streams for several decades (Connell 2007). In such circumstances there is effectively a culture of migration where most individuals at least contemplate migration at some time in their lives.

Yet migration is usually constrained in certain ways. Even for those with skills it is not always easy to cross political boundaries. Where political circumstances change, as in the case of the expansion of the European Union, enabling migration from poorer eastern states to those in the west, a substantial movement of doctors from the Czech Republic to the west quickly created gaps in the Czech health service (Mareckova 2004). Violence, coups, crime, warfare and persistent social unrest have predictably hastened migration from countries such as Zimbabwe (Chikanda, this book), Fiji and the Solomon Islands (Connell 2008), Lebanon (Kronfol et al. 1992) and earlier in Lusophone Africa (Luck et al. 2000). Many such migrants would prefer to stay.

The intention to migrate may occur even before entry into the health system. In the Philippines, for more than 20 years, at least some people sought to become nurses, partly and sometimes primarily, because that provided an obvious means of international migration (e.g., Ball 1996, this book; Choy 2003). By the end of the 1980s a medical degree at the Fiji School of Medicine was being widely seen as a "passport to prosperity" and in Kerala (India) "a nursing diploma is now considered as an actual passport for emigration where 'nursing for emigration' is common." Indeed in India nursing has moved from being something of a reviled and impure profession for poor people, to a preferred one as migration became possible: a migration opportunity "has become an actual strategy" (Percot and Rajan 2007:320; Thomas, this book). Nursing is a "portable profession" (Kingma 2006). More recently this kind of situation has become evident in other parts of the Pacific, Jamaica, India, Hong Kong, China and elsewhere, and becoming a health worker may be a means to migration at least as much as an end in itself (Connell 2008). Moreover specific careers may be chosen that optimise migration opportunities; in the Philippines male doctors have retrained as nurses, and fewer now choose a medical career, since nurses have superior migration opportunities (Brush and Sochalski 2007). The initial overseas destination may not be the intended final destination, especially for health workers in the Gulf, who seek to move on to the United States. Kerala nurses used their stay in the Middle East to save money and take advanced courses "to reach the much prized west" with the Gulf merely the first step in "the 'true' emigration" (Percot and Rajan 2007:321, 323). Health workers in the United Kingdom and Ireland also seek to move on the United States (Buchan and Yeates, this book). And migration is not just for SHWs; for Filipino nurses "nursing is seen as a way to move the whole family from the Philippines to the United States" (Ong and Azores 1994:173). As in so many other contexts the United States is the alluring, ultimate destination of step migration. This points to both accelerated migration and the frustrations of trying to develop an effective national workforce, when growing proportions of those being trained are intent on migration.

Migration is primarily a response to global uneven development, usually explained in terms of such factors as low wages, few incentives, or poor social and working conditions (Luck et al. 2000). Poor promotion possibilities, inadequate management support, heavy workloads, limited access to good technology including medicines have all been regularly cited as "push factors" (Buchan, Parkin and Sochalski 2004, Bach 2003, Kingma 2006). Such problems are intensified in rural areas, where health workers feel they and their institutions are too often ignored, victims of institutionalised urban bias in development policy (Dussault and Franceschini 2006), and have been similarly documented for thirty years (Mejia et al. 1979). Declining investment in health sectors has subsequently worsened working conditions in both origins and destinations (Stilwell et al. 2004, Pond and McPake 2006). Cultural factors have emphasised some migration flows. Tamil doctors have been more likely than majority Sinhalese to migrate from Sri Lanka for over thirty years. Recruitment, by both agencies and governments, has played a critical facilitating role, so much so that, in one recent study, 41% of all migrant nurses in Britain had come primarily because they had been recruited (Winkelmann-Gleed 2006:44). However, all these various, specific factors are embedded in the broader context of social and economic life, family structures and histories and broader cultural and political contexts.

## *Incomes*

Income differentials are invariably key factors in migration, as they are in decisions to join or later leave the health profession (Connell 2008). Income differences between countries are vividly evident. Nurses from the Philippines were reported to earn about $4,000 per month in the United States, about $180 in urban areas at home and about $100 in rural areas, while doctors earn between $300 and $800 per month (*Migration News*, nd). A Nepalese anaesthetist in New York, anticipating a starting salary of between

$225,000 and $250,000, compared with the $100 a month she earned at a government hospital in Kathmandu, observed "you have the answer to why thousands of doctors from the Indian subcontinent end up here" (Upadhyay 2003). A Kenyan nurse in an English nursing home routinely earned sixteen times what was possible in Kenya and with overtime thirty times (Baird 2005:10). Similar differentials are widespread, well known and widely reported as a major reason for migration whether for the personal benefit of the migrants or, more usually, their families (living or not yet even born, at home or going with them) (e.g., Awases et al. 2004). Econometric studies, at least from the Pacific island states, show that migration demonstrates considerable sensitivity to income differences (Brown and Connell 2004), but complicated by the structure of household incomes. Even in countries where there have not been specific surveys of migration anecdotal evidence and, in some cases, the rationale for strikes by health workers, emphasize the significance of wage and salary issues, though, at least in Ghana, significant wage increases have had little effect on reducing the extent of migration. Similarly the general movement of doctors, dentists and others into the private sector marks the quest for better incomes and conditions.

Health workers have not usually entered the profession solely for the income, but also out of some desire to serve and be of value in the community. However such feelings do not sustain a career, as workers become frustrated by low pay, poor (or biased) promotion prospects, especially in remote areas. In other words they find themselves unable to adequately meet the needs of the people they sought to help. One consequence is the reevaluation of nursing as a career and consequent attrition or migration. As, increasingly, people do join the health sector for economic reasons, migration becomes even more likely.

### Employment Conditions

After income the actual conditions of employment are influential for migration. Migrants, and potential migrants, frequently complain about the work environment in terms of insufficient support, whether directly through inadequate management (lack of team work, poor leadership and motivation, limited autonomy and support, and little recognition and access to promotion and training opportunities) or through the outcome of such poor "housekeeping" (limited access to functioning equipment and supplies) even extending to a lack of security.

The significance of income is firmly linked to the structure of careers and promotion that many health workers see as being more about "who you know than what you know"—nepotism and favouritism—and longevity in the system, rather than ability. SHWs have been strongly critical of the absence of an evident and transparent career structure, preferring to move to a meritocracy where skills and accomplishments will be rewarded. Where health workers are stationed outside the main centre the perception that they are being ignored for promotion is even stronger as many consider themselves to be "out of sight and out of mind." Reasonable and equitable opportunities for promotion are not always in place. Such concerns have been raised in several contexts, including Zimbabwe and elsewhere in sub-Saharan Africa (Gaidzanwa 1999, Awases et al. 2004), the Caribbean (Thomas-Hope 2002, van Eyck 2005), the Pacific islands (Connell 2008) and much of the Commonwealth (Commonwealth Secretariat 2001). Inadequate opportunities for promotion constitute not only an incentive to migration but a constraint to productivity and innovation in the health system.

Long hours of overtime, double shifts, working on the early morning "graveyard" shift or on weekends, especially when these do not receive proper income supplementation, influence migration. Shift work is a universal source of complaint, and particularly so in more remote places, where fewer staff are available and pressures on those remaining are greater. Nursing especially is both physically and mentally demanding with long working hours especially in emergency and intensive care units. In Latin America the expression *malestar de la enfermera* (discontent of the nurse) reflects the growing difficulty in coping with the heavy workload and demanding hours (Malvarez and Castrillon Agudelo 2005). While it is normal for some expectations to be unmet in most workplaces, especially where they are small and workers are expected to be flexible, in many workplaces there is considerable evidence of the lack of "good housekeeping" and management that should support skilled workers in challenging circumstances: "In many countries employers have failed to address long standing deficiencies related to hours of work, salary, continuing education, staffing levels, security, housing and day-care facilities" (Oulton 1998:126). Inadequate working conditions may also entail the risk of contracting disease. The rise of HIV/AIDs has made the nursing profession especially much less attractive than hitherto and, notably in Africa, has created a working climate that has become more difficult, as the workload has increased (Awases et al. 2004:44). Nurses have migrated from some countries, including Zimbabwe and Malawi, through concern over inadequate preventive measures against HIV/AIDS (Chikanda 2004, Palmer 2006) or because they too have HIV/AIDS (Kober and van Damme 2006). Thus in Malawi nurses moved overseas because working conditions and remuneration were the "poorest in various professions" hence "it is not so much the 'pull factors' that are attracting Malawian nurses to Europe, but rather 'push' factors are driving them out of the country" (Muula et al. 2003:436). While this may overestimate the "push", even without recruitment and overseas blandishments nurses and others are anxious to leave health sectors where their needs are unsatisfied.

SHWs, like other professionals in many developing countries, often feel and are isolated from trends in their profession and in the wider world and are conscious that they may miss out on skills that will enable their professional development (and perhaps migration in the future). In a group of

African countries the desire to acquire further training and gain extra experience was one of the most significant factors influencing migration (Awases et al. 2004:46).

In several developing countries economic restructuring, sometimes imposed from outside the region by international agencies, has led to reductions in the size of the public sector workforce and restrictions on the hiring of new workers. Changes in the health sector take place in a wider context where negative balances of payments and high levels of debt servicing place huge resource constraints on many developing countries. This has sometimes meant the deterioration of working conditions rather than the greater efficiency it was intended to encourage. Ironically, though half of all nursing positions in Kenya are unfilled, a third of all Kenyan nurses are unemployed, as IMF pressure encouraged national wage restraint (Baird 2005, Volqvartz 2004). In Jamaica in the 1980s, IMF imposed structural adjustment resulted in declining salaries and massive emigration of nurses (Phillips 1996). In several countries lack of resources, or alternative priorities, has resulted in low wages and poor conditions, with simultaneous vacancies, unemployment and migration. Overall, irrespective of any change in the international context, almost all the factors encouraging migration in source countries have tended to become more important over time.

It is usually the most educated who migrate first, and many migrants have left rural areas to take advantage of superior urban and international educational, social and employment opportunities. These factors reinforce each other, especially in the health sector. The widespread education bias enables young and skilled migrants, with fewer local ties, to more easily migrate. Most nurses, and many other SHWs, are women and face particular constraints related to partners' careers and family obligations, which may make remote postings and overseas migration difficult. In the Pacific islands, doctors are almost twice as likely to migrate as nurses, partly because wage differentials are greater but also because men tend to be the decision makers and most nurses are women (Connell 2008). Consequently, as in Senegal, the most likely migrants are young single workers followed by married workers without children (Awases et al. 2004:42). By contrast Indian nurses from Kerala migrated because their ability to earn and retain significant incomes gave them high status and the consequent ability to find high status partners in the "matrimonial market" (Percot and Rajan 2007:321; George 2000:152). Success in the United States gave Indian and Filipino nurses even higher status, downplaying the former relatively high status of their husbands, sometimes pejoratively called "nurse-husbands" in India, while households became more egalitarian (George 2005; Espiritu 2003, 2005). Subsequently and more recently many Kerala and Filipino men have taken up nursing careers as means of emigration. In many contexts gender relations have been restructured following migration. Social ties may result in pressure to migrate, to support the extended family, but may sometimes make migration more difficult to achieve.

## Recruitment

Recipient countries offer real alternatives to political and economic insecurity in many source countries. A high standard of living with higher wages, better career prospects, good education and a future for children are offered in recruitment campaigns, and often verified by those migrants established overseas. The structure of migration has become increasingly privatised through the expansion of recruitment agencies, and their regular use by recipient countries and by particular hospitals. Irrespective of any existing intent to migrate, active recruitment has put growing pressure on, and impressive opportunities in front of, potential migrants. Recruitment agencies smooth the way in attending to bureaucratic issues, satisfying concerns over different countries and cultures, and sometimes providing their own induction training in destinations.

Little information exists on the operations of recruitment agencies and therefore there is no evidence on whether they exaggerate the potential of overseas employment, but it is implausible that they do not increase its probability. For those who had emigrated from Cameroon, the single most important reason was recruitment (Awases et al. 2004), though obviously this would not have been successful unless other reasons existed. In this century there has been active recruitment of Fijian nurses for the United Arab Emirates, a country that few in Fiji would have had any knowledge of until then, and in the 1990s there was recruitment to work in several nearby countries, including the Marshall Islands (Rokoduru, this book). Concern over the activities of recruitment agencies is considerable (Rogerson and Crush, this book). In Mauritius the President of the largest Mauritian nursing union alleged that "The British send recruitment agents who discreetly make contact with nurses and directly negotiate the contracts. Last week, 26 nurses were lured away by a single recruiter" (quoted in *Afrol News*, 28 May 2004). In recruiting health workers for the United Kingdom many agencies engaged in some forms of exploitation (Buchan et al. 2005). Both in source and recipient countries agencies operate beyond the extent of effective regulation.

## Consequences of Migration

Migration of skilled health workers has diverse impacts, from more obvious effects on the delivery of health services and the economic consequences of the loss of locally trained skilled workers, to more subtle social, political and cultural impacts. Migrants tend to be relatively young and recently trained, compared with those who stay. Many leave after relatively short periods of work, but long enough to gain important practical experience. They often include the best and the brightest (Awases et al. 2004). Since migrants move to improve their own and their families' livelihoods, they are usually the key beneficiaries of migration. Recipient countries benefit from having workers who fill shortages in the health care system. Conversely sending countries and their populations, especially in remote areas, lose valuable skills unless those skills are an "overflow" or are otherwise compensated for.

## Health Care Provision

Migration affects the provision of health care both in quality and quantity. Logic and vast amounts of anecdotal data suggest strong links between migration and the reduced performance of health care systems, though actual correlations between emigration and malfunctioning health care systems are difficult to make, since it is impossible to quantify what is not there (Clemens 2007). However both India and the Philippines, both long-term providers of migratory health workers in circumstances initially described as an overflow (Oommen 1989), now appear to have become negatively affected (Brush and Sochalski 2007), while sub-Saharan and other states experience critical problems, but not simply or even primarily because of migration.

In certain circumstances the quantitative outcome of migration is obvious. The recruitment of several nurses from a cardiovascular unit in a provincial Filipino hospital effectively meant that the unit had to be closed down (Alkire and Chen 2004). In Malawi the loss of many nurses to the United Kingdom brought the near collapse of maternity services even in Malawi's central hospitals, with 65% of nursing positions being vacant (Palmer 2006). In the Lilongwe Central Hospital ten midwives sought to cope with delivering more than 10,000 babies a year, which meant that many births were not attended (Muula et al. 2003, Dugger 2004, Clark et al. 2006). Maternal health care has been similarly affected in Gambia and Malawi with increased workloads, waiting and consultation times and poorer infection control (Gerein et al. 2006). In Jamaica wards have been closed, male and female units have been merged, raising cultural issues, and immunization coverage and in situ training have both declined. In Zimbabwe by 1997 only 29% of all national positions were actually filled (Chikanda 2004) even before the most rapid international migration. While such data are fragmentary, and often depict worst-case scenarios, they point to difficult circumstances.

Reduced staff numbers mean that workloads of those remaining become higher, and less likely to be accomplished successfully. In Ghana and Zimbabwe the workload of midwives doubled in five years (Awases et al. 2004:35–37). Many anecdotal reports emphasise longer waiting times with the implication that this raises opportunity costs of medical care, and may also result in medical attention coming too late. In Zimbabwe over a quarter of health workers believed that longer waiting times had resulted in unnecessary deaths that prompt attention could have prevented (Chikanda 2004). Waiting times were problems in four African countries, and some health facilities had reduced opening times, especially in rural areas (Awases et al.

2004:50, 58). In Zimbabwe staff shortages resulted in patients being turned away from public clinics so that staff could carry on their private clinics without an excess workload, with obvious reductions in equity (Chikanda, this book). Health workers themselves stressed the decline in circumstances that had followed migration, in terms of such qualitative factors as respect for patients and care givers, attention given to patients and general communication between health workers and clients. Lack of staff also meant a decreased ability to get medication to patients effectively (Awases et al. 2004:50). Foreign aid programmes have recently expanded in sub-Saharan Africa, to provide drugs to millions affected by tuberculosis and AIDS, yet they have been hard to implement because of too few nurses to administer them effectively (Volqvartz 2005, Garrett 2007). In some contexts staff who remain have engaged in ethically and legally questionable activities, such as receiving "gifts" from patients and stealing drugs, in order to survive and achieve what they regard as appropriate incomes (Muula and Maseko 2006).

A further consequence of health worker migration is that of some patients travelling overseas for health care. Where such referrals are paid by the state the cost is considerable. Even where they are not, as is usually the case, resources are nevertheless transferred overseas. In a group of six African countries referrals have increased at the same time as health worker migration, resulting in "an unprecedented increase in both expense of care to fewer people and in the use of foreign currency, which could have been used for other development programmes or even for the motivation and retention of the country's health workers" (Awases et al. 2004:57). The lack of health personnel may not be the primary motivation for travelling overseas for treatment, but it nonetheless represents a substantial loss of scarce resources. Nigerians have been estimated to spend as much as US$1 billion a year on health costs outside Nigeria (Neelankantan 2003). Even in countries that are relatively well supplied with health personnel, the cost of referrals is considerable, making the task of financing local health systems and organising more labour intensive preventive health care more difficult.

### Rural and Regional Issues

The impact of emigration is usually most evident in remote regions, where losses tend to be greater (and where resources were initially least adequate), and has therefore fallen particularly on the rural poor (and sometimes therefore cultural minorities) who are most dependent on public health systems, further emphasising the "inverse care law." Equity has been further reduced. The impact of emigration is complicated and compounded by ubiquitous internal migration. This is even less well documented and it is primarily the evidence of inadequate stocks of health workers in the peripheries that suggest the extent of migration (and attrition) in remote areas. In Malawi for example two thirds of all skilled health workers are in urban areas whereas 85% of the population live in rural areas (Muula et al. 2003). Managua, the capital of Nicaragua, contains a fifth of the country's population but half the country's health workers. Centralisation in several Pacific and Caribbean states is even more extreme (Connell 2008). In Zimbabwe, even though less than 30% of national health positions were actually filled, the Harare Central Hospital had an excess of doctors over positions, while provincial hospitals were better staffed than district hospitals (Chikanda 2004). Chinese nurses are uninterested in moving to rural areas where needs are unsatisfied though cannot get jobs in what are regarded as "oversupplied" urban centres (Xu 2003). Internal migration exhibits a similar rationale to international migration (Awases et al. 2004, Connell 2008), but poses distinct problems where that internal migration is of those with particular skills, such as radiologists or pharmacists, where few are required hence the loss of even a small number may be crucial.

### Private Sector Growth

In most countries there is parallel movement between the public sector and the private sector. Where there are considerable income and other differentials (notably access to superior technology and working conditions) there may be substantial movement from the public sector thus disadvantaging its ability to provide services. "Migration" to the private sector has been particularly prevalent in African states because of superior salaries and working conditions, including better supplies of drugs and equipment (Awases at al. 2004). In Zimbabwe, in 1997, of the 1,634 doctors employed in the country just 551 (33.7%) were employed in the public sector, and a high proportion of nurses had also moved there, though unlike doctors they could not set up private practices on their own. So many nurses were working in the private sector that it was widely believed that "nurses in the public sector are engaging in a lot of part-time work in private clinics. By the time they come for their normal duties they will be too tired to work. That is why we get poor service when we visit the clinic" (quoted in Chikanda 2004). As a result of stress and higher workloads staff have tended to neglect public responsibilities to work in the private sector (Mutizwa-Mangiza 1998), especially where health tourism has emerged (Connell 2006). The movement of SHWs to the private sector has disadvantaged the poor, most of whom cannot afford higher private sector costs, alongside growing evidence of less adequate public sector services (Gerein et al. 2006).

### The Economics of Migration

Training SHWs is costly because of the long duration and high costs and is a burden on relatively poor states, whether directly or through scholarship provision. When trained workers migrate and the process is repeated costs mount further. However there have been few estimates of the costs of the ensuing brain drain, or the possible gain in skills through return migration, and a variety of methodologies and conclusions. Indeed the impact on health care provision of the emigration of doctors may be remarkably slight (Clemens 2007) compared with that of nurses.

The African Union has estimated that, if the cost of training a general practice doctor is estimated at $60,000 and that of other medical auxiliaries at $12,000, then low-income African countries subsidize high-income countries by about $500 million a year through the migration of these trained health workers (African Union 2003). Another estimate has suggested that there are three million health workers from developing countries in developed countries, and since it costs rich countries an estimated $184,000 to train one, the overall cost to developing countries has been $552 billion, about the same as the total overseas debt of these countries (Kimani 2005, Kirigia et al. 2006). Conversely, fragmentary data from developed countries indicate considerable cost savings involved in hiring overseas trained SHWs rather than training locally. By the 1960s it was estimated that training costs in Britain were roughly four times those of India and Africa, and for the United States were six times (Gish 1971:150). Such discrepancies have subsequently increased rather than decreased.

More complex calculations for Ghana suggest that because of migration Ghana has foregone around £35 million of its training investment in health professionals (Martineau et al. 2002), while Save the Children (2005) estimated that the United Kingdom has saved £65 million in training costs since 1998 by recruiting from Ghana alone. This has been described as a perverse and unjust subsidy from a relatively poor country to a relatively rich one (Mensah et al. 2005, Mackintosh et al. 2006). These estimates are based solely on the costs of training rather than additional costs based on foregone health care, lost productivity, the under use of medical facilities, etc. They also ignore possible remittances into Ghana (and their consequences). The United Kingdom has had its stock of health workers boosted and thus contributed to improved access to, and levels of, health care there—the converse of the impact in Ghana, again emphasising the impact of migration on equity.

### Return Migration

Where there is return migration of SHWs the relationship between income losses, return and the acquisition of human capital becomes unusually complex (Brown and Connell 2006, Connell 2008). Little good information exists on return migration, partly because the return of health workers is relatively limited in many countries, while aspirations to return are often weak (van Eyck 2004, Luck et al. 2000). If migrants return from overseas, with enhanced skills, knowledge, experience and enthusiasm (and perhaps also some capital), there might be major gains from migration. Sending countries could experience a positive transfer of technology (unless, as in the first phases of the brain drain, returnees came back with aspirations and demands for technology wholly inappropriate to local needs and budgets). However, significant return migration often fails to occur for the same reason that migration occurs; indeed, migrants are less likely to be tempted back by a system they left because of its perceived failings but often return for reasons that have nothing to do with health or because of problems in the destination. Any compensatory brain gain is slight.

If health systems improve then return migration occurs. Indian doctors have returned to India after new technology was introduced, and medical tourism took off (Connell 2006), and work in exclusive private hospitals with high salaries. But the overall number of return migrant doctors is modest, and they tend to return to senior positions in medical education or private practice. For Indian nurses from Kerala, working again as a nurse is "understood as a sign of failure" and only those who can get a superior position as a matron or a teacher work again after return (Percot and Rajan 2007:322). Health workers return to Pacific island states mainly because of perceived benefits—such as the ability to open a store—outside the health care system, which became at best mere supplementary employment (Brown and Connell 2004, Connell 2008). Unlike most others, Jamaican nurses have returned to work in the health sector, though the more qualified rejected this because of poor salary and working conditions (Brown 1997:206–209). Migrants thus rarely return because of conditions in the health sector, or out of a desire to return to work there.

### Remittances

A key reason for migration is usually expressed as the need or desire to help families remaining in countries and one of the most obvious and effective ways of doing this is through remittances.

The flow of remittances from SHWs is central to wider debates on their contemporary role, whether the resultant remittances are used for production or consumption, how they may contribute to inequality and ultimately whether they offset the loss of skills. In many contexts remittances are considerable, but few studies differentiate the remittances of SHWs from those of other migrant groups. However, a quarter of Jamaican nurses in the United States saved more than half their salaries and two thirds sent remittances home, around $2,000 each year, while most also sent goods (and a quarter brought home a motor vehicle). Remittances mainly supported their families, and enabled nurse households to become home owners, and over a third used them for investment (Brown 1997:208). A similar situation exists in the Pacific island states of Tonga and Samoa, hence the overall but limited evidence suggests that the remittances of SHWs substantially exceed training costs, benefit the private sector and do not contribute to greater equity, new training or improved health care provision (Connell and Brown 2004,

Connell 2008). Remittances tend to go to kin and thus the private sector, not directly to governments, hence do not directly compensate for the loss of skills that have mainly been produced by governments.

### Skill Loss/Brain Waste

A further outcome of migration can be a "skill loss when migrants with specific skills do not use them. This may result from failure to recognise qualifications, discrimination or a preference for jobs with better wages and conditions" (Luck et al. 2000, McNeil-Walsh, this book). Migrant doctors in Israel are directed into general practice rather than enabled to take up their previous specialisms (Shuval 1998). Filipina nurses in Vancouver had routinely become nannies and care-givers to secure migration opportunities, and had limited chance of regaining their old status (Pratt 1999). The most significant skill loss comes where nurses are employed as care-givers in nursing homes rather than working in hospitals. Expensive training is largely wasted and neither health systems, the migrants, nor their kin at home, who wait for remittances, make real gains.

## Social Costs

Few studies examine the social costs attached to the migration of skilled health workers, despite the fact that this is often of women moving as individuals and, in many cases, leaving families at home (Harper et al., this book). Yet many migrant workers, especially women within and outside the health sector, experience deprivation and discrimination. Recruitment agencies may impose unforeseen costs, and SHWs experience difficult circumstances, especially where cultures differ from those at home. Numerous examples exist of their experiencing racism in developed countries, and being ignored or experiencing reprisals when complaining of such problems, alongside being denied parity with local workers, promotion or wage gains (Hardill and Macdonald 2000, Robinson and Carey 2000, Hagey et al. 2001, Turrittin et al. 2002, DiCicco-Bloom 2004, van Eyck 2004, Kingma 2006, Likupe 2006, O'Brien-Pallas and Wang 2006, Percot and Rajan 2007). In some cases this has led to attrition, and return, and emphasises that this is emotional labour. Many migrants receive minimal cultural orientation in their new countries, and may be disappointed in their goal of working there at a higher level, appropriate to their education, experience and training (van Eyck 2004). Health workers are often recruited for, and directed into, positions and locations that are unattractive to local health workers, and peripheral geographical placement is common (Robinson and Carey 2000). Consequently new migrants are unlikely to be involved in specialist activities despite previous experience, and are most likely, at least initially, to be in the least attractive fields of specialisation and in outlying parts of the country. Compared with local health workers they are much less likely to be unionised and organised and be in a position to know and maintain their rights (e.g., Rokoduru 2002, this book) hence have reduced autonomy and authority.

There may also be stresses for the families of migrants. In the Caribbean the children of migrant nurses, sometimes referred to as "barrel children" (from the time when parents in the United Kingdom or elsewhere sent back goods to them in barrels), tend to be cared for by their grandparents. Since such children have to make multiple adjustments to new homes there is considerable stress on them, and potentially negative effects on child development and adolescent behaviour, through what in the Philippines has been called a "care deficit" (Parrenas 2002). However, in other contexts, as for Kerala nurses in the Gulf, the women and their families all gain in status through migration and its economic benefits without evident social cost (Percot 2005, Percot and Rajan 2007). Overall the outcome for many is probably much like that of Filipina workers in the United States a quarter of a century ago: "though work in the US presented many difficult and unexpected problems for the migrant groups, including the prejudice of other workers, assignments to onerous tasks, and distress from family separation, most migrant nurses were fairly satisfied with life and work" (Joyce and Hunt 1982:1223). After all, return migration was, and is, usually possible.

### Replacement

Migration of professionals has made it necessary for less or non-qualified people, such as nurses aides, to perform tasks that are normally beyond their ability. In several African countries "young recruits are often left alone to carry out work without supervision, at the risk of making incorrect diagnoses and prescribing inappropriate treatment, while unqualified personnel are left to perform duties that are specialized, and beyond their scope of practice which may endanger the lives of patients" (Awases et al. 2004:58). Alternatively patients have reverted to the informal sector with sometimes costly, uncertain and ineffective outcomes (Chikanda 2004, Mullan 2004). In extreme cases critical problems have arisen, as in the infamous case of "Dr. Death," a migrant doctor of Indian ethnicity, whose inadequacies, alongside poor management, caused the death of several patients in the small Queensland town of Bundaberg (Birrell and Schwartz 2005, Thomas 2007).

Where skilled workers leave relatively poor countries and are replaced, the cost may be very great, when the costs of both recruitment and salaries are substantially more than those of local doctors. Moreover, they may be less effective because of language and cultural differences, which restrict their ability to provide health services, contribute to training and enable sustainability. In some Pacific island states local workers have been replaced by Filipinos and Burmese, and most recently by Cubans and Taiwanese (Connell 2008), as part of the cascading global care chain.

POLICY DIRECTIONS?

It is often stated that mobility is a basic human right and thus should not be constrained, particularly for professionals with scarce skills. An open international market is said to offer efficiency and economic gains. However, gains in economic efficiency tend to be localised in receiving countries and, as the evidence of costs to national health, economic and social systems has mounted, there has been a greater interest in developing policies to diminish and mitigate the impacts of migration. Not all countries have sought to prevent migration, and some like India, Cuba, Egypt, China, Spain and the Philippines, purposefully export workers, including SHWs.

Many policy recommendations made by Gish (1971:122–128) nearly four decades ago, on the need for adequate, flexible, transparent and more rapid promotion opportunities, medical auxiliaries, adequate infrastructure, more rapid promotion and better access to training courses for those undertaking rural work, bonding, and even a bar on foreign recruiters have remarkable contemporary resilience. Various possibilities exist for more effective production and retention of SHWs, ranging from diverse financial incentives (inside and outside the health system), strengthening work autonomy and improving the status of health workers, increasing recruitment capacity, introducing intermediate categories of workers such as nurse practitioners, and ensuring an effective "fiscal space" for health services, but only rarely have these been effectively implemented in a concerted manner (Connell et al. 2007, Connell 2008). Similarly the SHW diaspora has only rarely been recruited for return.

Given the pressures on public sectors in less developed countries, and the very limited room for manoeuvre that exists where national economies are weak, the onus for a more equitable distribution of SHWs has gradually shifted towards recipient countries, where demand occurs. Few recipient countries have taken effective measures to increase recruitment and reduce attrition of SHWs, at a time of greater demand, either by increasing the number of training places or improving wages and working conditions (Pond and McPake 2006). Continued migration has thus led to renewed calls for ethical recruitment guidelines, adequate codes of practice binding countries and/or compensation for countries experiencing losses, yet compensation is inherently implausible and impractical, while ethical arguments confront blunt political realities (Bach 2007, Connell et al. 2007, Connell 2008). Better regulation, and more ethical recruitment, alongside bilateral relationships suggest some partial solutions, in terms of more effective managed migration.

THE FUTURE GLOBAL CARE CHAIN

Shortages of SHWs exist in most countries in the world, and have been remedied mainly by migration rather than by strategies for improved retention and recruitment, hence in the foreseeable future migration may well increase. Countries such as India and the Philippines, that previously exported an "overspill," are now experiencing adverse effects from their "export policies." Migration has tended to be problematic for relatively poor countries as the costs of mobility are unevenly shared, and the care chain becomes more global and hierarchical. International migration has become increasingly common—even though remarkably few people actually leave their home countries—and in many countries it is effectively becoming built into the socioeconomic system. Greater complexity increases the challenge of achieving more equitable outcomes.

The principal occupational flows of SHWs are primarily of nurses, where the evidence of losses in developing countries is substantial, however there are also parallel flows—but poorly documented—of every kind of health worker. Failures of governance, broadly the inadequate delivery of services, whether health, education or transport, constrain development. The international migration of SHWs has increased because perceptions of inadequate local conditions have grown, migrant "host" populations are generally increasing in metropolitan states, demand has increased and recruitment intensified, and because health skills are now valuable commodities in international migration. Yet, paradoxically, in many countries fewer people are being attracted to health careers. Wages and conditions are increasingly seen as deterrents to entry as other sectors become more attractive. Potential employees witness the frustrations of health workers and there is a wider range of job options. In both developed and developing countries careers in health are now less attractive, other than as a means to migration.

Sending countries have not always been able to discourage migration, which is widely perceived as a human right. Indeed several remittance-dependent countries, such as Cape Verde, have not challenged migration because of its economic role. Unions have supported the rights of members to better their circumstances by migration while also pressing governments to act locally to improve working conditions. Individual voices in some states have even called for the greater export of health workers—in pursuit of the "Philippines model"—to generate remittances. Migration is increasingly embedded in national and international political economies. There is little sign of any presently recipient country taking realistic steps to increase national market supply, and any solution requires multilateral consensus rather than a national or bilateral approach. Migration, and its often critical consequences, will surely continue.

## REFERENCES

Adkoli, B (2006) Migration of health workers: Perspectives from Bangladesh, India, Nepal, Pakistan and Sri Lanka, *Regional Health Forum*, 10, 49–58.

Alkire, S and Chen, L (2004) 'Medical Exceptionalism' in International Migration: Should Doctors And Nurses Be Treated Differently?, Joint Learning Initiative Working Paper 7-3, Harvard University.

Anand, S and Barninghausen, T (2004) Human resources and health outcomes: Cross country econometric study, *Lancet*, 364(9445), 1603–1609.

Awases, M, Gbary, A, Nyoni, J and Chatora, R (2004) *Migration of health professionals in six countries*, Brazzaville: WHO Regional Office for Africa.

Bach, S (2003) *International migration of health workers*, Geneva: ILO Working Paper No. 209.

Bach, S (2004) Migration patterns of physicians and nurses: Still the same story?, *Bulletin of the WHO*, 82, 624–625.

Bach, S (2007) Going global? The regulation of nurse migration in the UK, *British Journal of Industrial Relations*, 45, 383–403.

Baird, V (2005) Out of Africa, *New Internationalist*, 379, June, 9–28.

Bhutta, Z, Nundy, S and Abbasi, K (2004) Is there hope for South Asia?, *British Medical Journal*, 328, 777–778.

Birrell, B and Schwartz, A (2005) The aftermath of Dr. Death: Has anything changed?, *People and Place*, 13(3), 54–61.

Bower, F and McCullough, C (2004) Nurse shortage or nursing shortage: Have we missed the real problem?, *Nursing Economics*, 22, 200–203.

Brown, D (1997) Workforce losses and return migration to the Caribbean: A case study of Jamaican nurses, in P Pessar, (Ed), *Caribbean circuits: New directions in the study of Caribbean migration*, New York, Center for Migration Studies, pp. 197–223.

Brown R and Connell, J (2004). The Migration of Doctors and Nurses from South Pacific Island Nations, *Social Science and Medicine*, 58, 2193–2210.

Brown, R and Connell, J (2006) Occupation-specific analysis of migration and remittance behaviour: Pacific Island nurses in Australia and New Zealand, *Asia Pacific Viewpoint*, 47, 133–148.

Brush, B and Sochalski, J (2007) International nurse migration: Lessons from the Philippines, *Policy, Politics and Nursing Practice*, 8, 37–46.

Buchan, J, Parkin, T and Sochalski, J (2004) *International nurse mobility: Trends and policy implications*, Geneva: WHO, ICN & RCN.

Chen, L and Boufford, J (2005) Fatal flows—Doctors on the move, *New England Journal of Medicine*, 353, 1850–1852.

Chikanda, A (2004) *Skilled health professionals' migration and its impact on health care delivery in Zimbabwe*, Oxford: Centre on Migration, Policy and Society Working Paper No. 4.

Choy, C (2003) *Empire of care: Nursing and migration in Filipino American history*, Durham, Duke University Press.

Clark, P, Stewart, J and Clark, D (2006) The globalization of the labour market for health-care professionals, *International Labour Review*, 145, 37–64.

Clemens, M (2007) *Do visas kill? Health effects of African health professional emigration*, Center for Global Development Working Paper No. 114, Washington.

Clemens, M and Pettersson, G (2007) *New data on African health professionals abroad*, Center for Global Development Working Paper No. 95, Washington.

Commonwealth Secretariat (2004) *Migration of health workers from commonwealth countries*, London: Commonwealth Secretariat.

Connell, J (2006) Medical tourism: Sea, sun, sand . . . and surgery, *Tourism Management*, 27, 1093–1100.

Connell, J (2007) Local skills and global markets? The migration of health workers from Caribbean and Pacific Island States, *Social and Economic Studies*, 56, 41–66.

Connell, J (2008) *The global health care chain: From the Pacific to the world*, New York: Routledge.

Connell, J and Brown, R (2004) The remittances of migrant Tongan and Samoan nurses in Australia, *Human Resources for Health*, 2(2), 1–21.

Connell, J and Brown, R (2005) *Migration and remittances: A Pacific overview*, Manila, Asian Development Bank.

Connell, J and Stilwell, B (2006) Merchants of medical care: Recruiting agencies in the global health care chain, in C Kuptsch, (Ed), *Merchants of labour*, Geneva: ILO, pp. 239–253.

Connell, J, Zurn, P, Stilwell, B, Awases, M and Braichet, J-M (2007) Sub-Saharan Africa: Beyond the health worker migration crisis?, *Social Science and Medicine*, 64, 1876–1891.

DiCicco-Bloom, B (2004) The racial and gendered experiences of immigrant nurses from Kerala, India, *Journal of Transcultural Nursing*, 15, 26–33.

Dugger, C (2004) An exodus of African nurses puts infants and the ill in peril, *New York Times*, 12 July 2004.

Dumont, J and Meyer, J (2004) The international mobility of health professionals: An evaluation and analysis based on the case of South Africa, in OECD (Ed), *Trends in international migration*, Paris: OECD, pp. 150–205.

Dussault, G and Franceschini, M (2006) Not enough there, too many here: Understanding geographical imbalances in the distribution of the health workforce, *Human Resources for Health*, 4(12), 1–16.

Engels, B and Connell, J (1983) Indian doctors in Australia: Costs and benefits of the brain drain, *Australian Geographer*, 15, 308–318.

Espiritu, Y (2003) *Home bound: Filipino American lives across cultures, communities and countries*, Berkeley, University of California Press.

Espiritu, Y (2005) Gender, migration and work: Filipina health care professionals to the United States, *Revue Européenne des Migrations Internationales*, 21, 55–75.

Findlay, A and Stewart, E (2002) *Skilled Labour Migration from Developing Countries*. ILO International Migration Papers No. 55, Geneva, ILO.

Folbre, N (2006) Nursebots to the rescue? Immigration, automation and care, *Globalizations*, 3, 349–360.

Garrett, L (2007) The challenge of global health, *Foreign Affairs*, 86(1), 14–38.

Gaidzanwa, R (1999) *Voting With Their Feet: Migrant Zimbabwean Nurses and Doctors in the Era of Structural Adjustment*, Research Report No. 111, Uppsala, Nordiska Africainstitutet.

George, S (2000) "Dirty nurses" and "Men who play": Gender and class in transnational migration, in M Burawoy (Ed), *Global ethnography: Forces, connections and imaginations in a postmodern world*, Berkeley: University of California Press, pp. 144–174.

George, S (2005) *When women come first: Gender and class in transnational migration*, Berkeley: University of California Press.

Gerein, N, Green, A and Pearson, S (2006) The implications of shortages of health professionals for maternal health in sub-Saharan Africa, *Reproductive Health Matters*, 14(27), 40–50.

Getahun, S (2006) Brain drain and its impact on Ethiopia's higher learning institutions: Medical establishments and the military academies between 1970s and 2000, *Perspectives on Global Development and Technology*, 5, 257–275.

Gish, O (1969a) Emigration and the supply and demand for medical manpower: The Irish case, *Minerva*, 7, 668–679.

Gish, O (1969b) Foreign born midwives in the United Kingdom: A case of the skill drain, *Social and Economic Administration*, 3, 39–51.

Gish, O (1971) *Doctor migration and world health*, London: Bell.

Gish, O and Godfrey, M (1979) A reappraisal of the "brain drain" with special reference to the medical profession, *Social Science and Medicine*, 13C, 1–11.

Hagey, R, Choudhry, U, Guruge, S, Turrittin, J, Collins, E and Lee, R (2001) Immigrant nurses' experience of racism, *Journal of Nursing Scholarship*, 33, 389–394.

Hagopian, A, Ofosu, A, Fatusi, A, Biritwum, R, Essel, A, Hart, L and Watts, C (2005) The flight of physicians from West Africa: Views of African physicians and implications for policy, *Social Science and Medicine*, 61, 1750–1760.

Hagopian, A, Thompson, M, Fordyce, M, Johnson, K, and Hart, L (2004) The migration of physicians from sub-Saharan Africa to the United States of America: Measures of the African brain drain, *Human Resources for Health*, pp. 2(1).

Hardill, I and Macdonald, S (2000) Skilled international migration: The experience of nurses in the UK, *Regional Studies*, 34, 681–692.

Horn, J (1977) The medical brain drain and health priorities in Latin America, *International Journal of Health Services*, 7, 425–442.

Ihekweazu, C, Anya, I and Anosike, E (2005) Nigerian medical graduates: Where are they now? *The Lancet*, 365, 1847–1848.

Iredale, R (2001) The Migration of Professionals: Theories and Typologies, *International Migration*, 39, 7–26.

Joint Learning Initiative (2004) *Human Resources for Health. Overcoming the Crisis*, Cambridge: Harvard University Press.

Joyce, R and Hunt, C (1982) Philippine nurses and the brain drain, *Social Science and Medicine*, 16, 1223–1233.

Kimani, D (2005) Brain Drain Robs Africa's Health Sector of $552 bn, *The East African*, 7 February

Kingma, M (2006) *Nurses on the move: Migration and the global health care economy*, Ithaca: Cornell University Press.

Kirigia, J, Gbary, A, Muthuri, L, Nyoni, J and Seddoh, A (2006) The cost of health professionals' brain drain in Kenya, *BMC Health Services Research*, 6(89).

Kober, K and van Damme, W (2006) Public sector nurses in Swaziland: Can the downturn be reversed?, *Human Resources for Health*, 4(13), 1–11.

Kronfol, N, Sibai, A and Rafeh, N (1992) The impact of civil disturbances on the migration of physicians: The case of Lebanon, *Medical Care*, 30, 208–215.

Lanfranchi, P and Taylor, M (2001) *Moving with the ball: The migration of professional footballers*, Oxford, Berg.

Likupe, G (2006) Experiences of African nurses in the UK National Health Service: A literature review, *Journal of Clinical Nursing*, 15, 1213–1220.

Lowell, B. and Findlay A. (2002) *Skilled Labour Migration from Developing Countries*, ILO International Migration Papers No. 56, Geneva, ILO.

Luck, M, Fernandes, M and Ferrinho, P (2004) At the other end of the brain-drain: African nurses living in Lisbon, *Studies in Health Service Organisation and Policy*, 16, 157–169.

Mackintosh, M, Mensah, K, Henry, L, and Rowson, M (2006) Aid, restitution and international fiscal redistribution in health care: Implications of health professionals' migration, *Journal of International Development*, 18, 757–770.

Malvarez, S and Castrillon Agudelo, C (2005) *Overview of the nursing workforce of Latin America*, Geneva: International Council of Nurses, Issue Paper No. 6.

Mareckova, M (2004) Exodus of Czech Doctors Leaves Gap in Health Care, *The Lancet* 363 (9419), 1443–1446.

Martineau, T, Decker, K and Bundred, P (2002) *Briefing note on international migration of health professionals: Levelling the playing field for developing country health systems*. Liverpool: Liverpool School of Tropical Medicine.

Mejia, A, Pizurski, H and Royston, E (1979) *Physician and nurse migration: Analysis and policy implications*, Geneva: WHO.

Mensah, K, Mackintosh, M and Henry, L (2005) *The "skills drain" of health professionals from the developing world: A framework for policy formation*, London: Medact.

Millar, J and Salt, J (2007) In whose interests? IT migration in an interconnected world economy, *Population, Space and Society*, 13, 41–58.

Mullan, F (2004) *A legacy of pushes and pulls: An examination of Indian physician emigration*, Bethesda: George Washington University.

Mullan, F (2005) The metrics of the physician brain drain, *New England Journal of Medicine*, 353, 1810–1818.

Mutizwa-Mangiza, D (1998) *The impact of health sector reform on public sector health worker motivation in Zimbabwe*, Partnerships for Health Reform Working Paper No. 4, Bethesda: Abt Associates.

Muula, A and Maseko, F (2006) How are health professionals earning their living in Malawi?, *BMC Health Services Research*, 6(97).

Muula, A, Mfutso-Bengo, J, Makoza, J and Chatipwa, E (2003) The ethics of developed nations recruiting nurses from developing countries: The case of Malawi, *Nursing Ethics*, 10, 433–438.

Neelankantan, S (2003) India's global ambitions, *Far Eastern Economic Review*, 6 November.

O'Brien-Pallas, L and Wang, S (2006) Innovations in health care delivery: Responses to global nurse migration—A research example, *Policy, Politics and Nursing Practice*, 7(3), 49S–57S.

OECD (2005) *Trends in international migration*, Paris: OECD.

Ong, P and Azores, T (1994) The migration and incorporation of Filipino nurses, in P Ong, E Bocacich and L Cheng (Eds), *The new Asian immigration in Los Angeles and global restructuring*, Philadelphia: Temple University Press, pp. 164–195.

Oommen, T (1989) India: "Brain drain" or migration of talent, *International Migration*, 27, 411–422.

Oulton, J (1998) International trade and the nursing profession, in S Zarrilli and C Kinnon (Eds), *International trade in health services*, Geneva: UNCTAD and WHO, pp. 125–133.

Palmer, D (2006) Tackling Malawi's human resources crisis, *Reproductive Health Matters*, 14(27), 27–39.

Parrenas, R (2002) The care crisis in the Philippines: Children and transnational families in the new global economy, in B Ehrenreich and A Hochschild, (Eds), *Global woman: Nannies, maids and sex workers in the new economy*, New York: Metropolitan Books, pp. 39–54.

Percot, M (2005) Les infirmières indiennes émigrées dans les pays du Golfe: de l'opportunité à la stratégie, *Revue Européenne des Migrations Internationales*, 21, 29–54.

Percot, M and Rajan, S (2007) Female emigration from India: Case study of nurses. *Economic and Political Weekly*, 42, 318–325.

Phillips, D (1996) The internationalisation of labour: The migration of nurses from Trinidad and Tobago, *International Sociology*, 11, 109–127.

Pond, B and McPake, B (2006) The health migration crisis: The role of four Organisation for Economic Cooperation and Development countries, *Lancet*, 367, 1448–1455.

Pratt, G (1999) From registered nurse to registered nanny: Discursive geographies of Filipina domestic workers in Vancouver, B.C., *Economic Geography*, 75, 215–236.

Robinson, V and Carey, M (2000) Peopling skilled international migration: Indian doctors in the UK, *International Migration*, 38, 89–108.

Save the Children (2005) *Whose charity? Africa's aid to the NHS*, London: Save the Children.

Shuval, J (1998) Credentialling immigrant physicians in Israel, *Health and Place*, 4, 375–381.

Stilwell, B, Diallo, K, Zurn, P, Dal Poz, M, Adams, O and Buchan, J (2003) Developing evidence-based ethical policies on the migration of health workers: conceptual and practical challenges, *Human Resources for Health*, 1(8), 1–13.

Thomas, H (2007) *Sick to death*, Sydney: Allen and Unwin.

Thomas-Hope, E (2002) Skilled Labour Migration from Developing Countries: Study on the Caribbean Region, International Migration Papers No.50, Geneva, ILO.

Turrittin, J, Hagey, R, Guruge, S, Collins, E and Mitchell, M (2002) The experiences of professional nurses who have migrated to Canada: cosmopolitan citizenship or democratic racism?. *International Journal of Nursing Studies*, 39, 655–667.

Upadhyay, A (2003) Nursing exodus weakens developing world, *IPS News*, (www. Ipsnews.net/migration/stories/exodus) accessed 5 April 2005.

Van Eyck, K (2004) *Women and International Migration in the Health Sector*, Ferney-Voltaire, Public Services International

Van Eyck, K (2005) *Who cares? Women health workers in the global labour market*, Ferney-Voltaire, Public Services International.

Volqvartz, J (2004) The brain drain, *The Guardian*, 11 March.

Vujicic, M and Zurn, P (2006) The dynamics of the health labour market, *International Journal of Health Planning and Management*, 21, 101–115.

Winkelmann-Gleed, A (2006) *Migrant nurses: Motivation, integration and contribution*, Oxford: Radcliffe.

World Health Organization (2006) *Working together for health*, WHO: Geneva.

Wuliji, T (2006) FIP global pharmacy workforce and migration report: A call to action, *International Pharmacy Journal*, 20(1), 2–4.

Xiang, B (2007) *Global "body shopping": An Indian labor system in the information technology industry*, Princeton: Princeton University Press.

Xu, Y (2003) Are Chinese nurses a viable source to relieve the US nursing shortage?, *Nursing Economics*, 21, 269–274.

Zurn, P, Vujicic, M, Diallo, K, Pantoja, A, Dal Poz, M, and Adams, O (2004) Planning for human resources for health: Human resources for health and the production of health outcomes/outputs, *Cahiers de Sociologie et de Démographie Médicales*, 45(1), 107–133.

# 2 Globalised Labour Markets and the Trade of Filipino Nurses

## Implications for International Regulatory Governance

*Rochelle E. Ball*

Nursing is the one of the most feminised and increasingly globalised professions. A growing volume of nurses from developing nations, such as the Philippines, are using their portable skills globally, migrating to fill the demand created by real or induced shortages of nurses in a number of countries. This migration either as contract labour migrants or, for the more fortunate, as semi-permanent or permanent migrants, is fundamentally based on global inequalities in levels of development, income and opportunity. The massive migration of nurses from poor nations such as the Philippines is much more than a large migration of nurses, but it is also about development, fostering long-term underdevelopment of labour exporting nations (through undermining important areas of capacity building such as the health care system) within an unregulated global movement of highly skilled labour. The globalisation of nursing has resulted in an unprecedented and acute brain drain from major nurse exporting nations, evident early on in the Philippines (Joyce and Hunt 1985). Outcomes of globalisation may thus be divergent for nations at either end of the development spectrum.

The contemporary global migration of Filipino nurses is migration of the highly skilled. However, this migration in many instances exhibits the characteristics of contract labour migration—a concept most frequently applied to the global, temporary and contracted migration of the unskilled. Since the rise of institutionalized, state managed and promoted labour migration in the early 1970s, the Philippine state has played an aggressive role in seeking out international markets for all workers and particularly their nurse nationals. In the 1960s the brain drain of nurses from the Philippines occurred principally through permanent migration to the United States (Ball 2004). By the 1980s and 1990s the main nation of demand for Filipino nurses as contracted labour, often recruited and placed by the Philippine government, was Saudi Arabia—which accounted for two thirds of Filipino nurse migrants. Since the 1970s the supply of Filipino nurses has expanded both numerically and geographically, to the extent that about 250,000 Filipino nurses are employed globally. The development of a sophisticated system of nurse export from the Philippines has been facilitated by government policy (Ball 1996, 1997, 2006) and the use of temporary employment contracts and visas.

Contemporary labour export has wrought massive changes on Philippines economy and society. The economic effects of the labour export industry, in terms of worker remittances on the macro economy of the Philippines, has been widely acknowledged (Ball 1997, 2006; Tan 2000; Tyner 2004). Above all, it is migration's tremendous hard currency earning capacity that has won it the active support of the state (Ball 1996, 1997; Piper and Ball 2001). The combination of a state policy promoting labour export, the country's economic decline, and a burgeoning international demand for a range of labour services, has inevitably had an effect on individuals and households in terms of their career decisions, labour market participation and survival strategies (Ball 2000). Relatively little research has been conducted on industry and labour specific sectors, or on skilled migration of Filipino women. What research has been done on women OCWs (overseas contract workers) has largely centred on the situation of domestic helpers and entertainers (Chant and McIlwaine 1995; Yeoh and Huang 1998; Pratt 1999; Barber 2000; Tyner 1996, 2004) This chapter analyses changes in the nature of skilled migration of Filipino nurses, by employing a 'supply' and 'demand' approach to explore the nature of international labour market relationships in the global nurse trade from a poor underdeveloped nation to two economic powerhouses in the global economy: the United States and Saudi Arabia.

This chapter contextualizes the massive and ongoing export of nurses against the background of the phenomenal growth of international contract labour migration from the Philippines, and the economic impacts of remittances on the economy. The major impacts of this highly organized and ongoing global migration of nurses on the Philippine health care sector and labour markets over the last thirty years are then examined. The discussion first analyses how individuals and their families respond to both local and global labour market dynamics in the choice of nursing as an investment decision in a globalising world. It then examines the supply side nurse labour market in detail: the extent of nurse migration from the Philippines and its relationship to the local labour market, nurse–patient ratios, wages and condition of employment and the impacts of nurse migration on the Philippine health care system. The chapter then examines the demand side of the global nurse trade. Using the example of two major labour markets for Filipino nurses the chapter explores the differences in the nature of demand for nurses in the United States and Saudi Arabia. Finally, the chapter concludes by exploring how understanding the dynamics of these globalised labour markets provides the base from which we can identify potential areas for developing governance mechanisms between nurse exporting and importing nations that address the highly unequal impacts embodied in this trade.

## CONTEXTUALISING NURSE MIGRATION: CONTEMPORARY DIMENSIONS OF PHILIPPINE LABOUR EXPORT

The Philippines is one of the major contemporary countries of migration—perhaps even the largest migrant nation—with Filipino migrants found in more than 181 countries. As a labour exporting nation the Philippines ranks second in the world, next only to Mexico (Carlos 2002:81). For more than 30 years since the OPEC oil crisis of 1973, the Philippines has been a labour exporting nation which has supplied workers to labour-deficit and/or capital-rich nations. While the export of labour was promoted by the Philippine state as a temporary measure, for more than 30 years it has both persisted and greatly expanded (Ball 2006).

The growth of the overseas employment industry has been remarkable. International contract labour migration from the Philippines has wrought substantial changes on Philippine society and economy. Exactly how many Filipinos are working abroad is unclear (Ball 2006). In 2004, the Commission on Filipinos Overseas and the Philippine Overseas Employment Administration (POEA) estimated that more than 8 million Filipinos live abroad. Of these the majority (3.6 million) are temporary overseas contract workers, followed by 3.2 million permanent migrants and 1.3 million undocumented migrants (such as overstaying tourists working illegally). Remittances from overseas workers are the premier foreign exchange earner for the Philippines, and the 'national' economy of the Philippines has become increasingly dependent on the hard currency remittances of migrants. Central Bank of the Philippines data reveal that in 2005, US$10.7 billion was remitted through formal channels; remittances through formal channels in 2003 (US$7.6 billion) accounted for 10% of GDP (ADB 2003). The remittances have contributed greatly to the country's foreign exchange earnings and were as much as 20% of exports and 5% of GNP in 1990–1998 (Tan 2001:380).

### Gendered International Labour Mobility

Until the mid-1980s labour export from the Philippines was heavily dominated by men, primarily in the construction sector, but for more than two decades, it been dominated by women (Tyner 1996, 2004). The economic contribution of women's overseas employment is vital: 'At the end of the twentieth century, Philippine gendered labour migration and its diaspora have become the primary means for servicing Philippine indebtedness' (Barber 2000:399). By the mid-1990s it was estimated that Filipinas working abroad contributed in legally and illegally remitted earnings nearly US$8billion yearly to the Philippines economy (POEA 1999). A decade onwards, these figure are even greater given the subsequent rapid growth of remitted income into the Philippine economy.

By the mid-1980s a combination of several key factors increased global demand for and employment of Filipino women: escalating economic decline in the Philippines; a rise in labour demand in the international service sector in both Asia and the Gulf; declines in (male) labour demand in the Gulf construction sector; and aggressive global labour marketing campaigns by the Philippine state (Ball 1997). Within a relatively short period the gender structure of the global Philippine migrant labour force was transformed. By 2001 Filipino women constituted 72% of migrant workers leaving the Philippines (POEA 2004). While male workers still typically dominate in the construction and shipping industries, Filipino women are employed in all tiers of service sector employment ranging from entertainment, prostitution and domestic service through to nursing, and in Southeast Asian, North American, European and Gulf labour markets (Barber 2000). Within the broad categorisation of 'service sector' there are wide-ranging employment vulnerabilities related to the intersection of occupation and country of employment. In addition, most Philippine women who are employed legally are generally overeducated for the forms of employment that they take on overseas, resulting in both a brain drain and a deskilling of the globalised and gendered Filipino labour market (Ball 1996, 2004, 2006).

Nursing, service and entertainment positions are heavily dominated by women, with 95% of domestic helpers and entertainers and 92% of nurses being women (Ball 1991:97). Women also tend to dominate labour flows to particular countries. For example domestic helpers migrate mainly to Hong Kong, Singapore, Taiwan, Italy and the Gulf; entertainers migrate mainly to Japan (Ball 1996:72) and nurses work primarily in Saudi Arabia and the United States, followed by Libya, the United Arab Emirates and Kuwait.

## THE TRANSNATIONAL LABOUR MOBILITY OF FILIPINO NURSES

The Philippines has had a substantive post-war history of international migration of health workers (Ball 2004). In its various phases this has responded to the dynamics of international demand, the success of Filipinos as individuals and the institutional apparatus of the Philippine government in responding to and meeting this demand. The Philippines leads the way in people thinking about global jobs and securing training just for that end (Ball 2000). The nursing component of the Philippine labour market has become particularly responsive to international labour demands and local stresses, and is no longer oriented to serving only national health care needs to the extent that the Philippines is now producing nurses overwhelmingly for international rather than national labour markets (Ball 1991, 1996, 2000).

Filipino women have had a long history of internal migration in search of employment, and are amongst the most domestically migratory women in Asia (Trager 1984, Findlay 1987). The massive growth in international migration of nurses is an extension of internal labour migration trends, where women and daughters play a central role in household income generation. In the Philippines, individuals and families are choosing nursing as a profession, in clear response to the growing international demand for nurses. Feelings of responsibility and obligation to family, and strong family expectations that single adult daughters will financially contribute to their households, have underpinned the choice of nursing as a profession for the majority of a group of 640 Filipino nurses (Ball 2000). The family plays a central role in influencing the choice of profession as an investment decision, and the decision to educate daughters to become nurses is substantially influenced by concern for returns on that investment. Not surprisingly then, the choice of nursing as a profession was a decision made by daughters and families, which for a substantial number were strongly influenced by overseas, rather than domestic employment opportunities. Furthermore, most nurses do not intend to work as nurses in the Philippines after returning from working overseas. This has changed the focus of the nurse labour market in the Philippines away from local needs. The Philippine nurse education and labour market, since at least the mid-1970s, has essentially become a training ground for overseas employers and the international trade in nurses, with potential longer-term consequences for the Philippine health care sector and the quality of health care delivery.

The success of individual nurses in obtaining overseas employment has historically varied with the level of government intervention and regulation. The relatively unorganized international supply of medical workers as permanent residents to the United States in the 1960s and 1970s (Ball 2004) underwent massive transformation through the development of a state apparatus centred on labour export as development policy (Ball 1997, Ball and Piper 2002). As a result, the export of nurses expanded in volume, elaborate organisation, and destination, on a contract basis in the late 1970s and 1980s. While there is some overlap between this second phase of the brain drain (Ball 2004) and earlier permanent emigration of Filipino nurses to the United States, it was not until the early 1980s that private and public sector systems governing the temporary contract migration of Filipino nurses became well developed. This changed the status and conditions under which nurses migrated to the United States and other nations. The Philippines now supplies nurses to the United States, the Gulf, East and Southeast Asian nations, and to Britain and other European Union states as the major global exporter of registered nurses.

## Contemporary Nurse Migration from the Philippines

The number of Filipino nurses that have migrated to work abroad has been extraordinary. Historical and contemporary data collection has been ad hoc, so it is difficult to assess the full extent of nurse migration from the Philippines. The following statistics, however, reflect the enormity of this process. In 1985, 26,560 medical workers and 21,000 nurses (POEA 1986) were deployed for overseas employment, accounting for about 15% of all Filipinos finding employment abroad in that year. Since the 1980s, the annual exodus of nurses has fluctuated markedly (Figure 2.1), but has always remained substantial to the extent that the Philippines has consistently been the largest global exporter of registered nurses. For example, in the 1990s, the annual deployment of nurses had dropped from the levels of the 1980s and did not exceed 7,000 annually, but in 2001, 14,000 nurses left the Philippines (Baguioro 2002:1).

The Philippine Nurses Association estimated that in the early 1990s, almost two thirds (61%) of the total number of trained nurses (which was 174,202 in 1990) were employed outside the Philippines (Ortin 1994:190). Manzano (2005) estimates that in recent years over 70% of the 7,000 Filipino nurses who graduate annually leave for overseas employment. This figure, combined with the migration of nurses employed in the Philippines, amounts to a yearly estimated supply of 15,000 nurses per annum to more than 30 countries. This outflow is more than double the average number of graduates from nursing schools (Baguioro 2002:1): a substantial brain drain. In a promotional statement, a major Philippine nurse recruiter has written:

> Filipino nurses can be found everywhere around the world—in the big cities of United States and England, in urban centers of Europe and

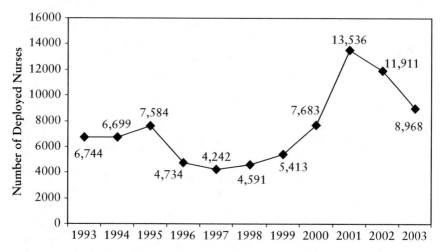

*Figure 2.1* Overseas deployment of Filipino nurse professionals.

*Source:* POEA, cited in Manzano (2005:12).

Asia, in the far corners of Africa and South America, in remote desert clinics in the Middle East, in offshore rigs on the China Sea.

(http://www.abbapersonel.com/nurses.html)

The top destinations of Filipino nurses are: Saudi Arabia, the United Kingdom, Kuwait, the United States, Ireland, and Singapore—the only ASEAN nation that is a primary destination (Table 2.1).

The labour migration of nurses from the Philippines is symptomatic of part of the overall shift of labour migration away from the migration of unskilled and semi-skilled workers, to skilled service sector workers that are used to sustain existing levels of development elsewhere. The dominance of the Gulf as the major nurse importing region increased in the 1980s when the United States' qualifying examination of the Commission for Graduate Foreign Nurses (CGFNS) was strictly enforced, resulting in fewer nurses being able to obtain work in the United States. Nevertheless, since then the

*Table 2.1* Deployment of Filipino Nurses by Country of Destination, 1993–2003

| | | Country of Destination | | | | | | |
|---|---|---|---|---|---|---|---|---|
| Year | Number of Deployed | Saudi Arabia | United States | U.K. and Ireland | United Arab Emirates | Kuwait | Libya | Rest of the World |
| 1993 | 6744 | 3762 | 1987 | 0 | 19 | 121 | 661 | 194 |
| 1994 | 6699 | 3032 | 2833 | 0 | 127 | 454 | 11 | 242 |
| 1995 | 7584 | 3015 | 3690 | 1 | 46 | 59 | 380 | 743 |
| 1996 | 4734 | 2711 | 270 | 0 | 50 | 269 | 809 | 645 |
| 1997 | 4242 | 3171 | 11 | 0 | 189 | 25 | 175 | 671 |
| 1998 | 4591 | 3473 | 5 | 63 | 268 | 143 | 34 | 605 |
| 1999 | 5413 | 3567 | 53 | 934 | 367 | 53 | 13 | 426 |
| 2000 | 7683 | 3888 | 89 | 2615 | 295 | 133 | 17 | 646 |
| 2001 | 13536 | 5045 | 304 | 6912 | 243 | 182 | 9 | 841 |
| 2002 | 11867 | 5688 | 316 | 4004 | 405 | 108 | 411 | 935 |
| 2003 | 8968 | 5740 | 196 | 1751 | 226 | 51 | 52 | 952 |
| Total | 87808 | 46153 | 11521 | 16280 | 2455 | 1877 | 2828 | 7064 |

Source: Philippine Overseas Employment Administration 2004

Philippines has provided a steady flow of highly trained and experienced nurses to both the Gulf and the United States.

### The Effects on the Philippine Health Care Sector

The impact on the Philippine health care sector of large annual outflows of nurses cannot be underestimated. This massive out-migration of nurses has created an under-supply of skilled nurses to the domestic health sector in the Philippines that has weakened the country's healthcare system. Since the mid-1980s there has been clear evidence that the country has lost many of its highly qualified and experienced nurses in both private hospitals and the public health care system (Ball 1996, 2004). As early as 1985, 47% of hospitals complained of being inadequately staffed, and extreme nurse–patient ratios existed—even as high as 1:120 in some larger hospitals (Venzon 1985:86, Quesada 1985). These serious nurse–patient ratios have been compounded by high staff turnover rates, again since at least the mid-1980s. In both private and public hospitals in Metro Manila, estimates of nurse turnover rates were 60% to 80% per year (Ball 1996). Hospital administrators and chief nurses all agreed that the quality of nursing care had been seriously affected by the rapid turnover of both junior nurses and the most experienced nurses. One of the consequences of understaffing was higher nurse-to-patient ratios, resulting in undue stress and widespread fatigue for nurses who receive no additional income for their higher workloads. The massive migration of nurses also led to serious geographical imbalances in the distribution of nurses. Of the estimated 35,744 nurses currently working in the Philippines, almost half are employed by national government hospitals and clinics, while 15% work in provincial and rural based hospitals operated by local government units (Manzano 2005). The scenario described above is magnified in rural areas, as many nurses migrate to Manila prior to obtaining overseas employment.

### Wages and Conditions of Employment

While the 1990s saw increased numbers of people undertaking nurse licensure examinations, the seemingly paradoxical situation of high overseas demand for overseas workers and domestic nursing shortages has not translated into improved wages and conditions domestically, as nurses are willing to endure poor wages and conditions in order to obtain the experience required for overseas employment (Ball 1996). Wage differentials between domestic and overseas employment (Table 2.2) indicate why nurses accept poor wages and conditions before seeking employment abroad. The average salary of nurses in the Philippines amounts to just almost P10,000 (US$215) per month, compared to the basic monthly salaries of Singapore (US$900), the United Kingdom (US$2600), and the United States (US$4600).

*Table 2.2* Salary of Nurses According to Position and Level

| Position | Tertiary Hospital | DOH Retained Government Hospital | Local Government Hospital | Private |
|---|---|---|---|---|
| Chief nurse | 20,415 | 19,729 | 16,864 | 19,293 |
| Assistant chief nurse/ division chief | 17,334 | 10,739 | 15,009 | 16,542 |
| Supervisor special unit | 13,715 | 15,009 | 13,857 | 13,065 |
| Supervisor ward unit | 13,715 | 13,357 | 13,357 | 13,065 |
| Head nurse | 12,206 | 11,888 | 11,888 | 11,466 |
| Staff nurse special area | 10,863 | 9,714 | 6,502 | 9,220 |
| Staff nurse ward | 8,605 | 9,714 | 6,502 | 9,220 |

Source: Manzano (2005). Salary in Philippine pesos.

It is not therefore surprising that for the majority of Filipino nurses, the major influencing factor on the choice of nursing as a career was the opportunity it provided for working overseas (Ball 2000). The international demand for nurses is so great that it has critically affected even the medical labour market of the Philippines: It is not uncommon for doctors to retrain as nurses, and more are opting for nursing over other medical fields, which has led to a decreased supply in other professions. Since nurses are willing to accept substandard wages in the Philippines—this leads to a feedback system which works simultaneously to depress nurses wages and encourage migration at the earliest opportunity. In short, the advent of systematic labour export of nurses has produced acute nursing shortages, rapid turnover of nursing personnel, declining standards in nurse education and health care, and the under-remuneration of nurses and nurse educators (Huno 1990; Ortin 1994; Ball 1996, 2004). With a global shortage of nurses becoming increasingly acute in the 1990s, labour market opportunities for Filipino nurses expanded into Asia and Europe to the extent that the Philippine Labor Secretary, Patricia Sto. Tomas stated that 'the country cannot comply with the industry demand for nurses abroad. There are simply too many job orders' (Dancel 2002).

The unparalleled 'success of the Philippines as an exporter of nurses,' has thus created a major crisis in health care delivery in the Philippines and raised serious questions over its long-term sustainability. Migration constitutes a massive loss of human capital: the Philippines bears the cost of training health professionals without fully utilising them for local needs (aside from the enormous revenues raised through remittances). The most junior and least well-qualified nurses remain in the health care system, hence the migrant nurses are the best educated and most experienced, and include many nurse educators, few of whom intend returning to nursing after working overseas (Ball 1996, 2000). The Philippines has become a training ground for nurses for an international market that can afford to provide the wages and working conditions that the Philippines cannot. These issues have serious transnational policy implications and major developmental impacts on the Philippines.

## THE DEMAND SIDE: IMBALANCES IN THE INTERNATIONL DISTRIBUTION OF NURSES— THE UNITED STATES AND SAUDI ARABIA

Acute imbalances in the distribution of nurses have led to substantial segments of developing country nurse labour markets becoming globalised to address increased demand for nurses in the oil rich states of the Gulf and in much of the rich world. Global demand for health services has aggravated human resource imbalances between first and third world nations (Bui 1987:88). Since the mid-1970s, rapid economic development in the Gulf States has been accompanied by commensurate growth in the health care industries of these countries, prompting the import of physicians and nurses (Mejia et al. 1979:49) The oil exporting nations experienced a spectacular increase in their total stock of foreign health workers primarily from India, Pakistan, Egypt, the Philippines and Korea (Bui 1987:91). Developed countries exploit the push factors from poor nations such as the Philippines, which, as discussed earlier, include low pay, severe understaffing, poor career structures and opportunities for further education. The following discussion analyses the demand dynamics of the two principal global employment destinations since the late 1970s for Filipino nurses: the United States and Saudi Arabia.

### The United States Market

The ongoing demand for nurses in the United States and much of the Western world is a complex combination of gender and labour market dynamics, the changing demography of the United States, and a restructuring of traditional methods of medical delivery. The United States nursing profession has experienced one of the most serious labour shortages since the 1980s. The national supply of registered nurses in 2000 was estimated to be 1.89 million, while demand was estimated at 2 million, or 6% more than needed, while demand grows at 1.7% annually (Anonymous 2002:24). The current shortage is more serious than previous shortages, as it is nationwide, is numerically greater, and affects all types of hospitals and nurses.

Explanations for the current and projected shortages included an 18% growth in the population, a growing population of elderly and medical advances. Widespread gender discrimination in nursing, as a female dominated profession, has depressed the attractiveness of nursing as a career. The financial rewards of nursing are not commensurate with the level of responsibility. Other occupationally based disincentives for people to become or remain nurses included: burnout; limited opportunities for upward mobility; insufficient authority and autonomy; increased work demands; and lack of participation of nurses in management decisions. While entry-level salaries for registered nurses are competitive with other professions, compression of the wage structure and relatively flat earning power creates severe retention problems (Aiken et al. 2001). Increasing dissatisfaction with nursing as a profession is also due to poor occupational prestige, shifts and weekend work. Most women want to work during the day, and may choose less interesting, less skilled, and lower paid jobs in order to do so. Nurses also perform many non-clinical, administrative, and management functions in hospitals, and the ratio of support personnel to professionals is substantially lower than in other industries.

Because fewer younger people are entering nursing and enrollments in nursing schools are declining, a third of registered nurses in the United States are more than 50 years of age and that proportion is rising, while turnover within hospitals is at approximately 20% per year, through dissatisfaction with increased workloads, low wages, and limited upward mobility (Dworkin 2002:23).

Demographic changes have intensified demand on nursing services. A rapidly aging population has expanded the proportion of population requiring health care, and hospitals in places with higher proportions of elderly (e.g., New York City, Miami and Texas) have experienced serious nursing shortages. Elderly patients require more intensive, longer term and complex care, and more labour-intensive nursing services. Hospitals are bearing the burden of providing a wider range of services to the growing elderly population, creating the need for more nurses (Dworkin 2002).

Changes in the form and philosophy of health care delivery have created new types of labour requirements. Medicare policies discourage in-patient and long-term hospital based care, which has meant an increasing emphasis on primary health care, especially amongst the elderly, and a move to home-based patient care. By contrast, hospitalized patients are sicker and require more care because of the reduction in discretionary admissions and the shorter average length of stay. The rapid growth of community-based health care organizations (e.g., home care, and walk-in medical treatment centres) offer professional nurses other choices of employment that often do not involve some of the less desirable aspects of hospital work including shift and/or weekend work.

## The Saudi Arabian Market

In rapidly growing oil-rich Middle Eastern nations such as Saudi Arabia, acute labour shortages have arisen for several reasons. Firstly, rapid economic development has taken place without the growth of an indigenous labour force to sustain and fuel such an expansion. Until the mid-1970s, many Saudi nationals were unable to take up employment in the modern sector. A politically motivated desire excluded most Saudi Arabians from the 'immorality' of modern sector employment. Despite a change in government policy encouraging an increased participation of nationals in the modern sector as part of a policy of 'Saudization,' both economic and social forces continue to work against full participation of nationals, particularly women, in this sector. In the health sector, a large infusion of capital has resulted in the rapid growth of health facilities to the extent that Saudi Arabia today boasts of some of the world's most advanced and sophisticated hospitals. A policy of free medical services and treatment for all citizens was first introduced during the reign of King Faisal (1964–1975). This resulted in rapid development of medical facilities for both preventative and curative health care. However, the growth in health facilities has not been accompanied by a corresponding rise of Saudi nationals to staff the health care sector. At the start of the 1990s some 92% of physicians, 92% of nurses and 73% of the technical staff were non-Saudi (Berhie 1991:821) though these proportions have subsequently declined considerably. Egyptians, Indians, Pakistanis and Filipinos mainly staff health services in base level nursing positions, and North Americans and British in senior or administrative positions. Studies on medical staffing in major institutions such as the King Faisal Specialist Hospital and Research Center indicated widespread employment dissatisfaction reflected in high staffing turnover rate with the average tenure among non-Saudi physicians and nurses being 2.3 years (Berhie 1991:821).

The acute shortage of nurses is also attributable to little enthusiasm among young Saudi Arabians for vocational training, combined with cultural and religious barriers that restrict female access to education and employment, especially in professions that require contact between men and women. Despite government policies to promote female education, social restrictions remain considerable, such that about half as many girls as boys attend school, consequently employment possibilities for women remain severely limited. Not surprisingly, Saudi Arabian women have very low labour force participation rates with less than one in ten actually employed in the paid workforce, and few of these (7.5%) are employed as nurses in the Kingdom's health care system although the number has been slowly increasing. The Saudi Arabian government thus depends heavily on expatriate nursing staff.

## GLOBAL IMBALANCES IN THE
## RIGHTS OF FILIPINO NURSES

Large imbalances occur in the international distribution of nurses. Sending nations tend to be Third World nations that supply capital rich nations with nurses, a situation that has exacerbated pre-existing imbalances in health care services in labour exporting nations. In both the United States and Saudi Arabia, Filipinos and nurses mainly from other Third World nations fill positions that nationals of receiving countries are unwilling to do, or are prevented from doing. Employment for Filipino nurses in the United States, the Gulf and elsewhere means the occupying of marginalised and racialised positions in the labour markets of both major nurse-importing regions. The labour migration of nurses to the Gulf is structured according to a racialised hierarchy of labour. According to the Hospital Corporation of America, principals recruiting workers for hospitals in the Gulf, and particularly in Saudi Arabia, recruit their labour according to the following racialised division of labour:

> *Americans and Europeans:* Senior hospital administrative, senior technical and supervisory positions, e.g., hospital administrators, doctors, head nurses.
>
> *Filipinos and Egyptians:* Middle status positions e.g., registered nurses and technical staff not in senior positions.
>
> *Sri Lankans, Pakistanis:* Low ranking positions—i.e., unskilled jobs, e.g., orderly and janitorial positions (Ball 1991:196).

Nurses, like other contract workers, are recruited and paid according to an international hierarchy, where more powerful and skilled positions are more readily accessible to workers from developed nations.

The degree to which Filipino (or any other) nurses employed in both nations have recourse to legal and institutionalised workplace practices to voice their concerns varies enormously between Saudi Arabia and the United States. In the Gulf, there are few mechanisms for nurses to lodge workplace abuse complaints, unless through the Philippine Embassy, which has little power to negotiate with employers on behalf of Filipino nurses. Nurses working in the Gulf are largely employed there due to their inability to obtain employment in the West, for financial reasons (such as recruitment costs) or due to the lesser quality of their qualifications. Filipino nurses often see their employment in Saudi Arabia as a mechanism to improve their practical and academic nursing skills as well as their financial capacity to sit the CGFNS or pay the recruitment fees necessary to obtain employment in the United States or more recently, in Europe. Employment in Saudi Arabia is simply a transition point to employment in western nations. Consequently, many Filipino nurses are willing to endure difficult, often abusive workplaces in order to accumulate the necessary capital and experience, and are much more reluctant to lodge complaints over racially based workplace abuse than they would elsewhere (Ball 1991).

In both major nurse-importing nations Filipino nurses report that they are often 'talked down to' by patients, colleagues and members of the public, and regularly experience racial abuse. They are more likely to be reprimanded for a minor misdemeanour that would be ignored by a Western nurse. As a result, in the United States, the confidence and motivation of many Filipino nurses is reported to be waning, despite widespread evidence of the capability of Filipino nurses to run large nursing departments. By contrast, there is an increasing incidence of lawsuits and class actions against employers that are discriminating against Filipino nurses in wages, assignments and other workplace conditions. For example, at the end of the 1990s, a legal suit filed with the U.S. Equal Employment Opportunity Commission against a hospital in Kansas by 65 Filipino nurses claiming discrimination based on their national origin, was recently successful resulting in a $2.1 million compensation payment.

The human rights position of migrant Filipino nurses varies. In Saudi Arabia, Filipino women occupy one of the lowest rungs on the ladder of racial tolerance: They are foreigners, Asian and women working in an industry which requires the crossing of major cultural taboos, such as contact between men and women outside of marriage. The vulnerability of Filipino nurses in this gendered and racialised hierarchy is mediated by the acute demand for nurses, which offers some non-institutionalised form of protection. Within Saudi Arabia there is a clear recognition of the need to retain nurses, hence greater attention has been given to job satisfaction and issues posed by the divergent backgrounds of nursing staff (Al-Ahmadi 2002). Such initiatives provide for the possibility of the development of institutional mechanisms that improve the labour and human rights of Filipino nurses and others from the developing world. In the case of the United States and other Western nations experiencing acute shortages of nurses, the fact that human and labour rights are integral to the rule of law, combined with the seriousness of nursing shortages provides a strong basis for increased institutional recognition of the rights of nurses. In addition, overseas Filipinos are well-known for their ability to network through NGOs and professional bodies within cities and through the internet, providing both the basis for information sharing as the basis for legal action, and the lobbying of Federal and State bodies responsible for regulating employment and workplace practices. The considerable divergence in the rights and ability to mobilize, alongside links with supportive NGOs (Ball and Piper 2002), emphasises the perceived hierarchy of destination states, and the particular distinction between the United States and Saudi Arabia.

## CONCLUSION

Labour export and the use of foreign labour is, at its most general level, generated by the requirements of capitalist accumulation, and is highly selective. Even amongst the 'unskilled' it is the most able, highly motivated, fit and youthful workers that successfully weave their way through a myriad of obstacles to obtain overseas employment. International labour migration and the large-scale movement of workers from less-developed countries to rapidly expanding economies have relatively recently been acknowledged as significant components of divergent globalisation (Castles 2000, Ball 2004, Ball and Piper 2006). The characteristics of the labour supply and the terms under which that labour is supplied reflect a sending nation's role in the world economy, the strength of its political ties and dependencies, and the degree of economic necessity to find employment for its nationals abroad. The contemporary global migration of Filipino nurses has intensified over the last thirty years to such an extent that there are now more Filipino nurses employed globally than within the Philippines. The scale of both the migration of Filipino nurses and its impacts on the health care system of the Philippines have increased to the extent that the Philippines government is challenged to control them. The Philippines is now producing nurses for an international rather than a national labour market, resulting in almost three decades of attrition of the Philippine health care system. While not ignoring the positive contribution of nurse migration for foreign exchange generation through remittances, this process of divergent development suggests the need for new dialogue between nurse supplying and importing countries.

This ongoing brain drain is also characterised by a weakening of the rights of nurses (as part of a global hierarchy of labour) in their contracted and globalised form. In both the two primary but very different nations importing nurses, Filipino nurses largely fill positions that for structural and cultural reasons nationals are unwilling to fill. This contributes to the marginalisation that many nurses experience, particularly in the Gulf, but also in the United States, where legal action is beginning to occur. However, there are no opportunities for legal recourse for nurses in vulnerable positions in the Gulf, hence broader transnational employment standards are required for international migrants alongside mechanisms for redressing institutionalised discrimination (see Ball and Piper 2002) for migrant nurses.

This expanding transnationalism of migration thus necessitates the parallel, but substantially belated, development of transnational methods of regulatory governance specifically oriented to improving equity between nurse labour supplying and importing nations in the terms of trade for nurses in the global labour market. Transnational regulations might include a continuum of approaches from intensive stakeholder dialogues, through persuasion to command and control mechanisms. Such regulatory governance to improve the developmental impacts and outcomes of labour migration can build upon existing models, frameworks and conventions that govern trade in commodities, refugee flows and regional multinational immigration systems. Multilateral organisations such as the WHO, the ILO and the International Organization for Migration are well placed to lead the way in addressing the hitherto unprecedented scale of migration of nurses and the global disparities it results in for nations such as the Philippines that are the providers of nurses, but not necessarily the beneficiaries of the process.

## REFERENCES

Aiken, L, Clarke, S, Sloane, D and Sochalski, J (2001) Nurses' reports on hospital care in five countries, *Health Affairs*, 20(3), 43–53.

Al-Ahmadi, H (2002) Job satisfaction of nurses in Ministry of Health Hospitals in Riyadh, Saudi Arabia, *Saudi Medical Journal*, 23, 645–650.

Anonymous (2002) HHS predicts growing nurse shortage, *Healthcare Financial Management*, 56(10), 24.

Asian Development Bank (2003) *Key Indicators: Education for Global Participation*, Manila: ADB.

Baguioro, L (2002) Emigration of nurses hurts Philippines' health services, *Straits Times*, 7 September.

Ball, R (1991) *The process of international contract labour migration from the Philippines: The case of Filipino nurses*, Unpublished Ph.D dissertation, University of Sydney.

Ball, R (1996) Nation building or dissolution: The globalization of nursing—the case of the Philippines, *Pilipinas*, 27, 67–92.

Ball, R (1997) The role of the state in the globalization of labour markets: The case of the Philippines, *Environment and Planning A*, 29, 1603–1628.

Ball, R (2000) The individual and global processes: Labour migration decision-making and Filipino nurses, *Pilipinas*, 34, 2000, 63–92.

Ball, R (2004) Divergent development, racialised rights: Globalised labour markets and the trade of nurses—the case of the Philippines, *Women's Studies International Forum*, 27, 119–33.

Ball, R (2006) Trading labour: Socio-economic and political impacts and dynamics of labour export from the Philippines, 1973–2004, in Kaur, A and Metcalfe, I (Eds), *Mobility, Labour Migration and Border Controls in Asia*, New York: Palgrave Macmillan, pp. 115–138.

Ball, R and Piper, N (2002) Globalisation of Asian labour migration: Implications for the nation-state, citizenship and human rights, *Political Geography*, 21, 1013–1034.

Ball, R and Piper, N (2006) Trading labour-trading rights: The regional dynamics of rights recognition for migrant workers in the Asia-Pacific, in Hewison, K and Young, K. (Eds), *Transnational Migration and Work in Asia*, New York: Routledge, pp. 213–234.

Barber, P (2000) Agency in Philippine women's labour migration and provisional diaspora, *Women's Studies International Forum*, 23, 399–411.

Berhie, G (1991) Emerging issues in health planning in Saudi Arabia: The effect of organisation and development of the health care system, *Social Science and Medicine*, 33, 815–824.

Bui, D (1987) Health manpower imbalances in the '90s: A worldwide panorama, In Z Bankowski and A Mejia (Eds), *Health Manpower Out of Balance: Conflicts and Prospects*, Geneva: IOM, pp. 81–92.

Carlos, R (2002) On the determinants of international migration in the Philippines, *International Migration Review*, 36, 81–102.

Castles, S (2000) *Ethnicity and globalization: From migrant worker to transnational citizen*, London: Sage.

Chant, S and McIlwaine, C (1995) *Women of a lesser cost: Female labour, foreign exchange and Philippine development*, London: Pluto Press.

Dancel, J (2002) Demand for Filipino nurses high in the international job market, *The Manila Times*, March 2.

Dworkin, R (2002) Where have all the nurses gone? *Public Interest*, Summer, 148, 23–36.

Findlay, S (1987) *Rural Development and Migration: A Study of Family Choices in the Philippines*, Boulder: Westview.

Huno, R (1990) *A study on the state of nurse education in the Philippines*, Association of Deans, Philippine College of Nursing, Presented at The Convention of Deans, The Midtown Hotel, May.

Joyce, R and Hunt, C (1985) Philippine nurses and the brain drain, *Philippine Quarterly of Culture and Society*, 13, 297–318.

Manzano, G (2005) "Quantitative dimensions: Professional manpower demand, supply and migration trends," Preliminary draft, Philippines Country Report.

Mejia, A, Pizurki, H and Royston, E (1979) *Physician and Nurse Migration: Analysis and Policy Implications*, Geneva: WHO.

Ortin, E (1994) The remuneration of nursing personnel in the Philippines. In *The remuneration of nursing personnel: An international perspective*, Geneva: ILO, pp.183–227.

Philippine Overseas Employment Administration (POEA) (1986) *Annual Report*, Manila: Department of Labor and Employment.

Philippine Overseas Employment Administration (POEA) (1999) Unpublished Data, Manila: Department of Labor and Employment.

Philippine Overseas Employment Administration (2004) Deployed new hire land-based workers by sex, 1992–2002 (http://www.poea.gov.ph/html/statistics.html) accessed 11 November 2004.

Piper, N and Ball, R (2001) The globalisation of Asian migrant labour: The Philippine–Japan connection, *Journal of Contemporary Asia*, 31, 533–554.

Pratt, G (1999) From registered nurse to registered nanny: Discursive geographies of Filipina domestic workers in Vancouver, BC, *Economic Geography*, 75, 215–236.

Quesada, M (1985) The Economics of Nursing, *Philippine Journal of Nursing*, 55 (4), 98-101.

Tan, E (2000) Labor market adjustments to large scale emigration: The Philippine Case, Paper Presented at the APEC HRD Taskforce on International Migration, Academic Sineca, Taipei, October.

Tan, E (2001) Labor Market Adjustment to Large Scale Emigration: The Philippine Case, *Asian and Pacific Migration Journal*, 10, 379–400.

Trager, L (1984) Family strategies and the migration of women: Migrants to Dagupan City, Philippines. *International Migration Review*, 18, 1264–1277.

Tyner, J (1996) The gendering of Philippine international labour migration, *The Professional Geographer*, 48, 405–416.

Tyner, J (2004) *Made in the Philippines: Gendered discourses and the making of migrants*, London: Routledge.

Venzon, L (1985) Nurses rapid turnover: Effects on quality nursing care, *Philippine Journal of Nursing*, 55(3), 84–90.

Yeoh, B and Huang, S (1998) Negotiating public spaces: Strategies and styles of migrant female domestic workers in Singapore, *Urban Studies*, 35, 583–602.

# 3 New Opportunities
## United Kingdom Recruitment of Filipino Nurses

*James Buchan*

This chapter examines the dynamics and policy context of the international migration and recruitment of nurses from the Philippines to the United Kingdom (UK). The Philippines has a long history of 'exporting' nurses and other health professionals to other countries and regions, such as the United States (US) and the Gulf; more recently it has become a major source for other English speaking countries (e.g., the UK and Ireland), and it is currently developing a bilateral agreement with Japan for recruitment of nurses. The Philippines is thus one of the most important national players in the global healthcare scene.

The chapter draws on previous research by the author (e.g., Buchan et al. 2005), to provide an overview of the linkage between the Philippines and the UK, within the broader context of flows to other English speaking countries. In particular, the rapid rise in inward recruitment from the Philippines to the UK is assessed—as is the subsequent rapid decline. The chapter then focuses in more detail on the profile and experiences of Filipino nurses in the UK.

## "TRAINING FOR EXPORT"?: THE PHILIPPINES AND NURSING

The Philippines is commonly regarded as one of the main global sources of English speaking nurses. Many nurses who train in the Philippines plan to move abroad as soon as they qualify, with the intention of remitting income to their extended families (Ball 2004). While there is no explicit policy in the Philippines that encourages migration of nurses, a number of government agencies facilitate the deployment and the protection of Filipinos abroad— the Philippine Overseas Employment Administration (POEA) and the Office of Workers Welfare Administration (OWWA, Lorenzo 2002, Lorenzo 2005), with the main underlying motivation being to stimulate inward flow of international currency to the country via remittances (Ball 2004).

The Philippines has a long tradition of 'training for export' of nurses and other female workers (Barber 2000). Initially the main destination countries for nurses were the US and the Middle East (Choy 2003, Ball 2004), and the nurse education system in the Philippines was primarily orientated to serve foreign labour markets (Hawthorne 2001, Ball 2004). In more recent years, the range of destination countries has broadened. Recent estimates suggest that some 70–85% of all employed Filipino nurses are working internationally, which amounts to more than 150,000 nurses (Aiken et al. 2004, Galvez Tan 2006), with 100,000 having left the Philippines in the period 1994–2003, as part of an upward trend (Galvez Tan 2006).

After stagnating in the mid-1990s, due to a reduction in demand from 'traditional' destination countries, particularly the US (Galvez Tan 2006), the annual outflow of nurses in recent years began to increase again in the late 1990s (Figure 3.1) . Demand for Filipino nurses from other countries has varied markedly over time, with a huge outflow to the US and the Gulf in the 1980s but lower demand from these countries in the 1990s.

Galvez Tan (2006) suggests that the most recent 'top five' destination countries have been the US, the UK, Saudi Arabia, Ireland and Singapore, although trends up to 2003 highlight significant variations, with Saudi Arabia being the consistent main destination, the US dropping down in the period 1996–2002, and the UK and Ireland have a 'spike' of significance from 1999–2000 (Figure 3.2).

The reasons for Filipino nurses leaving the country were examined by Lorenzo (2005), using focus group discussions. This highlighted 'push' factors including low salaries, low expectations for career development, and limited employment opportunities, in contrast to perceived 'pull' factors of much higher earnings and career opportunities elsewhere. These push fac-

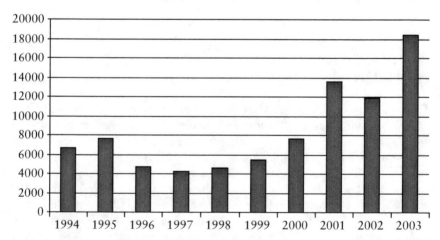

*Figure 3.1* Nurses leaving the Philippines, 1994–2003.

*Source:* Galvez Tan 2006 (note reported likelihood of undercounting and therefore underestimate of actual outflow).

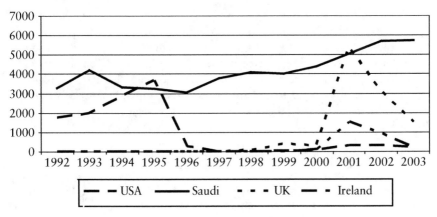

*Figure 3.2* Outflow of nurses from Philippines to selected countries, 1992–2003.

*Source:* Lorenzo 2005/POEA. (Note: likelihood of undercounting)

tors have also been reported by other authors (e.g., Ball 2004; see also Ball, Kelly and D'Addorio, this book).

Remittances can represent a significant source of hard currency for developing countries (International Organisation for Migration 2004), and nurses from the Philippines are important generators of funds for their home countries. A recent study of international nurses working in London (Buchan et al. 2005) found that Filipino nurses reported remitting the highest level of their income, of any nationality of nurses surveyed. Lorenzo (2005) has however noted that the remittances sent back do not directly benefit the health system.

Whilst the POEA facilitates international recruitment by supporting the work of recruitment agencies and by developing bilateral agreements (e.g., with the UK), not all nurses recruited from the Philippines are channelled through the POEA. Buchan and Seccombe (2005) reported that UK government sources indicated that only 186 Filipino nurses had been recruited to the UK via the bilateral agreement—whilst in the single year 2003–2004 more than 5,000 Filipino nurses were first registered in the UK. This suggests the bilateral agreement was of only limited relevance, other than being an enabling agreement, and that many other nurses from the Philippines were being recruited directly by employers or agencies. More recently, Galvez Tan (2006) has noted that US based hospitals have been directly recruiting nurses from the Philippines, by-passing the POEA system.

The role of recruitment agencies in facilitating the move of Filipino nurses to other countries has been highlighted—and criticised—as a means of exploitation of nurses and their families: It may be said that such contractualization provides an opportunity for workers in the developing countries to earn more while their countries also benefit

from additional foreign exchange earnings through their wage remittances. But the placement agencies which subcontract the recruitment
actually take advantage of high unemployment rates and demand for
jobs in order to charge exorbitant placement fees. Such demand for
survival forces Third World families to mortgage properties or go to
loan sharks in order to cough up the large sums demanded. In effect,
placement agencies take a share of the future wages of the contract
workers

(Tujan 2002)

The rapid growth in the provision of nurse education in the Philippines,
in response to demand for training places, has been met primarily by the
private sector. The total number of nursing schools has grown from about
40 in the 1970s, to 251 in June 2003, to 470 in July 2006 (Galvez Tan
2006). Lorenzo (2005) reported that annual output from nurse education
in the Philippines has risen sharply in recent years, to 10,000–15,000. Most
education is provided in private sector institutions, and nurses pay for their
education. This rapid growth also makes the sector vulnerable to any shifts
in the level of demand for nurses from other countries (Ball 2004).

The growth in numbers has also been associated with an overall decline in
pass rates in the national licensure examination for nurses—from 80–90%
in the 1980s, to 61% in 1994 and 42% in 2006 (Galvez Tan 2006). Moreover the national nurse licensing examination in 2006 in the Philippines
was hit by scandal, with allegations that some board members were bribed
to 'leak' questions to some candidates prior to the examination. This led to
re-organisation of the board and concerns being expressed that the drive to
obtain a nursing licence (and hence an overseas job) led nursing students to
fall victim to such scams, while the quality of nurse education in the Philippines was consequently suffering (*Asia-Pacific Post*, 2006).

Another aspect of the growth in provision of nurse education as a 'ticket'
out of the country is the phenomenon of Filipino doctors retraining as
nurses. Doctors find it much more difficult to migrate and maintain their
profession than do nurses, so many decide to retrain to make it easier to
move abroad. Galvez Tan (2006) reported 45 schools in the Philippines
offering the retraining course, with up to 80% of government employed
physicians doing part-time re-training.

Whilst the Philippines is often regarded as a major 'exporter' of nurses,
this is not a reflection of the country's health system being well staffed with
nurses (Ball 2004). The low staffed, poorly paid and funded situation for
nurses in the country, contrasts with that in the Gulf, Europe and North
America. Lorenzo (2005) estimated that in 2003, only 29,000 nurses were
working in the Philippines, compared to approximately 164,000 Filipino
nurses working abroad. Galvez Tan (2006) has highlighted low staffing
ratios in the Philippines (1 nurse to 40 or 60 patients in rural hospitals),

relatively low funding for the health sector, and a decrease in health service coverage because of out-migration.

In the next section, the connection between the Philippines and the UK is examined in greater detail. As noted earlier, the UK was not a traditional destination for Filipino nurses until the late 1990s. The section thus reports on trends in the inflow of nurses to the UK, and examines their experiences there.

## FILIPINO NURSES IN THE UNITED KINGDOM

The UK was highly active in the international recruitment of health professionals from 1999 until 2005. The new NHS Plan, introduced in the aftermath of the election of Tony Blair's Labour government in 1997, led to planned and funded expansion of the National Health Service (NHS), and the identified need to increase rapidly the numbers of nurses and doctors working in the NHS. National targets were set for workforce growth in the NHS, which drove the process, with significant increases in funding.

Whilst public sector investment was channelled into increasing the number of UK based training places for nurses, it was evident that this would not provide the 'quick fix' that was required. Four years was too long, for the policy makers charged with the increased staffing of the NHS. Therefore, as one means of achieving rapid workforce growth, over the period 1998–2005, there was an explicit policy emphasis on international recruitment of nurses (see Department of Health 2004).

Whilst reliance on nurses from other regions, such as Ireland, the West Indies and other Commonwealth countries, was well established in the NHS, what distinguished developments at the end of the 1990s was the high level of resources devoted to co-ordinated recruitment activity, to rapidly 'scale up' the workforce in the NHS, and meet the staffing targets. This period also coincided with growth in the Irish economy and health system which changed Ireland from being a net 'loser' of nurses to a country that was itself active in international recruitment. One traditional source market for nurses had largely disappeared. Other possible source countries, particularly in Africa, had become politically, and ethically, more problematic. Whilst aiming for rapid growth in international recruitment of nurses, the UK government was also aware of the negative media coverage that ensued when recruitment was targeted at understaffed developing countries, particularly in Anglophone Africa. It also came under pressure over 'poaching' staff, from African politicians, including Nelson Mandela.

In order to attempt to head off controversy, international recruitment of nurses and other health professionals to the NHS in England was codified within a so-called ethical approach. Guidelines for NHS employers were first established in 1999; a Code of Practice of international recruitment for NHS employers was introduced in 2001, and updated in 2004 (Department of Health, 2004). This code required NHS employers not to actively recruit from developing countries unless there is a government-to-government agreement that this is acceptable. The list was determined on the basis of level of economic development, and covers more than 150 countries. A request can be made by the government of the source developing country that they wish to be removed from the list. Such working agreements exist with only three developing countries—China, India, and the Philippines—all others being effectively designated as 'no-go' areas for active NHS recruitment.

The code does not stop individual health professionals from these countries applying for jobs, or travelling to the UK for training. Neither has it stopped 'back door recruitment'—where UK private sector employers (not covered by the code) internationally recruit nurses from developing countries on the list, and these nurses then move rapidly (within a matter of weeks in some cases) to jobs in the NHS (Buchan et al. 2005). The code did concentrate greater recruitment attention on the designated source countries of 'ethically acceptable' nurses, including the Philippines.

Initially this NHS led international recruitment activity was uncoordinated, undertaken by individual employers with, or without, recruitment agency support (Buchan 2002). The NHS then set up a network of regional international recruitment co-ordinators, to minimise overlap of recruitment effort and achieve economies of scale. The NHS in England also established a website dedicated specifically to recruitment from the Philippines (http://www.nursinguk.nhs.uk) though this no longer operates.

How significant has been the flow of nurses into the UK from the Philippines and from other countries? UK registration data give some idea. Any nurse from a non-EU (European Union) country who wishes to practice in the UK must apply for, and be admitted to, the register of the Nurses and Midwives Council (NMC). Unlike the US, where international nurses are required to sit a national examination and a State Board licensure, there is a 'one stop' process in the UK: nurses apply to the NMC and if their educational qualifications and career history are judged appropriate are accepted onto the register. In many cases, overseas nurses may be required to work a period of supervised practice or adaptation to remedy any identified deficiencies in their skills and competencies. This period of adaptation is normally two or three months. More recently, in September 2006, the NMC introduced new requirements that overseas nurses complete a 20-day Overseas Nurses Programme (ONP), which reduced inflow because of the time and cost incurred in finding and taking this UK based course.

NMC data make it possible to assess the relative size of each country source of 'new' nurses working in the UK. Figure 3.3 shows the total number of international nurses registering annually with the NMC between 1998–1999 and 2005–2006, with the number from the Philippines identified separately (the NMC registration 'year' is 1st April–31st March). It illustrates both the rapid growth in numbers of nurses from other countries registering to practice in the UK over the period up to 2003, and that

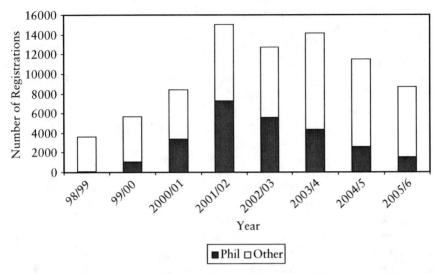

*Figure 3.3* Admissions to the UK nurse register from the Philippines and from all other non-EU countries, 1998/89–2004/5.

*Source:* Nurses and Midwives Council, UK.

the numbers registering from the Philippines rose dramatically, from 52 in 1998–1999 to 7,235 in 2001–2002, but by 2005–2006 this figure had dropped back to 1,541. In the period between 1998–1999 and 2005–2006, more than 24,000 nurses from the Philippines were registered in the UK. In the years 2000–2001 to 2003–2004 the Philippines was the single most important non-UK source of nurses for the UK register. (India has since become the leading source country.)

The reason for this rapid growth in the inflow of nurses from a country that did not have traditional links with the UK relates primarily to active international recruitment by the NHS, assisted, as noted above, by the relative reduction in employment opportunities for Filipino nurses in their more usual destinations—the US (Ball, this book). It is not just the UK that switched to the Philippines as a source of recruits: Large numbers of Filipino nurses were recruited to Ireland (Yeates, this book), and smaller numbers to other countries such as Norway (Buchan and Sochalski 2004).

The relative contribution of 'new' non-UK nurses peaked in 2001–2002, when more than half of all new nurses being registered in the UK came from non-UK sources, and has since declined. In 2005–2006 international nurses accounted for about 30% of new registrants, the lowest proportion since the late 1990s. The reason for the actual and relative decline in the contribution of international recruitment was the growth in numbers of new UK nurses coming out of UK based training in 2005 and 2006, combined with fiscal problems of some NHS employers in 2006. This led to local recruitment freezes and some redundancies (Health Committee, House of Commons 2006). With media stories of newly qualified UK nurses being unable to obtain jobs, the focus on active, nationally led international recruitment rapidly ended. In April 2006, general nursing jobs were removed from the list of 'shortage' jobs which were fast tracked for work permit applications, making it much less likely that Filipino nurses would be able to gain an employer/sponsor, and therefore a work permit to enter the UK.

Whilst NMC data can assist in tracking overall trends in the numbers of international nurses becoming eligible to practice in the UK, there is no complete and accurate published data available on where these nurses are located within the UK, or what type of work they are undertaking. The majority of working nurses in the UK are employed in the NHS (hospital and primary care), and the remainder are working in the independent (private) sector, in nursing homes and in the relatively small independent acute hospital sector. Both the NHS and the independent sector have been active in recruiting internationally. The Philippines Overseas Employment Administration listed the 'top ten' Filipino licensed agencies and direct recruiters of nurses for the UK, in 2003, just after the peak of recruitment activity (Table 3.1). Significantly the top eight UK 'employers' were in fact recruiting agencies.

Most of the limited published research on Filipino nurses working in the UK has focused on small scale cohort studies (Daniel et al. 2001, Withers and Snowball 2003, Parry and Lipp 2006). The first of these used two focus groups of Filipino nurses working in one UK hospital; one group had been in the UK for three months at the time of the research, the other had more recently arrived and were still undergoing the hospital orientation programme. The main reasons for both groups going to the UK were 'career prospects' and 'financial security.' The nurses felt that they had a heavy workload in the UK (in part at least because common practice in the Philippines was for patients' relatives to assist with care). Other features noted by the nurses were lack of respect for the elderly in the UK, differences in medical terminology (the nurses had been trained in American English which uses different words for some drugs, etc.), and greater specialization in UK nursing.

Withers and Snowball (2003) reported on some 120 Filipino nurses in one NHS trust in England, highlighting unmet financial expectations. Differences emerged between respondents' high expectations of nursing and living in the UK and their actual experiences. The majority described their financial expectations as being unmet. Though many experiences were positive, some faced problems during recruitment and in their clinical areas, and some perceived racial discrimination from patients and colleagues. Withers and Snowball concluded that the Filipino nurses had high expectations of earning more money, of having a higher standard of living and of gaining professionally, in coming to work in the UK, but that unmet expectations could lead to dissatisfaction, affect attitudes and behaviour and lead to eventual resignation from the organisation. However, where there have been

*Table 3.1* Recruiting Agencies and UK Employers 2003

| *Top 10 Licensed Agencies Deploying Filipino Nurses in UK* |
|---|
| 1. Add International Services Inc. |
| 2. Bison Management Corporation |
| 3. Arlimur Professional Services |
| 4. DHC International Recruitment and Consultancy, Inc. |
| 5. TCI Recruitment Corporation (TCI Overseas Placement Services) |
| 6. Warwick International Recruitment Agencies Philippines Inc. |
| 7. Vilman International Manpower and General Services |
| 8. Mariposa International Services Co. Inc. |
| 9. Bond Worldwide Inc. (for OGP Phils, Inc.) |
| 10. Manila Resources Development Corporation |

| *Top 10 Employers in UK Hiring Filipinos in 2003* |
|---|
| 1. Drake Personnel Limited |
| 2. Alliance Manpower Services |
| 3. Arlimur Professional Services (UK) Limited |
| 4. Abbot Healthcare Limited |
| 5. DHC International Recruitment (UK) Limited |
| 6. O'Grady Peyton Int'l (Europe) Limited |
| 7. Warwick International Recruitment Limited |
| 8. Mental Health Care (UK) Limited |
| 9. Barts and the London NHS Thrust |
| 10. The Royal Wolverhampton Hospital NHS Trust |

Source : POEA ( www.poea.gov.ph/country/uk.htm )

comprehensive and sensitive recruitment, induction and adaptation training programmes, as in the case of a small group of Filipino specialist nurses working in cancer care in a UK hospice (Parry and Lipp 2006), satisfaction and high retention rates have followed.

Further details of the experiences of Filipino nurses and other international nurses are covered in a recent survey of international nurses working in London (Buchan et al. 2005). The survey data, re-analysed here, assist in developing a better understanding of the profile and motivation of Filipino nurses. The survey was conducted in late 2004 with 380 respondents (40% response rate), all of whom had begun nursing in the UK within the previous four years. The 380 respondents came from more than 30 different countries of training; the Philippines was the most commonly reported, with 92 respondents, one in four of the total. Nigeria and South Africa were the other most commonly reported countries.

What had most influenced nurses to come to the UK, depended on source country. All the Australian, New Zealand and US nurses indicated that the main reason that they were in the UK was personal, linked to travel and experiencing a different way of life. Some nurses from Africa and India reported social reasons as being the main driver, primarily linked to joining family already in the UK. Nurses from the Philippines had primarily come for economic reasons. Nearly all Filipino trained nurses (96%) reported that a recruitment agency had been involved in their move to the UK. For the Filipino nurses that recruitment agency was usually based in their home country, but for most other nurses the agency was international, or based primarily in the UK. Nearly three out of every four nurses (72%) who reported using an agency had to pay for at least part of its services (i.e., the recruiting employer was not covering all the recruitment/registration/travel costs). Filipinos (74%) were more likely than any other nationality group to report that they had made payments to recruitment agencies. Two thirds (69%) of all the international nurse respondents were working in NHS hospitals in London, 13% were working in the private sector hospitals and 10% in private sector nursing homes (Figure 3.4). A higher proportion of Filipino nurses were working in NHS hospitals.

Most of the nurses were the major or sole 'breadwinner' contributing to household income. One third (37%) were contributing all of the household income, a further quarter (25%) contributed more than half, and a further one in five (20%) contributed about half. The pattern of responses from Filipino nurses was similar to the overall response (Figure 3.5).

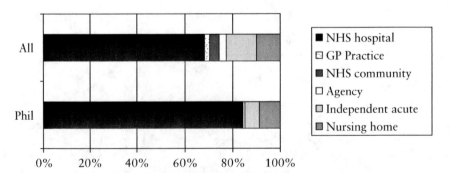

*Figure 3.4* Current employer, main job, by main regional groupings.

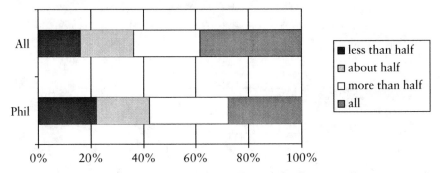

*Figure 3.5* What percentage of total household income do your earnings as a nurse represent?

More than half (57%) regularly sent remittances to their home country (Figure 3.6). However the pattern of remitting varied significantly by region of origin, with three quarters of Filipino nurses (73%) regularly remitting money home. They were also more likely to report that they remitted a high proportion of their income—about half of Filipino respondents were remitting at least a quarter of their income or more than 50% of their income (Figure 3.7). At that time (2004) the average full-time pay for a nurse in the UK was approximately £24,500 (though nurses in London earned more than the national average because of a regional supplement).

Respondents were asked to indicate how long they planned to remain in the UK as a nurse (Figure 3.8). The majority (60%), including the Filipino nurses, indicated that they intended to stay for at least five years, with a further quarter (25%) planning to stay between two and five years. Differences emerged when respondents were asked if they were considering a move to another country (Figure 3.9). Just under half (43%) said they were

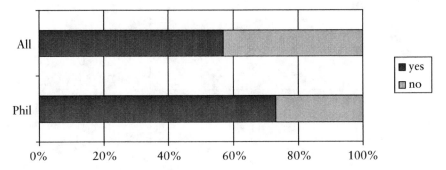

*Figure 3.6* Do you regularly send money to your country?

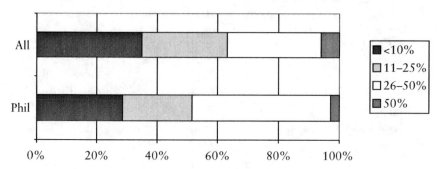

Figure 3.7 Proportion of earnings remitted home.

considering a move, but nearly two thirds of Filipino nurses (63%) were doing so, and nearly all of the Filipino nurses (83%) who were thinking of moving were intending moving to the US.

NMC data on outflow from the UK only show the possible destination of the UK registered nurses, but not their original source country, so cannot be used to assess the extent of onward (or return) movement of Filipino nurses. However, some additional evidence that the UK may be a staging post for some Filipino nurses whose ultimate goal is employment in the US is in data collated by the US based Commission on Graduates of Foreign Nursing Schools (CGFNS). The CGFNS screening examination can be taken in London, and is an early step towards applying for licensure to practice in the US. In 2005, more than 85% of the nurses who took the exam in London had not been educated in the UK. The majority of these were from the Philippines and India (Table 3.2).

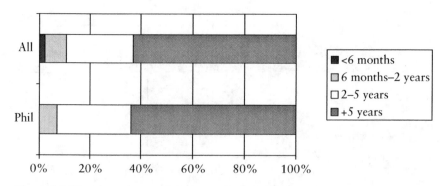

Figure 3.8 How long do you plan to stay in the UK as a nurse?

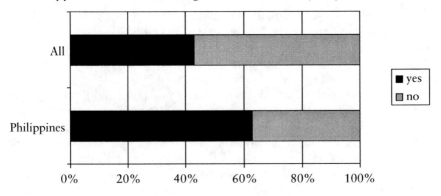

*Figure 3.9* Are you considering a move to another country?

## CONCLUSION

The Philippines is well established as the leading 'train for export' source country for nurses, although India is rising rapidly in prominence. The Filipino 'model' is predicated on nurse education primarily being provided in the private sector, with nurses paying for their education, with the expectation that they will be able to recoup the expense when they work abroad. Without the demand for foreign based employment, with the commensurate return to the Philippines of hard currency via remittances, the high levels of output from Philippine nurse education would not exist, as there would be neither the same level of demand for nurse education, nor the support of government agencies for migration.

The relatively low level of funding for the Philippines own health system, and associated low nurse to patient ratio, emphasises that the large scale of nurse education in the Philippines is largely independent of home based

*Table 3.2* Applicants Taking CGFNS Examination in London, by Country of Education, 2005

| Country of Education | Number of Test Takers (N = 265) |
|---|---|
| Philippines | 90 |
| India | 79 |
| UK | 36 |
| Nigeria | 22 |
| Other countries | 38 |

Source: CGFNS

demand for nurses. The growth in nursing schools in the private sector has occurred to meet overseas demand for nurses, rather than responding to national demand. The Philippines is a major exporter of nurses, not because there is any lack of need for more nurses in the Philippines, but because there is a lack of good employment opportunities.

The international nurse link between the Philippines and UK developed extremely rapidly in the late 1990s. The Philippines was a ready, 'ethical' source of English speaking nurses, and therefore an attractive option for NHS recruiters seeking to rapidly expand their workforce. Whilst there was no real previous link between the Philippines and the UK, the Philippines model, oriented toward the US, could easily be repositioned to meet UK requirements, particularly when the US was not actively recruiting.

The ability to undertake large scale active international recruitment was a key characteristic of the NHS in England from the latter part of the last decade. It has potential advantages of economy of scale in recruitment activity, scope to co-ordinate such activity, and inter-departmental opportunities to influence government policy on migration, which do not exist for individual private sector employers. The UK used these advantages in the period 1997–2005 to recruit large numbers of nurses from the Philippines. However, the number of nurses recruited to the UK has subsequently declined markedly, as staffing targets are met or exceeded, and as more home based nurses enter the workplace. UK recruitment efforts may have been assisted indirectly by reduced employment opportunities for Filipino nurses in the more traditional destination of the US, but survey evidence also suggests that, for many Filipino nurses, the UK may only be a stepping stone on the way to the ultimate goal—a job in the US.

## REFERENCES

Aiken, L, Buchan, J, Sochalski J, Nichols B, and Powell, M (2004) Trends in nurse migration, *Health Affairs*, 23(3), 69–77.
Asia Pacific Post (2006) *Filipino nurses' exam scandal*, 13 September, www.asia pacificpost.com accessed 21 September 2006.
Ball, R (2004) Divergent development, racialised rights: Globalised labour markets and the trade of nurses—the case of the Philippines, *Women's Studies International Forum*, 27, 119–133.
Barber, P (2000) Agency in Philippine women's labour migration and provisional diaspora, *Women Studies International Forum*, 23, 399–411.
Buchan, J (2002) *Here to stay?*, Royal College of Nursing: London.
Buchan, J, Jobanputra R, Gough P, and Hutt, R(2005) *Internationally recruited nurses in London: Profile and implications for policy*, London: Kings Fund.
Buchan, J and Seccombe, I (2005) *Past trends, future imperfect? A review of the UK nursing labour market in 2004 to 2005*, London: Royal College of Nursing.
Buchan, J and Sochalski, J (2004) The migration of nurses: Trends and policies, *Bulletin of the World Health Organization*, 82, 587–594.
Choy, C (2003) *Empire of care: Nursing and migration in Filipino American history*, Durham: Duke University Press.

Daniel, P, Chamberlain, A, and Gordon, F (2001) Expectations and experiences of newly recruited Filipino nurses, *British Journal of Nursing*, 10, 254–265.

Department of Health (2004) *Code of practice for the international recruitment of healthcare professionals*, London: Department of Health.

Galvez Tan, J (2006) *The mass migration of Filippino health professionals*, unpublished paper, Ateneo-Harvard Project for Asia and International Relations, Manila.

Hawthorne, L (2001) The globalisation of the nursing workforce: Barriers confronting overseas qualified nurses in Australia, *Nursing Inquiry*, 8, 213–229.

Health Committee, House of Commons (2006) *NHS workforce planning*, London: House of Commons.

Lorenzo, M (2002) *Nurse supply and demand in the Philippines*, Institute of Health Policy and Development Studies, University of the Philippines, Manila.

Lorenzo, M (2005) *Philippine case study on nursing migration*, unpublished paper presented at Bellagio meeting, July 2005, www.academyhealth.org accessed 17 August 2005.

Parry, M and Lipp, A (2006) Implementation of an adaptation programme for Filipino nurses in a UK adult cancer hospice, *International Journal of Palliative Nursing*, 12(2), 83–89.

Tujan, A (2002) Health professionals migration and its impact on the Philippines. *Asia-Pacific Research Network*, 6, March, www.apinet.org/index accessed 17 August 2005.

Withers, J and Snowball, J (2003) Adapting to a new culture: A study of expectations and experiences of Filipino nurses in the Oxford Radcliffe Hospital NHS Trust, *Journal of Nursing Research*, 8, 278–290.

# 4 Here to Stay?
## Migrant Health Workers in Ireland

*Nicola Yeates*

This chapter traces the changing position of Ireland within international health care labour markets from the nineteenth century to the present day, with particular reference to nurses. Renowned as a major exporter of nurses, over the last decade Ireland also began to import nurses. Initially these nurses were mainly 'sourced' from 'core' countries, but they are now drawn from a diverse range of countries worldwide. In this context, Asia has proved a significant source region in the most recent period and the discussion focuses on Filipino and Indian nurses whose presence in the Irish health care system has increased rapidly since 2000. The discussion highlights a number of key issues connected to the migrant nurses' general social protection and welfare, and reviews the policy responses to this migration as well as the forms of political activism on the part of the nurses themselves.

## NURSE EMIGRATION FROM IRELAND

Ireland has long been recognised as a major source of migrant labour globally. This history is best viewed as a series of movements since the sixteenth century, but during the last 200 years Irish migration has been massive and sustained. Levels of emigration from Ireland declined during the twentieth century, but remained high by European standards (Sexton 2002, Delaney 2002). During the nineteenth and twentieth centuries, unskilled emigrants predominated in this exodus from Ireland but emigration by skilled workers and graduates was also significant (Delaney 2002). Emigration included considerable numbers of the Irish nursing workforce. Indeed, this workforce has always had a sizeable contingent on the move, whether migrating abroad for training or employment, or returning from abroad after training to work in Ireland (Daniels 1993; O'Connor and Goodwin n.d.; Scanlan 1991; Walter 1989, 2001; Walter et al. 2002). Some nurses emigrated on their own initiative; others travelled as part of special assignments arranged under the sponsorship of philanthropic or religious organisations, including the Catholic Church, to provide health and other types of care (educational, social) to Irish female emigrants and to local populations abroad (Diner 1993, Scanlan 1991).

The development of nursing in Ireland was from the earliest days closely intertwined with Ireland's status as a British colony. In the mid-nineteenth century, substantial numbers of Irish nurses travelled overseas to provide health care for the British army (around one-third of which was comprised of Irishmen) at war in the Crimea. England also became a principal destination for nurse training and employment. During the period 1890 to 1900, half those accepted for further nurse training in Ireland had previously been trained in England (Wickham 2005). This migration continued after partition in 1922. As nurse training was apprenticeship training, with learning taking place 'on the job,' trainee nurses were also junior members of hospital staff. In the thirty years following (partial) independence from Britain, one in ten of all nurses registered in Ireland over this period were working abroad, mainly in England, Scotland and Wales and Northern Ireland (Yeates, 2008). Britain consistently drew on Ireland for supplies of trained and intending nurses (and midwives) prior to, during and after World War II. Flows of nurses to Britain were spurred by unemployment among Irish nurses, a large wage gap between nursing in England and Ireland (Table 4.1) and severe nursing labour shortages in British hospitals caused by a failure to address what was perceived by British women as a poorly paid and unattractive career option. Between 1949 and 1974 some 30% to 40% of Irish-registered nurses were trained abroad, most of whom would have been trained in Britain (Yeates 2008).

Assisted by historical and colonial ties between Britain and Ireland, and by labour networks that channelled and sustained Irish migration to Britain, Irish nurses forged a niche position in the British nursing labour force and maintained this position for most of the twentieth century. The concentration of Irish-born women working as nurses in the NHS persists to the present day (O'Connor and Goodwin n.d.; Walter 1989, 2001; Walter et al. 2002).

*Table 4.1* Rates of Annual Pay, Ireland and England, 1930s

| Grade | Ireland | England |
|---|---|---|
| District nurse | £52–£80 | £140–£200 |
| Hospital nurse | £60–£85 | £120–£140 |
| Ward sister | £75–£80 | £130–£200 |

Source: Scanlan, 1991: 136, citing *Irish Nurses Magazine* XII (September 1943)

While Britain was the major target of Irish nurse migration, Irish nurses migrated to many other countries for training and employment. Mostly these were English-speaking countries in North America, Africa, Asia and Australasia, but the historical connections between Ireland and France in respect of nurse training were not insignificant. The global migration patterns of Irish nurses were consolidated from the late 1950s. In the late 1950s South Africa and in the mid-1960s Rhodesia and the Middle East were added to the range of destinations (Yeates 2008). By the mid-1980s—when half as many nurses emigrated from Ireland as graduated from nursing school every year (Nowlan 1986)—most Irish nurses still went to Britain and the US, but they were also emigrating to European Union countries other than Britain and to other English-speaking countries such as Canada, South Africa, New Zealand, Australia, Kenya and Saudi Arabia where they compensated for these countries' nursing shortages.

Throughout the most recent period—1990s to the present day—a period of unprecedented economic growth and prosperity, Ireland has continued to export its nurses in significant quantities. During the period 1993 to 2005, between 5.4% and 7.1% of the stock of Irish-registered nurses were working abroad, with the United Kingdom and Australia accounting for the vast majority of nurses abroad (Yeates 2008). Recent international demand has been for Irish nurses with specialist skills, particularly in fields such as midwifery, intensive care and surgical operation and theatre work, and other 'peripheral' countries are now supplying the general nursing labour that Ireland formerly supplied in such massive quantities. One aspect of this nurse migration, then, is its exposure of the international hierarchy of countries, exemplified by which countries are exporting general nursing labour and which countries are exporting specialised or highly skilled nursing labour.


## MIGRATION OF NURSES INTO IRELAND

Although the predominant direction of the migratory flow was outward, Ireland has always been an importer as well as an exporter of nursing labour, even if the labour being imported was labour that had previously been exported. In the early twentieth century, the first Jubilee public health nurses included those same nurses trained in the United States who subsequently returned to Ireland; nurse training in France by the Bons Secours religious order also led to return migration to Ireland. For the 1950s and 1960s, nurses registered in Ireland came from American, Australian and Canadian states, as well as from Britain, Italy, the Netherlands, Nigeria and Zambia (Scanlan 1991).

The last fifteen years overshadow previous periods of nurse migration into Ireland in terms of the scale of the immigration, the geographical spread of nurse suppliers, and the ethnic composition of the nurse migrants. This period in Irish migration history is something of an historical exception.

Fuelled by relatively high rates of economic growth, inward migration increased and outward migration declined, resulting in only the second decade since records began of positive net migration (the first was the 1970s but the reversal was on a far smaller scale). While part of the immigrant population consists of returning Irish emigrants and/or their families, non-nationals coming to Ireland to work or study comprise a growing proportion of the gross inward population flow, and they are increasingly originating from countries other than Britain, the United States, Canada or Australia (Sexton 2002, Walter et al. 2002). Over the period 1995 to 2002, the number of work permits issued or renewed to non-European Union nationals increased ninefold, and such permits were awarded to nationals from over eighty countries in all continents (not including nationals from the European Economic Area (EEA)). The health (medical/nursing) sector accounted for a relatively small share (7%) of all work permits issued or renewed in 2002, but it was the single largest welfare sector for which work visas were issued (Sexton 2002).

A key trend during this period was the increased reliance of the Irish health system on overseas nurses. Two-thirds of the nurses recruited were of foreign origin (compared with 52% for the United Kingdom, 28% for Norway and 3–4% for the United States), and about two-thirds of these were from high and upper middle-income countries (Buchan et al. 2003). Of these, most were from the European Union, or more precisely, the United Kingdom—thereby reversing the traditional direction of nurse migration between Ireland and the United Kingdom. Thus, Ireland's place in the international division of nursing labour was changing, but the change accompanied the continuation of pre-1990s migration patterns by Irish nurses; that is, regional divisions of labour continued to operate alongside a changed global division of labour. This trend continued throughout the 1990s into the 2000s, with the numbers going from Ireland to the United Kingdom dropping to one fifth the level of the mid-1990s, and the numbers going from the United Kingdom to Ireland doubling (Buchan et al. 2003, Simoens et al. 2005).

While the migration that was occurring up to 2000 was more indicative of 'developed to developed' country migration than of the 'developing to developed' country migration that typifies U.K. nurse recruitment, from the year 2000 'developing to developed' country migration began to be of increasing importance in sourcing nurses for nursing work in Ireland. The proportion of nurses registering in Ireland who were trained overseas (European Union countries plus 'Other') increased from 35% to 84% of all newly registered nurses in Ireland, while nurses who were trained outside the European Union increased tenfold over the decade (Table 4.2). By 2002, non-European Union sources of supply had overtaken European Union sources, and in 2005 nurses registering from non-European Union countries were approaching three times the numbers registered in European Union countries.

*Table 4.2* Newly Registered Nurses by Place of Qualification

| Year | Ireland | EU | Other | Total Non-Irish | Total |
|------|---------|-----|-------|-----------------|-------|
| 1995 | 1675 | 675 | 237 | 912 | 2587 |
| 1996 | 1774 | 777 | 252 | 1029 | 2803 |
| 1997 | 1660 | 920 | 299 | 1219 | 2879 |
| 1998 | 1560 | 1157 | 357 | 1514 | 3074 |
| 1999 | 1504 | 1211 | 466 | 1677 | 3181 |
| 2000 | 1332 | 1559 | 612 | 2171 | 3503 |
| 2001 | n/a | n/a | n/a | n/a | n/a |
| 2002 | 1657 | 1193 | 1765 | 2958 | 4615 |
| 2003 | 1787 | 942 | 832 | 1774 | 3561 |
| 2004 | 1851 | 707 | 1075 | 1782 | 3633 |
| 2005 | 507 | 851 | 2154 | 3005 | 3575 |

Source: www.nursingboard.ie, acc. 6/12/03 and 23/5/06. n/a = not available.

In this latter period, the geographical spread of countries from which overseas nurses were recruited had considerably broadened but Asia had come to dominate in terms of the volume of nurses being supplied. Beginning in the late 1990s, the Philippines was targeted as a major reservoir of nursing labour. In 2000 the Philippines supplied 90% of non-European Union overseas trained nurses (HSEA 2004), and by 2002 Ireland was the third largest importer of Filipino nurses, after Saudi Arabia and the United Kingdom (Siazon n.d., Buchan et al. 2003). This use of overseas labour in Irish nursing was further consolidated over the following years as the numbers of overseas recruited nurses increased and the spread of countries from which they were 'sourced' widened. Thus, in 2000, Ireland recruited nurses from 9 countries; in 2002, it was recruiting from 22 countries, and by 2005, it was recruiting from 49 countries. The search for nurses extended as far as the People's Republic of China, but most recently, India has emerged as a major supplier, accounting for 41% of non-European Union nurses in Ireland in 2004. India's importance for the supply of nurses continued to grow and Indians constituted the majority of the 3,000 nurses recruited from abroad in 2005. Ireland's diversification of its recruitment continues. In 2006, Bahrain and Singapore were targeted for this indirect stock of Indian and Filipino nurses, as well as India and the Philippines themselves (Quinn 2006).

Table 4.3 provides a useful indication of the geographical spread of the country of registration of nurses working in Ireland in 2006, and also an indication of Ireland's shifting position in the international division of labour, in that of the 10,335 overseas nurses, 33% are from low income countries (India, Nigeria), 37% are from lower-middle income countries (the Philippines) and the remaining 30% are from upper-middle and high income countries. Ireland may therefore be shifting toward the United Kingdom's overseas recruitment model, which relies more extensively on low-income countries for its supplies of nurse labour.

Ireland has long been established as a major global nursing labour reservoir, providing a cheap and plentiful supply of nurse labour across both short and long distances. Nurse training has been one of the key means by which these internationalisation patterns and connections have developed, while return labour and remittances flowing back into Ireland from Irish nurses overseas have been among the more tangible material returns to Ireland from this export business. While much of this migration has been tied up with Ireland's colonial history and its close geographical, linguistic and cultural proximity to England, it is not entirely reducible to such relations since Irish nurses forged migratory routes to a range of countries around the world. While Ireland has always been both an importer and exporter of nurse labour, developments over the past fifteen years have been a particularly significant chapter in Ireland's migration history, as Ireland repositioned itself within the international division of nursing labour. Ireland still performs the function of a global care labour reservoir (mainly for developed countries

*Table 4.3* Top Ten Countries of Registration of Nurses Working in Ireland, 2006

| Ireland | 52,123 |
| --- | --- |
| Philippines | 3,831 |
| India | 3,215 |
| UK | 2,154 |
| USA | 256 |
| Nigeria | 233 |
| South Africa | 212 |
| Australia | 209 |
| Germany | 154 |
| New Zealand | 71 |

Source: *Irish Independent* 26/4/06:16.

such as Britain, the United States, Australia and the Middle East), but it now also increasingly recruits from other global care labour reservoirs, notably the Philippines and India.

Remarkably similar processes occur in these migration dynamics. Thus, just as Australian, American and British women enjoy better working conditions and career prospects outside nursing or outside their own countries' health systems, so Irish nurses can earn more in the immediate and longer term by working in these countries' health systems. In the same way, Filipino and Indian nurses can also earn more by working in Ireland than in their home countries. It is worth noting that the links between the Philippines and Ireland are essentially of the same order as those that historically linked, and still link, Ireland to Britain, the United States and many other countries. Monthly wages for nurses in the Philippines in 2000 were IR£160–200, while nurses in Ireland start at a basic salary of IR£15,762 (monthly IR£1,314) rising to IR£23,014 (monthly IR£1,918) (*Irish Times* 18/07/2000). The remittances that these nurses send home to their families constitute a tangible material link between these labour-importing and exporting countries and fulfil the same functions as remittances from Irish migrants to Ireland in the previous period. At one level, Ireland is just another country to which Filipino and Indian labour is exported, but the religious and cultural connections are not insignificant. Like Ireland, the Philippines is a Catholic country, and many Filipinos were educated by emigrant Irish Catholic nuns and priests. Similarly, migrant Indian nurses in Ireland are predominantly Christians from Kerala.

## STATE STRATEGIES

The importance of the state in steering these nurse migration patterns cannot be underestimated. Indeed, Filipinos' presence in Ireland is set to continue as nursing is one of the few occupations exempt from the new policy whereby Ireland should fulfill all its immigration requirements from European Union accession countries from May 2004. This exemption, together with the targeting of Indian nurses in India and elsewhere in Asia in the most recent period, may be taken as an indication of the tensions around the Irish government's regionalist (nurse) labour migration policy. Despite the advantages that the accession of ten new member states into the European Union brings, there are major institutional, professional and linguistic barriers that currently hinder the mobility of trained and intending nurses from these countries to Ireland. It is no coincidence that both the Philippines and India have adopted an export-oriented model of nurse production, have advanced bureaucracies for managing labour migration and are proficient in the English language.

Indeed, the rapid increase in non-European Union nurses, specifically Filipinos and Indians, working in Ireland is the result of state strategies spanning several countries. At one level, the Irish situation reflects a change in destination for Filipino nurses to 'new' English-speaking countries following retrenchment in the U.S. nursing market as a result of funding constraints and health system restructuring in the United States during the 1990s (Buchan et al. 2003). On the Irish side, the Irish government's international recruitment drive launched in the late 1990s was highly significant. Shortages of nursing labour had reached a critical point due to decades of under-investment in the Irish nursing workforce which was leading Irish trained nurses to either leave the nursing profession or emigrate to practice nursing abroad. Thus, in addition to the 4,000 qualified nurses working abroad, 15,000 qualified nurses in Ireland were not working in the health service. Mirroring the findings of research studies in the United States (e.g., Lafer 2005), many of these nurses would return to work if wages and working conditions improved and if nurse-to-patient ratios are at a level at which they believe they can provide professional care. Rather than improve the attractiveness of nursing as a career option, the government instead opted to search overseas for supplies of nursing labour—not as a temporary stop-gap measure as it initially claimed but as a labour strategy over the longer term.

The government policies of both of the main supply countries are also significant in this regard. The Philippines' export-oriented model of nurse training, adopted in the early 1970s, has made a global nurse reservoir of that country that has resulted in about 85% of employed Filipino nurses working abroad; the export of this 'surplus' labour is supported by one of the most advanced bureaucracies in the world for managing labour migration (Tyner 1999). India also has an established history of nurse emigration (e.g., to Britain, the United States and the Middle East), but its response to the global nurse shortage has entailed stepping up nurse 'production' for export and various Indian states have overseen a rapid expansion of nurse training and education courses and institutes oriented toward the export market (Yeates 2008).

These government policies have been carried out in partnership with a range of for-profit and not-for-profit agents: recruitment agencies, employer bodies, trade unions and professional associations. Thus, the Irish recruitment drive in China in 2001, for example, was a joint operation of state organisations and recruitment agencies, hospitals and labour unions. Representatives from a number of Irish Health Boards (semi-state organisations responsible for health care in designated geographical areas) and Dublin hospitals visited Beijing and ShenYang in China. This campaign was facilitated by a Dublin recruitment agency, EuroCollege, which had taken advice from the trade union SIPTU and the Irish Department of Health to agree salary scales for the fully registered staff nurses and nursing assistants being recruited in advance of their arrival in Ireland. The operation was also facilitated by the fast-track nurses visa scheme introduced in March 2000 as part of the Irish governments' international nurse recruitment strategy (*Sunday Business Post* 10/9/2001).

The Filipino policy operates in close conjunction with the private sector. In the mid-1990s there were 1,200 recruitment agencies in the Philippines in 2004 (900 for land-based jobs and 300 for sea-based jobs) with combined annual revenues exceeding $400m (Martin et al. 2004). The Indian strategy has been more of a private sector-led strategy involving American and local healthcare experts and entrepreneurs urging Indian states to increase nurse 'production' (Vaidyanathan 2005). Underpinned by foreign investment, this has entailed a significant expansion in nursing education, and a growth in both private nursing colleges and private sector recruitment companies operating in India. The organisation of industry interests is also evident here, with the Overseas Healthcare Staffing Association (OHSA) being set up in India in October 2003 to represent companies in the industry.

The expansion of the Irish economy over the last two decades has been dependent on continued supplies of foreign labour both at the top and bottom of the labour market. This is no less true of the health care system. These state-led dual nurse import-export processes have resulted not only in an increasing presence of migrant nurses among the national nursing labour forces, but an increasing dependence of the Irish health system on them for its basic operation. Surveys of nursing resources by the Health Service Employers Agency (HSEA) illustrate the extent of this dependence: In the survey covering the year to September 2002 overseas nurses accounted for 91% of the additional nursing posts created in Ireland that year and 32% of nurses recruited into the health sector overall (HSEA 2002). The trend continued into 2005, with 34% of nurses recruited being recruited from abroad (HSEA 2005a, 2005b). Nurses from the Philippines account for one in five of the nursing staff in Irish hospitals (McDonagh 2003), and, according to an Irish Nurses Organisation submission of June 2006, some units in Dublin hospitals had 'well in excess of 50% of the staff comprising foreign recruits on short term contracts' (INO 2006).

## THE EXPERIENCES OF OVERSEAS NURSES IN IRELAND

The chapter now turns to examine some of the issues raised by nurse migration in the Irish system. It covers working conditions and social welfare issues pertaining to the nurses and their families, as well as the trade unions' response to migrant nurses. Some of the issues raised by nurse migration outlined in this section—integration, development of multiculturalism in the workplace and exploitation of work permit holding workers—affect the whole health sector and other sectors as well.

### Working Conditions

In recent years the working conditions of overseas' workers, including nurses, have emerged as a major concern for agencies combating transnational

crime in recent years. In many cases women are recruited with false promises of legitimate jobs with good pay and conditions: When they arrive in
the host country, the promises are revealed to be false (Redfoot and Houser
2005). In Ireland, these same issues are also arising. A spokesperson for the
INO stated that:

> [I]n the INO, we receive phone calls daily from overseas nurses whose
> rights are being abused. Many find the promises recruiters made are
> reneged on as soon as they arrive here. Rogue employers force them
> to work for long shifts in succession without appropriate breaks, and
> some nurses are not paid Sunday, bank holiday or night duty premium
> rates of pay.

(McAnenly, quoted in *Irish Independent* 9/7/01)

Don Brenock of the Filipino-Irish Association confirmed that such exploitation was rife:

> Cases of young nurses being packed six to a room in very unsatisfactory
> accommodation, for which they were charged exorbitant prices as part
> of their contractual obligations are thankfully becoming less common.
> However, cases of exploitative work practices in the private nursing
> sector are common. I recently helped bring a case to the Labour Com-
> mission in which a nurse was working over 40 hours a week and was
> told there was no such thing as overtime in Ireland.

(Miller 2002:72–73)

The general perception is that these problems are greater in the private
system than the public one, and that there are more problems in nursing
homes than hospitals. While positive examples of investment in induction,
diversity training and mentoring for migrant and Irish nurses can be found,
these tend to occur in hospitals. Alongside this needs to be placed the fact
that migrant nurses in private hospitals and nursing homes in particular have
called in trade unions to address breaches of contract, minimum working
conditions, non-payment of wages and harassment (Conroy 2003). These
observations are supported by an ILO-sponsored study which observed that
'there are frequently differences between the experiences of employment in
a nursing care/aged care environment compared to a hospital setting. . . . It
is in private nursing that some of the worst abuses have been documented'
(Bach 2003:19).

Wage levels have emerged as a key issue, especially in the private sector.
The chairwoman of the Federation of Irish Nursing Homes confirmed in July
2001 that Filipino nurses were paid 30% less than the market rate for their
first year working in Irish nursing homes: 'It costs £3,500 to bring in every

employee . . . [the nurses] are paying back some of the cost of bringing them in' (*Sunday Business Post* 27/5/01). Officials from Ireland's largest union, SIPTU, have been particularly critical of the nursing home sector where many qualified overseas nurses are employed. Pointing out that the recruiting firm, C F Sharp, which had recruited a Filipina beautician to work on an Irish Ferries boat for a wage of one Euro an hour was also, through its nursing staff subsidiary International Quality Manpower Services (IQMAN), in partnership with the Irish Nursing Home Organisation (INHO), one SIPTU health official said the union had reports of 'well over 100' Filipino workers and over 600 foreign nursing home staff being paid less than the minimum wage. 'There are nursing homes paying under the minimum wage but non-nationals are afraid to report it because they're afraid their permits will be withdrawn' (Paul Bell, cited in Leahy 2005).

As early as 2002 the INO was expressing concern about how the work permit system leaves overseas nurses open to exploitation as the employer owns the permit, not the employee (*World of Irish Nursing* October 2002). These and other problems with the work permits scheme have led to proposed new legislation, the Employment Permits Bill, which provides for more flexible working arrangements for highly-skilled non-EEA workers (Quinn 2006:15). One basic problem, though, is that most attention so far has been directed at the more qualified nursing workforce rather than care assistants where greater exploitation would be expected. There is only some anecdotal evidence for the existence of one problem that has been observed internationally, namely the deskilling of foreign nurses through their placement as care assistants. There is urgent need for more research in this area.

Finally, while most of the examples of exploitative behaviour reported relate to the private sector, the public sector is not immune. One recent scandal relates to the National Maternity Hospital, Holles Street, in Dublin, where in February 2006, management attempted to force sixteen nurses from India and the Philippines to sign different contracts to those they had previously been offered under threat of losing their jobs, visas and repatriation. INO official Philip McAnenly, describing this as 'a new low for the health service,' condemned 'the efforts to threaten, intimidate and frighten a vulnerable group of nurses into signing inferior contracts' (Anon 2006). Following trade union intervention in this matter management apologised for the threats and reinstated the original contracts.

There is little evidence available on the racial and ethnic contours of the Irish nursing workforce. It is worth noting that complaints to and cases taken up by the Equality Authority show an increase from minority and ethnic workers, but evidence of racist attitudes and practices in Irish hospitals is anecdotal. At the INO conference in 2004 foreign nurses reported being 'undervalued' by hospital managers and senior nurses in charge of wards, being passed over for temporary responsibility posts in favour of less experienced Irish nurses (*Irish Times* 8/5/2004). The Irish state, cognisant of its dependence on migrant labour for the continued success of the economy, has initiated various anti-racism policies and programmes, which include the state health system in their remit.

## Rights of Family Members

Immigration has revealed the limits of Ireland's familist social policy in a number of ways over the last half decade. The 2004 constitutional amendment that removed the rights of children born into families such as those of migrant workers is the most obvious instance of institutional racism. The 27th Amendment to the Irish Constitution of 24 June 2004 removed the automatic granting of citizenship to all children born in Ireland, which had existed in law since 1922. Importantly, it was over this issue that the first public political position was taken by Filipinos in Ireland, with the League of Filipino Nurses criticising the proposed referendum on June 8th 2004 as discriminatory and racist (O'Keeffe 2004).

A related issue concerns family reunification and the rights of migrant workers' spouses/partners and children to access the same social standards that Irish citizens and European Union migrants currently enjoy. One problem involves the provision of work permits for spouses of migrant workers. Until 2004 the spouses of non-European Union nurses were allowed entry into Ireland but they were not permitted to take up paid work. This policy has meant that the majority of spouses of Filipino nurses in Ireland remain in the Philippines, while for the minority of spouses accompanying their wives to Ireland this policy amounts to state-enforced dependency of (male) spouses on their (female) partners. Following lobbying by the INO and other migrant and social welfare groups, the government—ever aware of its reliance on migrant nurses for the continuing operation of the health care system—changed this policy in February 2004 to attempt to retain Filipino nurses who, it was feared, would otherwise migrate to countries providing more adequate social benefits for their families (O'Halloran 2004). The following comment from the director of nursing at the Mater Hospital, Dublin, illustrates the importance of social provision for migrant workers and their families as a factor of international competition between states and health systems:

> We are going to be competing in particular with the UK and Australia for these nurses now, and the conditions of their visas are very attractive to the overseas nurses because they are giving their partners a work permit as well . . . in Australia, they provide guaranteed free education for their children. Obviously it's very difficult for us to compete with countries where their partners get work permits.

(*Irish Times* 12/7/2003)

## Trade Unions

The organisation of migrant labour forces has been of growing importance to trade unions across industrialised OECD economies. In some countries trade union growth is now seen as being dependent on the unions' abilities to organise migrant labour. Accordingly, major efforts have been made to extend trade union organisation to hitherto unorganised economic sectors where migrant labour predominates. One feature of this is the recognition that migrant workers have particular requirements, and for this reason, among others, some unions organise their migrant members separately. Internationally, the INO's support for a semi-autonomous section to represent and deal with overseas nurses is exemplary in this regard because it allows nurses to undertake both trade union work and more general political lobbying work. The INO first supported the formation of a League of Filipino Nurses in 2001 and, after commissioning research on the subject in 2003, formed the Overseas Nurses Section, whose inaugural meeting of took place in November 2003, to provide a venue for overseas nurses to discuss, reflect upon and solve problems and issues unique to them.

In addition to exemplifying how trade unionism can develop in a multicultural society (Kevin Glackin, SIPTU, cited by Miller 2002:74), this form of union organisation can bring benefits which extend beyond the usual benefits of collective bargaining over pay and working conditions. The INO became involved in migrant nurses' rights shortly after the arrival of the first group of Filipino nurses, when thirty of them were provided with unsafe, unsanitary and overcrowded accommodation. Despite the nurses not being INO members, the union intervened to alert local council officials to the fire and safety hazards in the building and pressurise health authorities to immediately place the affected nurses in alternative accommodation (Cassidy 2001). A further example of the wider effects of the section is the INO's contribution to bringing about change in the legislation allowing the spouses of overseas nurses to legally work in Ireland. Problems still remain, however, regarding union representation of migrant health workers. Partly this is due to the uneven scale of unionisation across the health care system. In particular, levels of unionisation are lower outside the main teaching hospitals, and lowest among private nursing homes where migrant workers are most vulnerable to exploitation (Fitzgerald 2002:27).

## CONCLUSIONS

While Ireland has continually exported nurses and other categories of skilled health workers to other countries over the last century, since 1990 it has imported migrant nurses on an unprecedented scale, with the result that the operation of Ireland's public health system is now dependent on migrant labour. These migrant nurses first came from other 'developed' countries, particularly the United Kingdom, but since 2000 'developing' countries, particularly India and the Philippines, have become major suppliers of nursing labour to Ireland. These developments resulted from state and non-state internationalisation strategies across several countries. With Ireland still adjusting to its new position as an importer of labour, problems related to the exploitation of these migrant nurses have arisen. Autonomous organisations within the trade union movement have emerged and been instrumental in campaigning for improved labour and social rights. Government responses to these injustices have taken the form of new legislation changing the existing work permit scheme for nurses and the provision of work permits for nurses' spouses, perhaps thereby ensuring that Ireland retain and expand its place in the global care chain.

## REFERENCES

Bach, S (2003) *International migration of health workers: Labour and social issues*, Geneva: ILO Working Paper No.209.

Buchan, J, Parkin, T and Sochalski, J (2003) *International nurse mobility: Trends and policy implications*, Geneva: International Council of Nurses.

Cassidy, M (2001) No place like home, *The World of Irish Nursing*, May, 16–17.

Conroy, P (2004) *Migrant workers and their experiences.* Equality Commission of Northern Ireland/National Consultative Committee on Racism and Interculturalism, North/South roundtable on migration, Belfast, 5 February, pp.2–3.

Daniels, M (1993) *Exile or opportunity? Irish nurses and midwives in Britain*, Occasional Papers in Irish Studies No. 5, The Institute of Irish Studies, The University of Liverpool.

Delaney, E (2002) *Irish emigration since 1921*, Dublin: The Economic and Social History Society of Ireland.

Diner, H R (1983) *Erin's daughters in America: Irish immigrant women in the nineteenth century*, London: John Hopkins University Press.

Fitzgerald, K (2002) Recruiting overseas—how Dublin hospitals responded to the nursing shortage, *Industrial Relations News*, 25 July, 23–27.

Health Service Employers Agency (2002) *National survey on nursing resources*, November, Dublin.

Health Service Employers Agency (2004) *National survey on nursing resources*, October, Dublin.

Health Service Employers Agency (2005a) *National survey on nursing resources*, October, Dublin.

Health Service Employers Agency (2005b) *National survey on nursing resources*, December, Dublin.

INO (Irish Nurses Organisation) (2006) *Submission to the Labour Court: Eight claims in relation to pay and conditions of employment for nurses and midwives*, June, http://www.ino.ie/DesktopModules/articles/Documents/Submission%208 Claims%2020Jun06.doc accessed 4 September 2006.

Lafer, G (2005) Hospital speedups and the fiction of a nursing shortage, *Labor Studies Journal*, 31(1), 27–46.

Leahy, E (2005) Irish nursing homes "use underpaid Filipinos," *Sunday Times* 27 March, pp. 1, 5.

McDonagh, M (2003) Filipino nurses "may be lured away by better pay," *Irish Independent*, 3 June, p. 4.

Martin, P, Abella, M and Midgely, E (2004) Best practices to manage migration: The Philippines, *International Migration Review*, 38, 1544–1549.

Miller, S (2002) Workers' rights, Irish wrongs, *Magill Annual 2002*, pp.72–74.

Nowlan, D (1986) Nearly half of all nursing graduates emigrating, *Irish Times*, 7 May.

O'Connor, H and Goodwin, J (n.d.) *Locating Irish workers in the British labour force survey*, Centre for Labour Market Studies Working Paper No. 25, University of Leicester: Centre for Labour Market Studies.

O'Halloran, B (2004) New work permit will benefit 10,000: Scheme will allow spouses of non-nationals to apply for jobs barred to others, *Irish Times*, 19 February, p. 6.

O'Keeffe, C (2004) Filipino nurses call for referendum No vote, *Irish Examiner*, 9 June.

Quinn, E (2006) *Managed migration and the labour market—the health sector in Ireland*, Dublin: ESRI/European Migration Network.

Redfoot, D L and Houser, A N (2005) *"We shall travel on": Quality of care, economic development, and the international migration of long-term care workers*, Washington, DC: AARP. www.mecf.org/articles/AARP_immigrant.pdf, accessed 9 November 05.

Scanlan, P (1991) *The Irish nurse: A study of nursing in Ireland—history and education 1718–1981*, Manor Hamilton, Leitrim: Drumlin Press.

Sexton, J (2002) *Ireland, SOPEMI report for 2002*, Dublin: Economic and Social Research Institute.

Siazon, D (n.d.) *Deployment of overseas Filipino workers (OFWs)*, Embassy of the Republic of the Philippines, www.philemb.org.uk, accessed 13 June 2003.

Simoens, S, Villeneuve, M and Hurst, J (2005) *Tackling nurse shortages in OECD countries*, Paris: OECD Health Working Paper No. 19.

Tyner, J (1999) The web-based recruitment of female foreign domestic workers in Asia, *Singapore Journal of Tropical Geography*, 20, 193–209.

Vaidyanathan, L (2005) India should gear up to fill global shortage of nurses, *Economic Times* 13 November 05, http://economictimes.indiatimes.com/articleshow/1293589.cms, accessed 2 May 2006.

Walter, B (1989) *Irish women in London: The Ealing dimension*. Ealing Women's Unit: London.

Walter, B (2001) *Outsiders inside: Whiteness, place and Irish women*. London: Routledge.

Walter, B, Gray, B, Almeida Dowling, L and Morgan, S (2002) *Irish emigrants and Irish communities abroad: A study of existing sources of information an analysis for the task force on policy regarding emigrants*, Dublin.

Wickham, A (2005) "She must be content to be their servant as well as their teacher": The early years of district nursing in Ireland, in Fealy, G M (Ed), *Care to remember: Nursing and midwifery in Ireland*, Cork: Mercier Press, pp.102–121.

Yeates, N (2008) *Migrant care workers in a global economy*. Basingstoke: Palgrave.

# 5 "Filipinos Are Very Strongly into Medical Stuff"

## Labour Market Segmentation in Toronto, Canada

*Philip Kelly and Silvia D'Addario*

The outbreak of Severe Acute Respiratory Syndrome (or SARS) in 2003 illuminated an interesting series of transnational connections linking Canada and Asia. The virus was thought to have spread from Guangdong and Hong Kong to Vancouver and Toronto, and from there back across the Pacific to the Philippines. This geography of transmission highlighted some of the key channels of human interaction between Canada and Asia—China and the Philippines were two of Canada's three largest sources of immigrants in the 1990s. But the viral transmission, which appeared to occur almost exclusively in hospital settings, also shed light upon the accentuated exposure of the Filipino community in Toronto. More than any other immigrant group, men and women from the Philippines are concentrated in the healthcare sector as nurses, personal support workers, clinical assistants and medical technologists. Even in non-health care positions in hospital settings, such as janitors and cafeteria staff, Filipinos are heavily represented. They were, therefore, at the front line of exposure to SARS, and indeed a Filipina nurse at Toronto's North York General Hospital was the first Canadian health care worker to die after contracting the virus.

This chapter seeks to provide explanations for the concentration of Filipino immigrants in the healthcare sector in Toronto in particular, but in the process we seek broader explanations for the repetition of this pattern in many places around the world. This sort of question, concerning occupational and sectoral segmentation, has been a staple of labour market studies for several decades. It is usual, however, especially in more recent versions of segmentation theory, to see the process as constituted at the scale of the urban labour market. By focusing on a particular instance of segmentation for one cultural group, however, we suggest that immigrant labour markets must be understood, in part at least, in terms of processes that transcend local and national scales and encompass transnational linkages forged through institutional, cultural, social and economic ties, usually through the household nexus.

Institutional processes guide Filipino migrants into certain occupations and labour market niches. In part this reflects regulatory biases in the

Canadian immigration apparatus: Preferences are given to certain professions or trades in the 'skilled worker' category, hence migrants are more likely to found in particular jobs, including nursing. This does not, however, explain why Filipinos in particular are employed in the healthcare sector in such numbers. The institutional basis for this phenomenon rests in the training infrastructure in the Philippines and, in particular, the massive expansion of nursing schools in recent years. This is the first transnational linkage that we explore. An institutional basis is, in many ways, a symptom rather than a cause. Integrated with institutional factors are a second set of processes operating in, and from, the Philippines, which can broadly be labelled the cultural contexts for nursing. Here, questions of femininity, parental discipline and the naturalization of migration in the life course are all central. The practicalities of migration and occupational channelling also require social networks, which form a third set of factors. Flows of labour market intelligence, as well as assistance in integration and job searching are processes that are constituted at a transnational scale. Finally, the economics of migration are such that flows of remittances are a crucial part of any migration strategy and career information or instructions are often transmitted with these remittances. All these factors suggest that labour market segmentation is not a set of processes contained within the urban or national context, but is constituted in multiple transnational linkages. Together they create circumstances where certain people are destined for certain jobs long before arriving in Canada.

The process of segmentation—the means by which certain groups are channelled and concentrated in certain occupational and sectoral niches— requires a qualitative understanding of the decisions and opportunities taken with respect to labour market participation, training, education, job searches, and, in this case, geographical mobility. Conventional quantitative measures of labour market segmentation represent only the starting point. From there we move on to qualitative interview and focus group data gathered in both Toronto and the Philippines. In Toronto, personal interviews were conducted with 21 individuals including nurses and other healthcare employees, as well as a small selection of employers. In the Philippines, 20 personal interviews were conducted with nursing school administrators, nurses and immigration agents/recruiters, as well as two focus groups with seven nurses who had worked overseas. Specific interviews illustrate themes that emerged consistently across the set of respondents.

The chapter starts with a brief overview of labour market theories as they pertain to segmentation and space. The following section uses statistical data to establish the nature of Filipino immigration and settlement in Canada, and labour market segmentation in Toronto in particular. The next four sections outline particular institutional, cultural, social and economic processes that contribute to an explanation for high levels of Filipino representation in the healthcare sector, and the nursing workforce in particular. The final section summarizes the way in which these processes come together to explain why Filipinos in particular are playing such an important role in Canada's healthcare system, and by extension, those of other countries around the world.

## THE "LOCAL" LABOUR MARKET

How people are allocated to occupations is the core question of labour market studies, but the answers are diverse. Orthodox human capital approaches view the market as an objective sorting of individuals, with varying skills and education, to appropriate functions in the division of labour (Becker 1993). Any inequalities in the labour market, based on gender or ethnicity for example, would be seen as reflecting prior discrimination in the training or educational system, thereby limiting the human capital of certain individuals. However, a labour market is in fact a 'socially constructed and politically mediated structure of conflict and accommodation among contending forces' (Peck 1996:5). Various axes of identity, such as gender, ethnicity and immigrant status, have affected labour market experiences. Three central arguments have been that labour markets are shaped by institutional forces and power relations; different segments of the labour market operate according to different sets of rules; and the labour market is not blind to gender, ethnicity, etc., but rather these dimensions of difference are central to its operation (Waldinger and Lichter 2003, Bauder 2006).

While labour market segmentation theory has been sensitive to the interaction between social reproduction and demand-side issues, less attention was paid to the complex spatialities of local labour markets. The localization of labour market studies opened up a rich terrain for research, but it has also imposed certain implicit limitations. By emphasising the localness of labour market operation, studies have tended to consider processes at the urban scale, or, at most, within national regulatory spaces. Increasingly, and in certain places more than others, such analytical boundedness has begun to look untenable. A burgeoning literature on transnationalism has demonstrated the ways in which immigrants and others construct their lives in multiple places and across national boundaries. This occurs in the realms of cultural belonging, or political organization, but also in entrepreneurial activities, job searches, information circulation and household finances (Levitt 2001, Espiritu 2003, Guarnizo 2003).

This purpose of this chapter is to explore the ways in which a specific example of labour market segmentation can be understood in the context of such transnational linkages. Thus, the processes leading to labour market segmentation in the Canadian urban labour market are enmeshed in processes partly rooted in other sites, and especially the place of origin of new immigrants. In the case of Filipino immigrants, this spatially unbounded perspective on the labour market helps to open up explanations for the high levels of concentration in the healthcare sector.

## FILIPINO IMMIGRATION AND LABOUR
## MARKET SEGMENTATION

In the 2001 census, just over 223,000 people in Canada were recorded as immigrants with Filipino ethnic identities. This large increase from previous censuses emphasised that the Philippines had been Canada's third most important source of immigrants in the 1990s (after China and India). Filipinos as a group are, therefore, relatively recent arrivals and a rapidly growing community. In 2001, more than three quarters of all Filipinos in Canada had arrived since 1980, and more than half since 1990 (Kelly 2006).

A second distinctive feature of migration from the Philippines has been the importance of special immigration categories for domestic workers (see Figure 5.1). During the 1990s, the Live-In Caregiver Programme (LCP) accounted for around a quarter of all Filipinos gaining immigrant status in Canada. The LCP allows caregivers to enter Canada on work visas and apply for permanent residency after 2 years. This has had a major influence on the experiences of Filipinos in the Canadian labour market and on the gender composition of the Filipino community; overall, women comprised almost 60% of immigrants from the Philippines in the period 1980–2001 (see Figure 5.2).

The geography of Filipino settlement is decidedly urban and concentrated in just a handful of gateway cities. Of the 308,575 people who declared themselves to be of Filipino ethnicity in the 2001 census (including both immigrants and Canadian-born), 133,675 (43%) were in Toronto. Many of the rest were in Vancouver (18%), Winnipeg (10%) and Montreal (6%). Filipinos have, therefore, tended to settle in Canada's urban centres, with

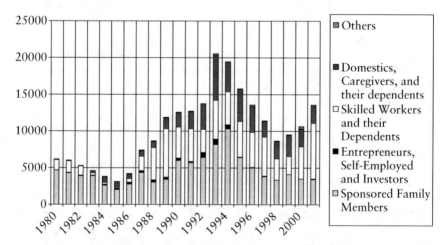

*Figure 5.1* Landing categories of Philippine-Born immigrants to Canada, 1980–2001.

*Source:* Citizenship and immigration Canada, Landed Immigrant Data System.

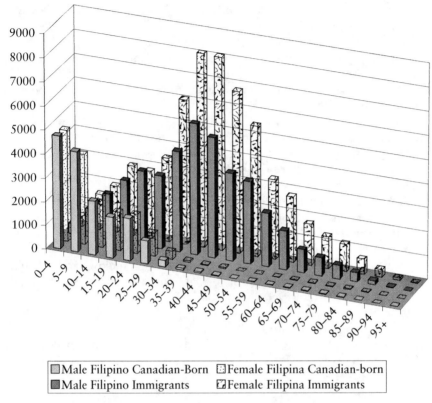

Male Filipino Canadian-Born ▣ Female Filipina Canadian-born
Male Filipino Immigrants ▨ Female Filipina Immigrants

*Figure 5.2* Demographic profile of ethnic Filipinos in Toronto, 2001.

Source: Statistics Canada, 2001 Census.

Toronto the single largest destination. Within Toronto and Vancouver, however, Filipinos are remarkably dispersed. Statistically, Filipinos have one of the lowest levels of segregation of any visible minority group in Canada (Bauder and Sharpe 2002). Almost 57% of Filipino immigrants residing in Toronto in 2001 had some university-level education. This compared with 33% for all immigrant groups, and just under 35% for all residents of Canada. Moreover, this education was gained from institutions in the Philippines that were, in many cases, established during the American colonial period (1898–1946) and modelled on U.S. educational institutions. Most Filipinos in Canada therefore arrive with a strong command of English and familiarity with North American culture and institutions.

Despite this human capital, Filipinos as a group tend to occupy marginal socio-economic positions upon arrival in Canada. Many are successful in integrating with the mainstream waged labour force (participation rates for men and women are high, and self-employment is low), but wage levels are anomalously low. Census figures show Filipino men and women earning significantly less than the average for immigrants, let alone the population as a whole (see Figure 5.3).

The feature of Filipino integration of most relevance here, however, is the concentration in relatively few labour market niches. Healthcare and manufacturing, in particular, are prime destinations for working Filipinos, and within these sectors there is a tendency toward concentration in lower status occupations (see Table 5.1).

The pattern of segmentation is especially accentuated in the healthcare sector, although when absolute numbers are substituted for location quotients this segmentation is far more common for women than men. For male Filipinos, only manufacturing jobs actually ranked in the top ten occupations by absolute numbers employed in Toronto. For female Filipinas, however, all the healthcare occupations listed in Table 5.1 featured in the top ten list of occupations by absolute numbers.

The importance of Filipino and other internationally trained healthcare workers becomes apparent when the demand side of the labour market is examined. It is estimated that 50% of Canadian nurses employed in 2001 will have retired by 2016—a shortfall of 113,000 nurses. In a context of public healthcare provision, however, this shortfall is not an accident of demographics, but reflects a failure to fund the system in such a way that nursing and other healthcare professions are attractive as career options, and that nurses are not lured away to more lucrative positions in the United States. Between 1991 and 2001 the Immigration and Naturalization Service in the United States issued

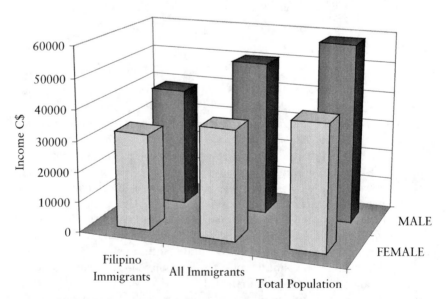

*Figure 5.3* Average employment income in Toronto, 2000.

Source: Statistics Canada, 2001 Census.

*Table 5.1* Selected Occupational Location Quotients for Filipino Immigrants in Toronto, 2001

| LQ | MALE Filipino Immigrants | LQ | FEMALE Filipina Immigrants |
|---|---|---|---|
| 5.4 | Nurse supervisors and registered nurses | 4.1 | Child care and home support workers |
| 5.3 | Assisting occupations in support of health services | 3.3 | Assisting occupations in support of health services |
| 3.6 | Child care and home support workers | 2.7 | Nurse supervisors and registered nurses |
| 3.0 | Assemblers in manufacturing | 2.2 | Technical and related occupations in health |
| 2.9 | Technical and related occupations in health | 1.8 | Assemblers in manufacturing |
| 2.5 | Machine operators in manufacturing | 1.7 | Mechanics |
| 2.1 | Labourers in processing, manufacturing and utilities | 1.4 | Machinists, metal forming, shaping and erecting occupations |
| 0.4 | Judges, lawyers, psychologists, social workers, ministers of religion, and policy and program officers | 0.3 | Senior management occupations |
| 0.4 | Construction trades | 0.3 | Technical occupations in art, culture, recreation and sport |
| 0.3 | Professional occupations in art and culture | 0.3 | Professional occupations in art and culture |
| 0.2 | Professional occupations in health | 0.2 | Teachers and professors |
| 0.2 | Teachers and professors | 0.0 | Construction trades |
| 0.2 | Senior management occupations | 0.0 | Heavy equipment and crane operators, including drillers |

The Location Quotient is calculated by dividing the percentage of Filipino immigrants in an occupational category by the percentage of the total population in the category.
Source: Statistics Canada, 2001 Census.

33,901 visas to Canadian Registered Nurses (Blouin et al. 2004). Clearly then, the problem is one of nurse retention, and the global shortage of nurses, to which Canada contributes, is a product of institutional circumstances.

Meanwhile, between 1980 and 2001, some 14,702 qualified Registered Nurses entered Canada (see Table 5.2). The Philippines represented the

Table 5.2 Healthcare Workers Immigrating to Canada by Source Country 1980–2001

| | Philippines | UK | USA | Poland | China | India | Hong Kong | Other | Total |
|---|---|---|---|---|---|---|---|---|---|
| Registered Nurses | 2008 | 1851 | 1303 | 813 | 393 | 293 | 1127 | 6914 | 14702 |
| Nurse Aides & Orderlies | 482 | 373 | 206 | 557 | 142 | 73 | 53 | 3452 | 5338 |
| GPs and Family Physicians | 116 | 362 | 135 | 297 | 153 | 272 | 80 | 3455 | 4870 |
| Med Lab Techs & Pathologists' Asst | 985 | 104 | 94 | 71 | 923 | 458 | 229 | 1795 | 4659 |
| Pharmacists | 257 | 148 | 73 | 90 | 168 | 405 | 162 | 2879 | 4182 |
| Specialist Physicians | 51 | 340 | 201 | 220 | 235 | 329 | 56 | 2511 | 3943 |
| Other | 1496 | 1994 | 1866 | 1639 | 1029 | 1124 | 1072 | 13058 | 23278 |
| Total | 5395 | 5172 | 3878 | 3687 | 3043 | 2954 | 2779 | 34064 | 60972 |

Source: Citizenship and Immigration Canada, Landed Immigrant Data System.

largest single source of RNs and a significant source of several other categories of healthcare workers.

These patterns of immigrant flows are also reflected in figures for the stock of internationally trained nurses in Canada, with the Philippines representing the single largest source of all foreign-trained nurses. In 2005, there were 19,230 foreign-trained registered nurses in the Canadian RN workforce of 251,675. Of these just over 30% were trained in the Philippines (see Table 5.3).

The Philippines in particular, then, provides the single largest source of foreign trained nurses for the Canadian healthcare system—a system that is becoming increasingly dependent on this source of labour. To the question of why Filipinos in particular have become such an important source of nursing labour for Canada we now turn. A conventional explanation would look at the qualifications that Filipinos bring to the labour market. In the case of a regulated profession such as nursing, there is some value in paying attention to this issue. We might also look at changing Canadian immigration regulations over time. Neither of these approaches explains why Filipinos in particular dominate this sector. What are the wider institutional and social factors that guide Filipinos (and Filipina women in particular) into nursing and support occupations in the healthcare sector? The question

*Table 5.3* Foreign-Trained RNs Working in Canada in 2005 by Place of Initial Graduation

| Country of Graduation | Total | Per cent of Foreign Graduates |
|---|---|---|
| Philippines | 5,830 | 30.3 |
| United Kingdom | 3,610 | 18.8 |
| United States | 1,245 | 6.5 |
| India | 1,013 | 5.3 |
| Hong Kong | 960 | 5.0 |
| Poland | 642 | 3.3 |
| Australia | 395 | 2.1 |
| Other Foreign | 5,535 | 28.8 |
| Total Foreign Trained | 19,230 | 100 |

Source: CIHI (2006)
Note: This take does not include those who qualify or re-qualify as RNs after arriving, so the total number of immigrants in the RN workforce is higher.

can only be answered in the context of transnational institutions, cultural signifiers, social networks and financial flows.

## THE INSTITUTIONS OF LABOUR
## MARKET TRANSNATIONALISM

Trained workers do not simply materialise without an institutionalised infrastructure in place. But this infrastructure need not be physically present in the local labour market where demand for skilled workers exists. The educational and training infrastructure for a labour market may extend around the globe to encompass the sources of migrants. Similarly, migrations do not happen spontaneously on a personal whim. Here, too, a regulatory and institutional structure, as well as an information network, is needed to supply labour. In this section we highlight the institutional foundations of training and labour supply for the Canadian healthcare sector, but we focus on the components of that infrastructure that exist in the Philippines (see also Ball, this book). An important part of the healthcare segmentation puzzle is thereby put in place.

An extensive and rapidly expanding infrastructure exists in the Philippines for the training of nurses. As various countries have expanded their recruitment of foreign nurses, that training infrastructure has similarly expanded. A wave of recruitment in the 1960s and 1970s to both the United States and to the oil-rich economies of the Middle East saw a dramatic expansion of healthcare training in the Philippines, with the number of nursing schools doubling in both decades. A second expansion has taken place since 2001 (see Figure 5.4).

The expansion of nursing colleges has been mirrored in the number sitting the nursing board examination in the Philippines, which grew rapidly in the early 1990s before declining again (see Figure 5.5). It seems likely, however that this number will climb steeply again as current students sit the board exam.

Most nurses trained in the Philippines are not, however, destined for the Philippine healthcare system. Of the 354,154 nurses who passed the qualifying board exam between 1970 and 2004, only 27,150 (in 2002) were actually employed as nurses in the Philippines (17,547 in government institutions, 7,535 in private institutions, and 2,078 in nursing education). Thus, more than 300,000 nurses trained in the Philippines have either left the profession or left the country. Indeed, in the early 1990s, the Philippines was licensing enough nurses each year to entirely replace its domestic workforce. Clearly, the expansion of the training infrastructure for nurses is geared toward the export of nursing labour.

Directors and deans of nursing schools interviewed in Manila confirmed this. Most estimated that 80–90% of their graduates would eventually go overseas and this was the primary motivation for many to enter the nursing

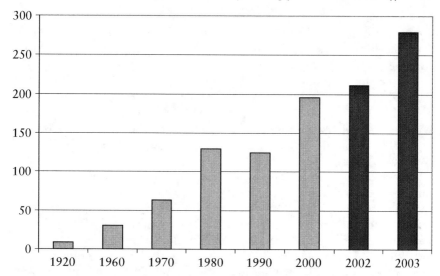

*Figure 5.4* Nursing colleges licensed in the Philippines, 1920–2003.
*Source:* Tan (2003).

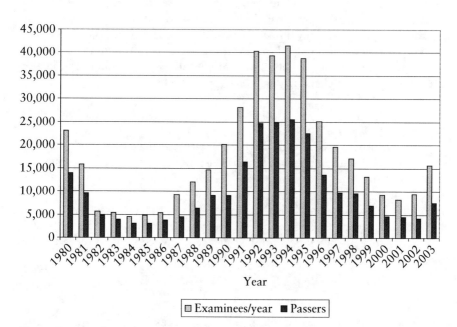

*Figure 5.5* Numbers of examinees and passers of Nursing Board Exam, 1980–2003.
*Source:* Philippine Nurses Association data 2004.

profession in the first place. They attributed the expansion of nursing in the 1980s and in the last 2–3 years to expanding demand in the United States, Canada, Middle East and Europe, and foresaw it continuing for many years to come.

The economic rationale for migration is clear. Even after a substantial increase in pay in 2002, nurses in Philippine government hospitals earned around P13,000 (US$650) per month in Manila, while in a private hospital wages were half that. In the provinces, wages can be lower still—as little as P2,500 a month, roughly equivalent to the wages of a domestic maid in Manila.

The orientation of nursing education to overseas work is explicit in a number of ways. Several colleges market themselves as preparing students for the global labour market. Centro Escolar University, for example, tags itself in brochures and other material as 'Your Link to a Global Career.' Curriculum offerings, too, are directly targeted at overseas employment. One Dean noted that English was emphatically enforced as the language of instruction: 'Because eventually they will be going abroad, right? So they have to learn, and the only way to learn a language is to speak it' (Dean 1, Interview, Manila, 2004). Another commented that the curriculum is 'patterned' for U.S. and U.K. nursing practices. An article in the *Philippine Journal of Nursing* strongly endorses this 'global' approach to nursing education:

> I think instead of lamenting the fact we are losing our graduates to foreign employee [sic], we should look at the positive side of it. The global market for our nurses demands that our nursing students should be educated not only [in] our local health systems, practices, and problems. . . . Our students should be taught about various cultures, health practices and beliefs they will be exposed to.

> (Barcelo 2001)

One Dean was asked whether the issue of staying in the Philippines is ever discussed with students. Her answer amounted to an endorsement of overseas work:

> Of course, we always do that. Every subject that we teach, we always tell them about the importance of staying in the country for at least 2 years so that they'll be equipped with experiences and so they will not be behind when they go abroad.

> (Dean 2, Interview, Manila 2004)

The effects of overseas migration of nurses are felt in the Philippine healthcare system. Paradoxically, while the country has a huge infrastructure for training nurses, local hospitals face a shortage of qualified personnel, and nursing schools have difficulty in retaining faculty (PCIJ 2005).

> The effect is that our nurses are depleted. The hospitals are now understaffed because many nurses go abroad. For example in the colleges nowadays what is our problem? Faculty. We have very rapid turnover and then we lack faculty. Not just in our school but almost in all schools. Plus nursing service. It's hard nowadays to get sick because it's hard to get a nurse. It scares me, and that's true.
>
> (Dean 3, Interview, Manila, 2004)

Ramos-Conde (2001) points to the example of one the country's most prestigious schools of nursing at Universiti Santo Tomas (UST). Of 50 supervisors in the teaching hospital, administrators estimated that four would resign within 4–6 months, 14 would go within 8–14 months, and a further 26 were contemplating departure. Only 6 had explicitly decided against migration. Nurses, too, are turning over at an alarming rate. Of 478 nurses at UST hospital, 414 are in the 20–29 age bracket, 362 are single, and 334 have fewer than 2 years of experience. Many Philippine hospitals are therefore seeing a constantly circulating staff of inexperienced nurses, many just waiting for their migration papers to come through. A nurse in the Philippines also pointed to this phenomenon in a focus group discussion: 'Plenty of hospitals are now closing some wards like here in LaSalle UMC [De La Salle University Medical Centre]. Part of the medical ward was closed because of lack of staff. . . . They are working 12 hours per shift.' (Nurse, Focus Group Discussion, Philippines 2004).

These issues have led many to talk of a crisis in Philippine nursing. Nursing schools attract enrollment precisely because of the promise of overseas employment, and alumni overseas are sometimes generous supporters of their alma mater. Several deans noted that infrastructure purchases in their colleges had been financed through donations from overseas alumni. In one case, U.S. alumni had collectively donated P1 million (US$20,000) in 2003 in order to purchase computers for the school.

The first piece of the Filipino healthcare segmentation story, then, is in training institutions in the Philippines. Not only are students entering nursing colleges specifically with the intention of migrating overseas, those institutions themselves have strong incentives to encourage this process and their curricular offerings are tailored to the needs to international employment. Furthermore, such institutions have proliferated in recent years, so that the Philippines now has a large infrastructure for the training of nurses and their subsequent export. This has clear consequences for the Philippines healthcare system, but the various actors in that sector have little incentive to address the problem.

## THE TRANSNATIONAL TRANSMISSION
## OF CULTURAL VALUES

Why do so many Filipina women enter the proliferating number of nursing colleges in order to pursue the profession? As already noted, there is an economic rationale that is undoubtedly compelling in many cases, and nursing has the rare advantage of being a regulated profession that can be practised relatively easily overseas. But questions of cultural norms must also be considered. These relate less to the notion that nursing is an appropriate profession for young women, and more to the familial expectations resting upon young daughters, sisters and nieces.

Many older nurses described the status and prestige of the nursing profession and the sense of altruism that attracted them in the first place. There was also a strong sense that nursing represented an 'appropriate' profession for Filipina women/wives/daughters/mothers (see also Choy 2003). For most, however, this notion seemed antiquated. For younger nurses, the appeal of nursing was framed in terms of innate essences of *Filipino* femininity, rather than femininity *per se*. Typically, tropes relating to the caring, compassionate, humane Filipina were articulated, which 'naturally' leads toward certain professions:

> Most of the countries abroad prefer Filipino nurses because we are a very compassionate people. . . . We got this from the Spaniards or whoever had been to the Philippines. Our culture here is not of our very own but it's a conglomeration of other cultures, of those people who came and tried to discover our country. That is the plus factor of Filipino nurses: very compassionate, very understanding. Our humanitarian side dominates. That's why Filipinos take mostly health-related courses. I think that really makes Filipinos not only nurses but doctors or in other health-related courses—our being compassionate. That's my observation, I myself have been abroad and I try to compare myself with other nationalities, and I find that we are very compassionate [*maawain*] to other people, regardless of religion or anything.
>
> (Dean 3, Interview, Manila 2004)

While the passage above draws upon colonial history to explain Filipino 'character,' another respondent, this time a Filipina doctor in Toronto, explicitly identified the servitude that is implicit in such a 'caring' role. The non-assertive Filipino, she argued, gravitates toward secondary rather than leading roles:

> That is something that is non-existent: 'assertiveness.' There's no such word that matches that in any Filipino dialect. Because it's not a value, it's not seen as something that is positive, so what happens when they

come here a lot of the virtues like being obedient . . . often times as an adult it's seen here as being subservient and Filipinos don't even realize that.

(Filipina Doctor, Toronto 2003)

These characteristics were identified by several respondents as advantageous in the labour market in Toronto:

Nowadays if you are an Asian, a Filipino especially, you apply in all the service areas, not the management area level, the service area position . . . they'll probably get hired. Filipinos' reputation as a healthcare giver, we have a very good reputation, like we work hard, we work with quality and we are courteous and you very seldom find a Filipino that says the F-word or curses a lot, it's always with respect, so our reputation precedes us.

(Male Filipino hospital orderly, Toronto 2003)

This respondent succinctly summarises the positive but subservient tag that Filipinos have in the Canadian labour market. The identity this respondent sees himself as playing out for his employers is as a skilled worker, a respectful and unassertive employee, but always confined 'not [in] the management area level, [but] the service area level.' This crystallizes into a naturalization of Filipino employment in the healthcare sector, providing a strong cultural explanation for Filipino segmentation on the demand side:

I think, I don't really know, but I think if you were to apply for a job in a hospital, I think other cultures do realize that Filipinos are very strongly into medical stuff. I think they find that they are very reliable and that they can do the job and you know, just because there are so many people doing it. I mean there are tons of Canadians. . . . But if you do go into hospital you will notice there are just so many of them! Filipinos are populated [sic] in the hospital, honestly I think, I don't want to sound like we're great, but I'm just saying that they are well-known to be in the health-care system.

(Filipina medical technician, Interview, Toronto 2003)

In short, nursing and caring professions in general are read as being consistent with a sense of Filipino self-identity, and not exclusively a feminine/Filipina identity.

Beyond essentialized Filipino characteristics, many nurses identified parental or familial pressure as a key factor in taking up nursing.

Well, actually I took up nursing because of what my parents told me. . . . Nursing before was like the course that every one else is taking. My dad told me that if you don't take up nursing then we will not finance your studies anymore. Of course I want to study so I took up nursing. And then the reason why I took up nursing is because it's a good course. It's not just because of the possibility of leaving for work or for money, but you'll learn a lot with nursing courses. . . .

Q: Why would your parents want you to enroll?

You know why? Because my parents wanted me to go to the US. That is really their goal. It is not because you'll learn a lot and things like that, but because they wanted me to follow my sister. My sister is also a nurse, and a few years after she graduated she left for the States. And they wanted me to be the same—that I would also leave.

(Review Instructor for Nursing exam, Interview, Manila 2004)

When I was in high school, my aunts would always say . . . a lot of my aunts in the States are all nurses including uncles, they're all nurses, so every time we visited them, 'you should take nursing, you should take nursing it's really good, you can find a job anywhere, like in the US, in Canada, wherever. It's good to take.' So I had a lot of that pressure and I didn't want to do it because I was getting pressured so much and then I finally said you know what I guess maybe I do want to do it because I didn't know what else to take. But it was a lot of family influence.

(Filipina medical technician, Toronto 2003)

Most of the students are being sent to school by their relatives who are working abroad. That's why many of them take up nursing. And most of them don't like nursing but if they don't take up nursing, they won't be financed by their relatives. Most of them are being financed by relatives abroad. And since this is the right profession or the most practical profession to take, that's why there are many students who take up nursing.

(Dean 3, Interview, Manila 2004)

As these quotes indicate, familial pressure to enter the nursing profession can be intense, but the pressure is not necessarily based upon a sense of feminine roles—indeed many nursing colleges report a recent significant increase in their numbers of male students, in some cases up to 25% of the student body.

The identification of nursing with femininity should not therefore be overstated, and many see it as co-existing with a stronger set of economic motives. At most, then, there is a convergence between the cultural value attached to nursing for women and the fact that it is also a profession that opens doors to lucrative global contract work or migration. Perhaps more important than the notion of nursing as a feminine career, therefore, is the notion that overseas employment and the sending of remittances as an opportunity, even a duty, of daughters and sisters. This is evident in the pressure many felt from their families to enter the nursing profession in the first place—not as a culturally appropriate career, but as a culturally expected and normalized component of a family livelihood strategy. It is not just that the choice of nursing is considered appropriate, but also that working overseas is viewed as a natural and inevitable sacrifice for the family, and nursing is the way to do that.

> You know, when you are young you want adventure and you know when you take up nursing, like it's a visa to go to other places . . . basically you know when you become a nurse you're going to go abroad.
>
> (Filipina Nurse IL, Toronto 2003)

> Q: Why did you choose this line of work?
>
> A: To go abroad. . . . I was thinking I would just be a teacher but if I become a teacher how can I come here because the only way to come abroad is to work as a nurse, it's your passport. That's why you see lots of nurses here that are Filipinos because our purpose is to go abroad. It was already in my mind when I was in Grade 1.
>
> (Filipina Nurse AC, Interview, Toronto 2003)

> I did not like that course before. I wanted to be a teacher, but my mother didn't agree. She told me that I might as well become a nurse like my elder sister because my sister didn't find it hard to find a job. My sister also worked abroad so my mother had a good impression of her profession.
>
> (Company Nurse, Interview, Philippines 2004)

These quotes highlight the deeply embedded status of migration in the Philippines. For many it is more than a distant aspiration or a vague possibility; it is a definite goal to be worked toward. To get ahead, one has to get out.

The preponderance of Filipina nurses is not simply a product of a training infrastructure that exists to educate them prior to deployment into the global nursing labour market. Rather, the choice of nursing as a career fits with cultural expectations upon young Filipina women. These expectations are not, however, so much related to the traditional notion of nursing as an appropriately feminine profession, although the fit between healthcare professions and self-constructions of 'Filipino characteristics' is certainly apparent. Instead, it is the direct connection seen between nursing and lucrative overseas employment that satisfies cultural expectations that sisters and daughters will support other family members. This forms a part of a 'culture of migration' in the Philippines—a strong and growing sense that international migration represents the only way of achieving success, fulfilment and upward mobility (Asis 2006).

## TRANSNATIONAL SOCIAL NETWORKS AND THE LABOUR MARKET

While training institutions in the Philippines and a cultural identification with nursing and migration are critical ingredients in explaining occupational segmentation in the healthcare sector, what is missing is the practical knowledge and institutions to link trained nurses in the Philippines with the labour market in Canada. To create these practical linkages, social networks are needed that provide individuals with the information they need. Such information is not equally available to all potential immigrants globally and thus the topology of such networks is an important element in channelling Filipinos into the Canadian healthcare sector.

For some nursing students in the Philippines, these linkages are made by commercial recruiters and agents. Many visit nursing colleges directly to recruit students. More important, however, are the personal social networks that link trainee or practising nurses in the Philippines with job opportunities in Canada and elsewhere. Information flows about opportunities, procedures, circumstances, wages, costs, etc., in different destinations are widely discussed. One nurse explained how these connections worked in her case:

> I have a friend in Texas, her name is Lita. Once, she called me, I told her, 'Lita, life here in the Philippines is so difficult. The government is so shaky.' So, she told me, 'But, what are you doing there? You come here!' How could I go there? *Sabi ko*, [I said] 'I'm getting old, I have a small kid with me, I cannot leave him alone.' 'No, you just have to take the CGFNS. You have to pass the exam and you can bring your immediate dependents,' meaning my small kid and my husband. 'I still have a place [here for you]. I'll send you this reviewer, . . . don't stay bored and doing nothing there in the Philippines.' *Sabi niya* [She said] 'there's a lot of opportunity here.' She used to talk to me hours, 30 minutes to 1 hour over the phone. Imagine that, just to encourage me to start reviewing.'

> (Filipina Nurse, Focus Group, Philippines 2004—
> formerly in Saudi Arabia)

This nurse later went on to point out that Texas would be her preferred destination because of networks there: 'I want to go to Texas . . . because I have two friends there. Both of them are offering their houses to me. So, I already have a support.' As in the quote above, she also later emphasised that it was not only the knowledge of the opportunity that her friends provided, it was also an example to be followed, and in a sense, to be matched.

> I want to have a graceful retirement, and I believe I am still capable . . .
> *pero kung mananalo lang ako sa lotto, 'di ako aalis* [but if I won the lotto, I would not leave]. . . . There's this feeling inside me, that if my friends have worked there and apparently, they have succeeded, then why can't I?
>
> (Filipina Nurse, Focus Group, Philippines 2004—
> formerly in Saudi Arabia).

At the Canadian end of the process, transnational recruitment is often recognised by employers:

> I mean, it's funny! My aunt is a lab tech here; she works in Mississauga. Every time they are looking for somebody they will ask my aunt if she has family or whatever, you know they will like to hire from the inside first, and they will always ask my aunt because she has been there for long time but I guess they really trust your judgment or they know that obviously she is Filipino and like family-wise she can get somebody. She has gotten a couple of people just because they ask her and I guess they trust her
>
> (Filipina medical technician, Interview, Toronto 2003)

In some cases this recruitment through networks is even encouraged in the form of a 'finders fee':

> They always put it in our computer system and then they post it in the bulletin and then from there it becomes word of mouth, you call your friends and if they want a position and the good thing is that the hospital is giving you a finders fee. If a friend of yours got hired, you recommend him and the friend stays up to six months you will get a check for $500, so it's nice to recommend a friend. And you know Filipinos! Boom! My daughter is filling the application and is hired and I get $500.
>
> (Male Filipino hospital attendant EDAA, Interview, Toronto 2003)

The respondent above, an emergency room attendant without any health-care experience, found his own job through a similar network: a friend of his wife, employed as a housekeeper in the hospital, brought the position to his attention. This respondent estimated that there are around 70–75 Filipinos in a staff of 700 at the hospital. While illuminating the process through which jobs are frequently found, this also points to the cumulative effect of social networks that bring Filipino immigrants into the healthcare sector. When every employee is a source of new employees, the existing ethnic structure of the workforce is likely to be perpetuated in a process that might be called 'cumulative segmentation.'

A key point made by several respondents was that finding work for friends and relatives is not limited to those already in Toronto. Labour market intelligence flows back to the Philippines, and new arrivals are often met with the necessary contacts to find a job quickly. This is not, therefore, a social network that can be thought of as local and 'co-ethnic' in nature. Rather, it represents the transnational reach of familial and social ties, which become localised when the protagonists are all in Toronto.


## ECONOMIC DIMENSIONS OF TRANSNATIONALISM

Training for the nursing profession is widespread, as noted earlier, but it is not inexpensive. Fees in the Philippines can range as high as 40,000–60,000 pesos (US$800–1,200) per semester. A year of fees could be equivalent to approximately 8 months of post-graduation salary if a nurse were to find employment in a private hospital in the Philippines. With these kinds of costs, it is difficult for even financially secure middle class families to support a daughter or son through nursing college. Most, therefore, depend upon the support of overseas relatives. Several deans of nursing schools in Manila indicated that a majority of their students were supported financially in this way.

The cumulative concentration of Filipinos in the nursing profession is therefore attributable to more than just the social networks that guide them there. It is also a product of the need for an overseas relative to finance the necessary training. Indeed the two are connected, as students will usually seek to go to the overseas location where their benefactor is located:

> It's their relatives you know, if they were the ones who sent them to school, then naturally they have to go to the States. So, it depends where their relatives are stationed—in Canada or in UK. So, it doesn't really matter for as long as they can get out of the country and you know, earn dollars, U.S. dollars, any kind of dollars.

> (Dean 3, Interview, Manila 2004)

The growing supply of international nurses from the Philippines, then, is also part of a transnational circulation of money, in which overseas nurses (and other workers) fund the studies of their relatives back home. Migration, in this way, begets further migration. In the case of immigration to Canada, it is not simply the expense of training that must be shouldered, but also several thousand dollars in application fees, air tickets, landing fees, and possibly fees for courses upon arrival. The availability of support from relatives already abroad is therefore a crucial part of the process that explains why Filipino nurses in Toronto are joined by other Filipino nurses.

## CONCLUSIONS AND IMPLICATIONS

Immigrant labour market segmentation neither starts nor finishes at the scale of the local labour market in which it occurs. The preponderance of Filipino nurses in Toronto, and Canada as a whole, therefore needs to be explained with reference to processes that transcend urban labour markets and encompass transnational linkages with the Philippines, where nurses are being trained, socialised and acculturated with a particular set of skills and outlooks. As a culture of migration takes hold, the natural option is training that permits global mobility and a fulfilment of cultural expectations and obligations toward other family members. This is an obligation that is gendered, with expectations falling heaviest on daughters and sisters. Nursing also conforms to cultural expectations of femininity, although the increasing number of men enrolling in nursing schools indicates some flexibility in that respect. Alone, however, such cultural explanations are probably necessary but not sufficient conditions. An institutional infrastructure is needed to train nurses and deploy them overseas, and social networks are required to feed labour market intelligence back to sites of out-migration. Furthermore, an education that conforms to global standards is not cheap—thus remittances from relatives already overseas are needed in order to reproduce the next wave of nurse-migrants. In all of these ways, nursing labour, and healthcare workers in general, are reproduced not in the labour markets of their employment, but in the Philippines. The existence of these interrelated cultural, social, economic and institutional ties creates a potent framework to reproduce and deploy healthcare labour for Canada's hospitals and laboratories. It is, moreover, a system with positive feedback loops, such that information and remittance flows accentuate existing segmentation, creating a process of cumulative segmentation.

All of these features exist on the supply side of the labour market. But cultural identification and racialization is also at work on the demand side. Just as Filipinos present themselves as 'naturally' suited to caring professions, albeit in subservient, unassertive roles, so their employers re-create this discourse in their preferences for certain groups in certain occupations. And once it becomes known that Filipinos 'do' healthcare, the naturalization of the segmentation process is complete.

## REFERENCES

Asis, M B (2006) The Philippines' culture of migration, *Migration Information Source* http://www.migrationinformation.org/Profiles/display.cfm?ID=364 accessed 11 August 2006.

Barcelo, T I (2001) Internationalisation of nursing education, *Philippine Journal of Nursing*, 71(3–4), 16–18.

Bauder, H (2006) *Labor movement: How migration regulates labor markets*, Oxford: Oxford University Press.

Bauder, H and Sharpe, B (2002) Residential segregation of visible minorities in Canada's gateway cities, *The Canadian Geographer*, 46, 204–22.

Becker, G S (1993) *Human capital: A theoretical and empirical analysis with special reference to education*, (3rd ed), Chicago: University of Chicago Press.

Blouin, C, Gibb, H, McAdams, M and Weston, A (2004) *Engendering Canadian trade policy: A case study of labor mobility in trade agreements*, Ottawa: Status of Women Canada.

Choy, C (2003) *Empire of care: Nursing and migration in Filipino American history*, Durham: Duke University Press.

CIHI (Canadian Institute for Health Information) (2006) *Workforce trends of regulated nurses in Canada*, 2005, Ottawa: CIHI.

Espiritu, Y L (2003) *Home bound: Filipino American lives across cultures, communities, and countries*, Berkeley: University of California Press.

Guarnizo, L E (2003) The economics of transnational living, *International Migration Review*, 37, 666–699.

Kelly, P (2006) *Filipinos in Canada: Economic dimensions of immigration and settlement*, Working Paper 48, Centre of Excellence for Research on Immigration and Settlement, Toronto.

Levitt, P (2001) *The transnational villagers*, Berkeley: University of California Press.

PCIJ (Philippine Centre for Investigative Journalism) (2005) *Nursing the world: Filipinas in the global care industry*, Quezon City: Philippine Centre for Investigative Journalism.

Peck, J (1996) *Workplace: the social regulation of labor markets*, New York: Guilford.

Ramos-Conde, A (2001) Perspective on nursing shortage and strategies to nurture the nurses who stay, *Philippine Journal of Nursing*, 71(1–2), 37–44.

Tan, J G (2003) Realities and challenges for the global nursing community, *Philippine Journal of Nursing*, 73(1–2), 8–10.

Waldinger, R and Lichter, M (2003) *How the other half works: Immigration and the social organization of labor*, Berkeley: University of California Press.

# 6    Indian Nurses
## Seeking New Shores
### Philomina Thomas

This chapter examines the perspectives of nurses in New Delhi, India, on their working environment and the prospect of international migration. The first part examines the ongoing migration of Indian nurses from the perspective of the nurses themselves, and looks at why Indian nurses in general, and some particular groups among them, may migrate. It also identifies which countries they wish to migrate to. The chapter then looks at the implications of this migration for India's public health, and possible policy responses to the phenomenon. It is primarily based on a survey conducted by the author of 448 nurses in New Delhi, the capital of India (Thomas 2006).

A very large number of young, trained Indian nurses are planning to migrate. Although the tendency to migrate is at present more pronounced among nurses belonging to some particular regions, language groups and religious affiliations, which account for only a small proportion of India's population, the indications are that the desire and tendency to migrate is spreading very quickly to almost all young, well-qualified nurses. Given the persistent shortage of such nurses in rich countries, it is probable that, in the absence of suitable policies, India will, in the coming years, lose a large number of nurses to rich countries. This will inevitably have serious consequences for the health sector in India.

## THE MIGRATION INTENTIONS OF NURSES

The process of international migration of nurses can be divided into certain key parts: the initial aims of the nurses; the availability of contacts with friends and relatives abroad; their move to Delhi, whether for eventual international migration or not; the experience of work in Delhi, which would in some way affect their perceptions about migration; the process of making enquiries, deciding about destinations, and contacting agents; and finally the actual migration. Only the last stage cannot be discussed here, since that stage, for these nurses, lies in the future. The nurses were from four government and eight private hospitals, and eight schools and colleges of nursing in different parts of Delhi. Of the 448 nurses in the sample, 281

(63%) expressed their intention to migrate. While this percentage cannot be taken as indicative of the average propensity to migrate of all Indian nurses, or even of nurses in Delhi, these nurses constitute a substantial sample from a diversity of institutions.

As many as 134 out of 448 nurses in the sample said that they had joined the nursing profession in order to migrate. Of these just 17 had subsequently changed their mind about migration. On the other hand, of the 314 nurses who had joined the profession for reasons other than migration, more than half (164) had changed their views and were now planning to migrate. Some factor or group of factors had brought about a change in their ideas. About three quarters of the nurses were not originally residents of Delhi. A large proportion had come to Delhi for employment, and another large group had come for education, but many from both groups now wanted to go abroad. Delhi had become a potential stepping stone to onwards migration.

Given the large proportion of nurses who expressed their intention to migrate, it might be thought that levels of job satisfaction would tend to be low, but that was not actually true. The level of job satisfaction did not vary significantly across different grades of nurses, nor did it differ between nurses in private and in government employment. There was, however, a significant difference in the opinions of prospective migrants and non-migrants regarding their current jobs. Some 104 nurses were not satisfied with their present job, and of these, 90 nurses (87%) were planning to migrate. But it should not be thought that the migrating nurses were all dissatisfied with their jobs. As many as 344 of the 448 nurses in the sample said they were satisfied with their jobs, yet of these as many as 191 (56%) said that they were planning to migrate overseas. The reason for migration was not mere dissatisfaction with their jobs.

Why then were the nurses planning to migrate? A large number were generally critical of the approach of the government to their problems, though nurses in private sector employment were more critical than their government sector sisters. This may be due to their resentment at not getting government jobs, which in India, as in many other countries, are considered much more desirable than private sector jobs. It is possible that in the perception of the nurses it is primarily the government's duty to employ health service providers, and the government's failure to do so in sufficient numbers is one of their major grievances. The salary data clearly indicate that where the staff nurse in government employment was drawing an average salary of Rs.14,272 (US$350) per month, her counterpart in the private sector was drawing just Rs. 9,053 (US$220). The standard deviation of salaries was much higher for the lower paid private sector staff nurses, which indicates that a very large number of private sector staff nurses were drawing extremely low pay, which would certainly generate a sense of grievance against the government.

Pessimistic views regarding living conditions in India play an important part in influencing migration behaviour. Of the 165 nurses who felt that living conditions were becoming unmanageable, 116 (70%) said they were planning to migrate. But many nurses who planned to migrate were from the other group; of the 212 nurses who felt that living conditions were satisfactory, 120 (57%) still planned to migrate to some other country.

Pessimism among nurses regarding the possibility of fulfilling their professional goals was one of the most important factors influencing attitudes to international migration. About half the nurses in the sample said that it was not possible to fulfill 'the noble ideals of the nursing profession' while working in India, and a huge proportion of these (157 of 223: 70%) were planning to migrate. But, at the same time, many nurses (as many as 160) believed it was possible to fulfill the ideals of the profession while working in India, and yet 89 (56%) of them were still planning to migrate.

Unhappiness with prevalent social attitudes may be an important factor motivating international migration. Of the 448 nurses, a very large number (362) were unhappy with Indian society's attitude toward nurses and, of these, a large share (241 or 67%) of the nurses said they were planning to migrate. Only 70 nurses said they had no problem with Indian society's attitude toward nurses, and consequently a comparatively low percentage (46%) were planning to migrate.

Significantly, despite their higher pay scales and more generous service conditions, the government sector nurses were more critical of social attitudes toward their profession than the private sector nurses though the difference was not statistically significant at the 5% level. A possible reason for this could be the feeling amongst a large number of nurses belonging to 'forward' and 'middle' castes that their promotional avenues had been choked off as a result of reservation in promotion for nurses belonging to Scheduled Castes and Scheduled Tribes. (The Indian government's promotion rules provide for reservation of posts not only at the entry level, but also in promotions. Thus, a nurse belonging to a Scheduled Caste or Tribe may get two or three promotions within a span of 15 years, whereas her 'forward' or 'middle' caste colleague, senior to her in experience by 5 years and perhaps with more professional qualifications, languishes as her subordinate at the entry level post, and sees no prospect of promotion as the higher posts have been allocated to the 'Scheduled Caste' and 'Scheduled Tribe' nurses). Consequently there is a much greater propensity for 'forward' and 'middle' caste nurses to migrate compared with nurses from Scheduled Castes and Tribes.

An enormous sense of alienation existed among the nurses. Many seemed to regard the survey interview as a long-suppressed opportunity to voice their grievances. Some of the problems raised by them related to poor management, over-work, poor transport facilities, lack of recognition for their work and absence of opportunities for promotion or professional growth. In the private sector hospitals, the nurses complained that they received very low pay and had no means of collective expression. Unions were conspicuously absent in the private sector. Nurses complained that they were generally made scapegoats for every problem arising from deficiencies of medical treatment. They were also treated shabbily by the patients, many of whom were from elite sections of Indian society.

In the government-run hospitals, although nurses were better paid and usually enjoyed some degree of job security, the problems arising from the management style were, if anything, worse. A number of nurses complained that the doctors alone had a voice in the running of their institutions. Even the nursing superintendents and chief nursing officers were hardly consulted. At the ward level, the word of even the junior-most doctor carried much more weight than that of the nursing sister-in-charge. Some, nurses who had contacts with their colleagues who had migrated, knew that this kind of situation was, to a great extent, unique to India, and this made them even more bitter in their attitude toward management and doctors in general. Within a few minutes of the interview this bitterness would become apparent. The senior nurses said that they were staying on in India only because of family ties and a feeling that they were no longer employable outside. As one nurse put it:

> In other countries the nurses are able to work because they have a suitable work atmosphere. They have better facilities and better management practices and so the work is easier. We too work hard but the conditions are so bad that it is difficult to provide genuine relief to the patients. If we work this hard in a foreign country we would be paid much better, would get more respect and would have more job satisfaction. . . . I'm here because I've missed the bus.

In each government institution, when the matter of promotions came up, there were heated exchanges between nurses belonging to different caste groups. While the beneficiaries of reservation believed that the benefits they were receiving were just recompense for historical injustices done to them, the other group were vocal in their condemnation of the government's policy of reservation in promotion. Some of them pointed out that at the level of assistant nursing superintendent and deputy nursing superintendent the only 'General' category nurses were on the verge of retirement. The outcome would be that whenever the post of nursing superintendent became vacant the post would go to the reserved category candidates alone on the ground of longer duration of service in the 'feeder grade.' This situation was evident in many of the government institutions, which are increasingly dominated at the top by beneficiaries of reservation, while in private institutions, the number of Scheduled Caste and Scheduled Tribe nurses, whether at junior or senior levels, is miniscule.

Particular groups of nurses were much more likely to wish to emigrate than others. Younger nurses without strong ties were more likely to be interested. Of the 219 nurses in the age group 20 to 29 years, 179 (81%) intended to migrate compared with 102 of 229 (45%) in older age groups. Christian nurses also tended to be prospective migrants; of the 255 Christian nurses,

185 (73%) expressed their intention to migrate compared with 85 of 176 Hindu nurses (48%). Given that Christians constitute just 2% of the population of India, it is also apparent that Christians were much more likely to become nurses (Percot and Rajan 2007).

Of the various linguistic groups, Malayalam speakers were most interested in migration, with 184 of 255 (72%) expressing their intention to leave. Since Malayalam is the language of the state of Kerala, which accounts for only 3% of the population of India, it was evident that many of the Delhi nurses had first moved from there as a prelude to emigration. This was also linked to the availability of contacts abroad, though not necessarily in the nursing profession.

The preponderance of Christians from Kerala amongst those interested in migration was evident when combining Christianity and language. Of 213 Malayalam-speaking Christian nurses 160 (75%) were planning to migrate. And of 42 other Christian nurses, the least migration prone were the Hindi speakers, just 14 out of 29 (48%) wishing to migrate. Both Malayalam speaking Christians and Hindi speaking Christians had a migration propensity very similar to that of their non-Christian sisters speaking the same languages. Of the two influences, language was the decisive one as far as the tendency to migrate is concerned, indicating the significance of being from Kerala, the state most characterised by international migration. Whether Hindi or Malayalam speakers, Christians had more contacts abroad than others, again linked to a history of migration, and the number of social contacts overseas was correlated with interest in migration.

In Kerala, the state of origin of a very large proportion of Indian nurses and where Christian nurses once constituted an overwhelming majority, non-Christians are opening nursing schools and colleges and enrolling for nursing training in large numbers. This is because other communities, which once shunned nursing as a low-grade occupation fit for subordinate social groups, have now realized that out-migration of women as nurses can open up paths to economic development and even the migration of entire families to more prosperous countries. Marriage to a nurse is now considered by many young men the easiest path to escaping the grip of Indian poverty and unemployment (Percot and Rajan 2007).

Those nurses who had come to Delhi from distant states were also more likely to wish to migrate internationally. All 13 nurses who received their nursing education in Tamilnadu state sought to migrate. Similarly, 35 out of 43 of those qualifying from Andhra Pradesh, and 40 out of 54 of those qualifying from Kerala, intended to migrate. By contrast, 125 out of 200 of those qualifying from Delhi and 13 out of 23 of those qualifying from Punjab said they were planning to migrate. Even smaller proportions of nurses qualifying from the states of Bihar, Uttar Pradesh, Maharashtra and Madhya Pradesh said they were planning to migrate. The association between migration intent and state of initial training was statistically significant. However many of those from states outside Kerala who sought to migrate

were also Malayalam speakers. As many as 12 of the 13 nurses who qualified from Tamil Nadu were Malayalam speakers, as were 39 of 43 of those
who qualified from Andhra Pradesh. Punjab was the only state from where
a significant percentage was planning to migrate, where the share of Malayalam speakers was low, being 4 out of 23. However Punjab too has been
a state with a tradition of migration, and a large share of those obtaining
nursing qualifications from Punjab were Christians.

Nurses with the more basic BSc (Bachelors Degree in Nursing, usually
acquired after Class 12) were keener to migrate. As many as 76 of the 97
nurses (74%) with the BSc said they planned to migrate. On the other hand,
a somewhat lower proportion (172 of 277: 62%) of the nurses with the
3- to 4-year 'General Nursing and Midwifery' (GNM) qualification sought
to migrate. Twelve of the 32 nurses (38%) with 'Post Certificate BSc' (Bachelors Degree in Nursing, acquired after some years of practice by a GNM-
qualified nurse) and 17 of 34 nurses (50%) with Masters in Nursing said
they planned to migrate. Nurses with the basic BSc have an advantage, being
younger, with fewer commitments and better job prospects, and hence they
are more interested in migrating than any other more educated group. It is
not therefore the most skilled and experienced who are most likely to wish
to migrate.

The three categories of nurses that dominated the sample were staff nurses,
clinical instructors and tutors, who numbered 308, 23 and 52 respectively.
Of these categories, 71%, 65% and 48% respectively said they planned
to migrate. Again, those most interested in migrating were in posts at the
lower levels, whether among nurse practitioners or among nurse educators,
whereas fewer assistant nursing superintendents, nursing superintendents,
lecturers and senior lecturers, said they planned to migrate. Thus, international migration is a phenomenon that disproportionately affects the base
of the nursing profession in India. While the relative economic gain from
migration was much more for junior staff, since they were drawing less pay,
this was probably of little significance given the massive gap between foreign and Indian pay scales at every level. Indeed during the study a number
of cases of lecturers and senior lecturers in nursing were encountered who
were in the process of migrating overseas to take up jobs at the lowest rungs
of clinical nursing. More significantly a large number of senior nurses indicated that they were 'tied down' because of age, families and children. Many
did not want migration to disrupt their family life.

Nurses in private employment were more prone to migration than those
in government employment. Seventy-eight percent of the nurses in private
employment expressed their intention to migrate as against 41% in government employment. This was partly due to the larger share of low-income
earners among the private sector nurses, but also because private sector
nurses tended to have less negative impressions about service conditions
overseas. Given the high level of job security and relatively relaxed work
atmosphere in government institutions, it was perhaps natural that nurses

working in government institutions were more apprehensive about their abilities to experience and cope with new conditions abroad. However, interest in migration was clearly linked to income, and the greater the potential gain in income, the greater the tendency to migrate. Of 152 nurses in the lowest-income bracket, as many as 135 (89%) expressed their intention to migrate. In higher-income brackets, the percentage intending to migrate fell. But even in the highest-income category, 13 of 38 respondents (34%) said they were planning to migrate. Treating total family income as the unit for such calculations, a similar result was found: The higher the family or husband's income, the lower the propensity to migrate.

Having personal contacts overseas, perhaps especially someone who was a fellow nurse, was strongly linked to interest in migration. Some 250 nurses in the sample knew an already migrant nurse, and of these 165 (66%) were planning to migrate. On the other hand of the 120 sample nurses who knew a non-nurse migrant, 75 (62.5%) were intending to migrate. This slight difference suggests that while it was important for a prospective nurse migrant to have contacts abroad, it was not necessary that they be from the nursing profession. The process of nurse recruitment for overseas migration has however developed to a point where personal contact with an already migrant nurse is no longer as important as it was in the past. This has followed the growth of Indian communities overseas, and the shift in the process of migration from individual decision making to recruitment.

Many nurses had started going through formal processes in order to migrate to foreign countries. As many as 197 (58%) of the nurses had contacted one or other agency or responded to newspaper advertisements concerning migration. Of the remaining 251 some 101 were still planning to migrate but had not made any formal contact with agencies or appeared for interviews. A large number of those who had reported that they were planning to migrate were still at an early stage in decision making, though the majority were taking at least preliminary steps.

By far the most popular destination was the United States, followed by the United Kingdom. The United States was the preferred destination for 205 of the nurses and second choice for another 38, while the United Kingdom was first choice for 53 nurses and second choice for 106 nurses. Gulf countries were low on the priority list, being first choice for three, second choice for four and third choice for four nurses. Australia, in contrast had a higher degree of visibility among the prospective migrants: first choice for 19 nurses, second choice for 57 nurses and third choice for 67 nurses. This contrasts with the existing situation of Kerala nurses overseas, which has tended to consist of a couple of years of work in India, followed by a much longer spell of up to 20 years working as a nurse in the Gulf, before moving again (Percot and Rajan 2007). Despite a tradition of Kerala nurses moving to the Gulf, many disliked some facets of life there and sought to move on. Percot and Rajan stated that 'in the coming years a social distinction would emerge between emigrant nurses coming from a more privileged milieu who reach western countries directly . . . and emigrant nurses who belong to more socially modest families that view the Gulf as a first goal or even the only possibility' (2007:324). Evidently, a new generation of nurses is beginning to look more directly to western countries, because of easier access, growing communities there and more information, Moreover, migration to the Gulf, apart from its known problems, also involves fairly large unrecorded, under-the-table payments to agents, while migration to the richer countries like the United States, United Kingdom and Australia does not involve such large payments. Together with the superior salaries on offer, and the possibility of family migration to these countries, a large number of nurses, not only from Kerala, but also from elsewhere, no longer find the Gulf attractive.

Many reasons were given by the nurses for their choice of destination. As far as the United States was concerned, pay was mentioned as an important consideration by as many as 86 out of 118 nurses who responded, but very often it was combined with factors like a better working and social environment, better status for nurses and more prospects for professional growth. The United States was considered to be a more suitable place for family migration and settlement, with nurses also very conscious of the greater possibility of their spouses getting suitable jobs. Another factor was the existence of links with previous migrants to the United States. Some 20 of the 118 nurses mentioned that one or more of their close friends or family members had already settled there. Broadly the same factors influenced choice of the United Kingdom: better salaries in combination with a better social and professional environment. Australia exercised a more nebulous fascination, beyond obvious income benefits.

## IMPLICATIONS AND POLICY RESPONSES

Most nurses were planning permanent migration, with their families, to rich countries like the United States, United Kingdom and Australia. Little interest was expressed by the nurses in ever returning to their homeland. While intentions are far from outcomes, this indicates that nurse migration may mean a permanent loss of valuable human resources.

Would this migration of nurses have an adverse effect on the Indian health service sector? Or is it the case that India has a surfeit of nurses, so that some out-migration is of no real consequence for the health care sector? The 2006 World Health Report included India among the countries having a 'critical shortage' of 'health service providers,' that is of doctors, nurses and midwives (WHO 2006: 12). To more adequately meet the WHO norm of 2.28 health care professionals per 1000 population for the Indian population of around 1,112 million in 2005–2006, some 2,535,360 health workers are required. However Government of India data indicate a total availability in 2005 of around 1,520,000 health care providers (865,135 nurses and 656,111 doctors; Government of India 2007), indicating a massive shortage.

According to the recommended norms of the Government of India's Expert Committee on Health Manpower Planning, Production and Management (also known as the Bajaj Committee), which used a norm of 1 bed per 1,000 population and one staff nurse per every three beds (plus 30% leave reserve), the requirements for 2000 came to 664,623 nurses for hospital nursing services. The committee also projected requirements of 78,491 nurses for community health centres, alongside 34,875 Public Health Nurses, 107,960 Health Supervisors and around 323,882 auxiliary nurse midwives/ health workers, making a total of 1,131,340. Projecting this onto 2006 population figures indicates a total requirement of around 1,269,475 nurses. Comparing this with the actual availability of nurses in India, there is a shortage of nurses of around a third. Debate over the means of calculating needs and availability might produce different numbers but would probably not really challenge the substantial deficit.

The implication of these calculations is that the out-migration of trained nurses is not a cost-less transfer of an otherwise unemployed, unnecessary resource. Very often it has been said that the loss from out-migration needs to be offset against the prospective gains from migration in terms of economic transfers from migrants to residents, and possible benefits from return migration. So long as out-migration of nurses was primarily short-term circular migration to the Gulf, the prospective gain from migration could be expected to be quite large. With the change in direction, and perhaps duration and family structure, of out-migration, prospective gains cannot necessarily be expected to be the same. Purely in terms of the economic loss of valuable human resources, out-migration of nurses must be considered as something harmful for India, emphasising that India is probably a net loser as a result of the migration of skilled workers (Khadria 2005).

Policy options available to the Government of India, that might reduce the loss, include entering into international agreements on proper recruitment methods with the countries to which nurses are migrating, as well as attempting to get destination countries to fund the opening of new nursing colleges in India (Aiken et al. 2004, Buchan and Sochalski 2004). To encourage more nurses to stay in India, the government must make the nursing profession more attractive to young people. A major improvement in pay scales for government sector nurses is called for, though this could not realistically reduce the international wage differentials for nurses. Given the enormous differentials that prevail (of the order of 15 to 1), a major wage revision for government sector nurses would actually be more valuable in terms of enhancing the social status of nursing. Nurses feel that their pay scales have suffered in comparison to categories such as junior doctors, operation room technicians, primary school teachers and junior engineers. This changing relativity in salaries has had a major influence on the morale of the nursing profession and their considerable alienation from government policies. It is not merely a matter of improving salaries of government sector nurses. Pay scales in the private sector have a close link with those in the public sector. A substantial improvement in government pay scales would have a positive effect on the pay scales and the morale of their sisters in the private sector.

Another effective measure would be to bring about improvements in living and working conditions (housing and travel allowances, etc.) as incentives to nurses to stay on at home (Vujicic et al. 2004, Zurn et al. 2005). Working conditions, such as more flexible shift timings, work autonomy, career development, and reduced violence in workplaces, are critical. Among other things, this would require a strengthening of nurses' representative organizations (Buchan et al 2005). Promotional avenues must be transparent and assured. Some method should be found to avoid the choking of promotional avenues for 'forward' and 'middle' caste nurses. Perhaps the most difficult (yet very necessary) step would be to allow nurses to practise. Remarkably, of all categories of nurses, only community health workers, who have a much lower level of knowledge and skill than the GNM, BSc (Nursing) or MSc (Nursing) nurses, have the legal right in India to prescribe medicines and provide treatment to patients. If nurses with higher-level qualifications are allowed to practise (of course, within clearly defined guidelines), then some of the more dynamic of them would see the scope for increasing their incomes as well as their social status while living in India, and this would have a positive effect on the entire nursing community in India. Similarly developing at least one progressive 'Magnet Hospital' in every major Indian city would provide a management style involving active nurse participation, well-prepared and qualified nurse executives, flexible working schedules for nurses, clinical career opportunities and facilities for in-service/continuing education. These could be the models for providing better working conditions for nurses as well as patients.

Many schools and colleges of nursing in India have emerged in the last two to three decades and charge very high fees to the students. Those who pass out from such institutions will naturally seek to recover the money they and their kin have spent on their education as quickly as possible. It would be very unfair to ask students who have spent a large amount on their education not to migrate. If more nurses are to be encouraged to stay on in India, it will be possible only if the government frames and implements guidelines on fee structures for both private and government nursing educational institutions, and puts in place a range of other structural changes. That may well depend on fundamental economic and political developments.

## REFERENCES

Aiken, L H, Buchan, J, Sochalski, J, Nichols, B and Powell, M (2004) Trends in international nurse migration, *Health Affairs*, 23, 69–77.
Buchan, J, Kingma, M and Lorenzo, F M (2005) *International migration of nurses: Trends and policy implications*, Geneva: International Council of Nurses.

Buchan, J and Sochalski, J (2004) The migration of nurses. *Bulletin of the WHO*, 82, 587–594.

Government of India (2007) *Economic survey 2006–07*, New Delhi.

Khadria, B (2005) Exporting health workers to overseas markets, in International Organization for Migration, *Health and migration: Bridging the gap*, Geneva: IOM, pp. 78–81.

Percot, M and Rajan, S I (2007) Female emigration from India: Case study of nurses. *Economic and Political Weekly*, 42, 318–325.

Thomas, P (2006) The international migration of Indian nurses, *International Nursing Review*, 53, 277–283.

Vujicic, M, Zurn, P, Diallo, K, Adams, O and Dal Poz, M (2004) The role of wages in the migration of health care professionals from developing countries, *Human Resources for Health 2004*, 2(3).

World Health Organization (2006) *Working together for health*, Geneva: WHO.

Zurn, P, Dolea, C and Stilwell, B (2005) *Nurse retention and recruitment: Developing a motivated workforce*, Geneva: International Council of Nurses.

# 7 The Migration of Health Professionals from Zimbabwe

*Abel Chikanda*

## INTRODUCTION: HUMAN RESOURCE CRISIS IN AFRICA

African countries are faced with a large and growing problem of the migration of skilled professionals. Such movements have induced a human capital crisis on the continent and pose a serious threat to sustainable economic growth and the attainment of the Millennium Development Goals (MDGs) (Wadda 2000). There is a general consensus in the discourse on economic development that the migration of skilled workers constitutes a drain on the sending country's human resources because its investments in human capital development will be utilised by the recipient country, although such movements are largely beneficial to the individuals concerned. The United Nations Commission on Trade and Development (UNCTAD) estimates that each migrating African professional represents a loss of US$184,000 to the continent (Leise 2004). Paradoxically, Africa spends nearly US$4 billion a year on the salaries of 100,000 foreign experts (Oyowe 1996).

Better wages and employment conditions, better information, recruitment, and cheaper transportation are encouraging skilled migrants to seek jobs in developed economies (Lowell and Findlay 2001). However the magnitude of the phenomenon is uncertain because of lack of reliable data sources (e.g., Adepoju 1995, Gaidzanwa 1999, Meyer and Brown 1999, Russell 1993). Where statistical data are available, they tend to be of poor quality, have numerous gaps and cannot be used as reliable sources.

Recent research has shown that the health sectors of several African states have been severely affected by the loss of skilled and experienced professionals (Huddart et al. 2003, Leise 2004). However, the reasons underlying the decision to migrate as well as the impacts of medical migration have not been adequately researched, a gap this chapter seeks to fill for Zimbabwe. The chapter draws on research conducted in 2002 that sought to assess the magnitude of the migration of health professionals from Zimbabwe, analyse the effects on health care delivery, and recommend ways of retaining skilled health personnel.

## MEDICAL MIGRATION FROM
## SOUTHERN AFRICA: AN OVERVIEW

Piecemeal attempts have been made to document the scale of medical migration from Africa. The most comprehensive study on health professionals' migration, conducted in 2002 under the sponsorship of WHO, took place in six countries: Cameroon, Ghana, Senegal, South Africa, Uganda and Zimbabwe (Awases et al. 2004) and the findings reported later on in this chapter are drawn from this survey (see also Chikanda 2005, 2006). The research was limited since some countries were unable to provide data on national staffing patterns in their health sectors. Clemens and Petterson (2005) subsequently established the number of African trained medical professionals working in nine major immigrant receiving countries, namely the United Kingdom, United States, France, Canada, Australia, Portugal, Spain, Belgium and South Africa; 36,653 African medical doctors were working abroad, with the United Kingdom (15,258) and the United States (12,813) being the leading destinations (Table 7.1). While South Africa has the highest absolute number of doctors practising abroad (7,363), countries with fewer professionals have recorded the most significant losses in proportional terms, with Angola and Mozambique having more than 70% of their doctors practising abroad. South Africa has received a large number of doctors from African countries such as Zimbabwe. Of the 1,459 immigrant African doctors working in South Africa in 2000, 643 were from Zimbabwe. South Africa also hosted 834 doctors born in the major immigrant receiving countries noted above.

In proportional terms, the loss of nurses from Africa has been less significant than that of doctors as the total population is almost three times that of doctors (Table 7.2). However, the absolute number of nurses migrating from Africa is slightly more than that of doctors. South Africa and Zimbabwe stand out as the two biggest exporters of nurses from Southern Africa. Again the United Kingdom and the United States are the major destinations for African nurses.

The figures in Tables 7.1 and 7.2 give a rough indication of the number of Southern African health professionals working in the major immigrant receiving countries. A new development over the past two decades has been the growth in the number of professionals moving to other countries within the continent, although the magnitude of such movements has yet to be established. Adoption of stringent immigrant controls by the major immigrant receiving countries and increased economic differentiation among African countries has facilitated the growth in movements within the continent (Gould 1988), but subsequent more relaxed controls facilitated the migration of health professionals. This has been a huge loss to most African countries that offer tertiary education at subsidised rates. Kirigia et al. (2006) have calculated the cost of training a medical doctor from primary school to university to be US$65,997, and note that, for every doctor who

*Table 7.1* Distribution of Doctors Trained in Southern African Countries in Nine Receiving Countries, 2000

| Sending Country | Domestic | Total Abroad | Percent Abroad |
|---|---|---|---|
| Angola | 881 | 2,102 | 70 |
| Botswana | 530 | 68 | 11 |
| Congo Republic | 670 | 747 | 53 |
| Democratic Republic of Congo | 5,647 | 552 | 9 |
| Kenya | 3,855 | 3,975 | 51 |
| Lesotho | 114 | 57 | 33 |
| Malawi | 200 | 293 | 59 |
| Mozambique | 435 | 1,334 | 75 |
| Namibia | 466 | 382 | 45 |
| South Africa | 27,551 | 7,363 | 21 |
| Swaziland | 133 | 53 | 28 |
| Tanzania | 1,264 | 1,356 | 52 |
| Uganda | 2,429 | 1,837 | 43 |
| Zambia | 670 | 883 | 57 |
| Zimbabwe | 1,530 | 1,602 | 51 |
| Sub-Saharan Africa | 96,405 | 36,653 | 28 |
| Africa | 280,808 | 64,941 | 19 |

Source: Clemens and Petterson, 2006

migrates, a country loses US$1,854,677 worth of investment in human capital. Therefore, there is a need to find an effective solution to the substantial outflow of health professionals from the continent.

## HEALTH WORKER MIGRATION FROM ZIMBABWE

Zimbabwe has become a leading source country for health professionals, with 51% of its medical doctors and 24% of its nurses practising abroad in 2000 (Clemens and Petterson 2006). The few remaining health professionals have to cope with heavy workloads in a country faced with a growing

*Table 7.2* Distribution of Nurses Trained in Southern African Countries in Nine Receiving Countries, 2000

| Sending Country | Domestic | Total Abroad | Percent Abroad |
|---|---|---|---|
| Angola | 13,135 | 1,841 | 12 |
| Botswana | 3,556 | 80 | 2 |
| Congo Republic | 4,933 | 660 | 12 |
| Democratic Republic of Congo | 16,969 | 2,288 | 12 |
| Kenya | 26,267 | 2,372 | 8 |
| Lesotho | 1,266 | 36 | 3 |
| Malawi | 1,871 | 377 | 17 |
| Mozambique | 3,664 | 853 | 19 |
| Namibia | 2,668 | 66 | 2 |
| South Africa | 90,986 | 4,844 | 5 |
| Swaziland | 3,345 | 96 | 3 |
| Tanzania | 26,023 | 953 | 4 |
| Uganda | 9,851 | 1,122 | 10 |
| Zambia | 10,987 | 1,110 | 9 |
| Zimbabwe | 11,640 | 3,723 | 24 |
| Sub-Saharan Africa | 414,605 | 53,298 | 11 |
| Africa | 758,698 | 69,589 | 8 |

Source: Clemens and Petterson, 2006

HIV/AIDS crisis. Poor salaries and deteriorating economic and political conditions are promoting the migration of medical doctors from Zimbabwe (Mutizwa-Mangiza 1998, Gaidzanwa 1999). Zimbabwe's inflation rate of 1,730% in February 2007 made it the highest in the world (Central Statistical Office 2007), while periodic political disturbances since the disputed 2000 elections created an intimidating atmosphere in the country. Hence, professionals wishing to escape the harsh economic and political conditions often see migration as a 'safety valve.'

Zimbabwe's public health care system is heavily dependent on government funding, but national support has been on a downward trend since the late 1990s. The government's expenditure on health as a percentage of total expenditure fell from 12.1% in 1998 to 9.2% in 2003 (WHO 2006). Meanwhile per capita government expenditure on health fell from US$91 in 1999 to US$47 in 2003. This was in large part a result of the growing isolation of the country from the international community which has seen external support for health falling from 17.5% to only 6.8% of total expenditure on health (WHO 2006). With poor funding, public health institutions have not been able to offer competitive salaries and a large number of professionals have moved to better paying private health institutions.

The United Kingdom is the leading destination for health professionals from Zimbabwe. There was a dramatic increase in the number of health professionals moving to the United Kingdom as political and economic conditions in Zimbabwe continued to deteriorate (Figure 7.1). From just 76 health professionals migrating from Zimbabwe in 1995 the figure increased to 2,825 in 2003.

Nurses comprised the majority of the health professionals migrating to the United Kingdom. Some 2,346 of the 2,825 work permits offered to Zimbabwean health professionals in 2002 in the United Kingdom went to nurses (Dovlo 2003). In the same year, Zimbabwe was the United Kingdom's fourth largest supplier of overseas nurses, after the Philippines, India and South Africa. Zimbabwe's Ministry of Health and Child Welfare (MoHCW) does not keep statistics on the number of professionals who migrate from the country. In order to review trends in the migration of health professionals, this research analysed changes in the number of registered professionals.

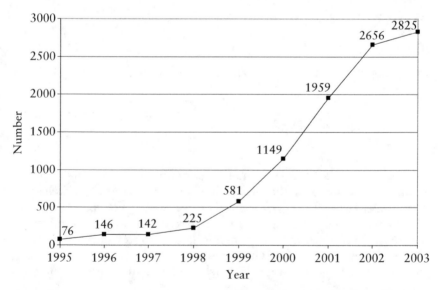

*Figure 7.1* Zimbabwean health professionals who were offered work permits in the UK, 1995–2003.

*Source:* House of Commons, 2004.

The data was obtained from the Central Statistical Office (CSO) and covered the period 1995–2000. This was correlated with staffing trends in the public sector, which is the principal provider of health services in Zimbabwe. This data was obtained from the MoHCW.

The number of registered medical practitioners countrywide increased slightly from 1,575 in 1995 to 1,629 in 2000 (a 3% increase) (Figure 7.2), despite the fact that the Medical School of the University of Zimbabwe trains between 80–90 doctors every year. There was an overall increase of only 54 doctors (rather than an expected 360 or so) over the four-year period, which suggests that emigration is at least partially responsible. The data also shows a general decline in the number of doctors employed in the public sector over time. For instance, the number of doctors employed countrywide in public health institutions fell from 742 in 1997 to 692 in 1998 (a loss of nearly 7%).

The total number of registered nurses in the country was stable up to the late 1990s, after which a significant decline was experienced (Figure 7.3). While there were 15,476 registered nurses in 1999, only 9,357 remained by 2004 (a total loss of almost 40% over a five-year period). Such a sudden decline is cause for concern and clearly a result of emigration. On the other hand, the number of nurses employed in the public health sector fell from a peak of 8,662 in 1996 to 7,007 in 1999 (a decline of 1,655 or 19.1%). This decline occurred during a period when 1,370 nurses were produced by the country's public training institutions. While some of the nurses might have left the public sector through attrition (such as retirement and death) or moving to the private sector, a significant proportion followed emigration.

Nurses have been moving into the private sector, evident as the number of nurses registered nationally rose only marginally from 15,096 in 1995 to 15,476 in 1999 (an increase of 2.5%), while the number of nurses employed in public health institutions declined from 8,635 in 1995 to 7,007 in 1999 (a decline of 19%).

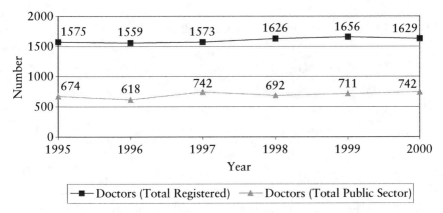

*Figure 7.2* Total registered medical doctors in Zimbabwe, 1995–2000.

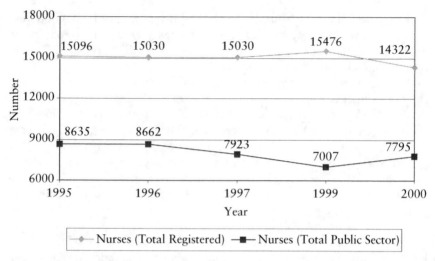

*Figure 7.3* Total registered nurses in Zimbabwe, 1995–2000.

The staffing crisis in Zimbabwe's public health sector is highlighted by the fact that even in 1997 the sector employed only 28.7% of its national requirements. Of the 1,634 doctors registered in the country in 1997, only 551 (33.7%) were employed in the public sector, with most of the remaining registered doctors employed in the private sector (Table 7.3). The problem was more severe for pharmacists, as only 18.7% of the posts were filled in the same year. The shortage of pharmacists, in particular, has been worsened by strong recruitment drives in developed countries, notably the United Kingdom. In early 2002 there were media reports of a planeload of pharmacists destined for the United Kingdom from Zimbabwe and a further planeload was expected to leave the country for the same destination later that year (Dzirutwe 2002). Emigration from the health sector was across the board.

*Table 7.3* Health Professionals Employed in the Public Sector, 1997

|  | *Number Registered in the Country | MoHCW Requirement (1997) | Approved Posts | *Filled Posts | Percent of Requirement Filled |
|---|---|---|---|---|---|
| Doctors | 1,634 | 1,851 | 676 | 551 | 28.7 |
| Nurses | 16,407 | 14,251 | 7,923 | 7,923 | 55.6 |
| Pharmacists | 524 | 198 | 59 | 37 | 18.7 |
| Dentists | 148 | 43 | 14 | 14 | 32.6 |

*Figures are for beginning of the year, while those in Figures 1 and 2 are for end of the year.
Source: Republic of Zimbabwe, 1999

## Surveying Zimbabwe's Health Care Institutions

To document the causes, extent and impacts of the migration of health professionals from Zimbabwe, a survey was conducted in the country's major health institutions. A total of 18 health institutions were selected; they included three central hospitals (Harare, Mpilo and Parirenyatwa), five provincial hospitals (Chinhoyi, Gweru, Marondera, Masvingo and Mutare), three district hospitals (Kadoma, Kariba and Nyanga), one mission hospital (Bonda), four training schools (Harare and Mpilo Central Hospitals and the University of Zimbabwe's School of Medicine) and three health centres (Epworth Poly Clinic, Waverly Clinic and Rimuka Maternity Clinic). Additional focus group discussions were held in Epworth, a suburb located just outside the administrative boundary of Harare, the capital. These discussions sought to document the impacts of the migration of health professionals on the community users of the health system, with participants including community leaders (12), adolescent users of health services (6 females, 6 males, ages 15–19 years) and adult users of health services (6 women of child bearing age and 6 men between 30 and 60 years). Lastly, a small sample of 25 emigrant health professionals, mostly doctors working in South Africa, were interviewed to find out the general causes of health professionals' migration from the country. The sample size was too low to allow much more than meaningful generalisations.

## MIGRATION INTENTIONS AND CAUSES OF MIGRATION

Examination of the migration intentions of in-country health professionals provides a useful indication of likely future brain drain patterns. The study also sought to establish their intentions of moving to the private sector. Although not as damaging as international migration, public to private sector migration has important implications regarding equity of access to health care services. In Zimbabwe, the majority of the country's population rely on medical services offered by the public sector and cannot afford to pay for the services offered by better equipped and well-staffed private health institutions. Private health institutions flourished in Zimbabwe following the deregulation of the health sector that occurred in the early 1990s as part of structural adjustment programme reforms (Mutizwa-Mangiza 1998).

The survey showed that as many as 68% of health professionals were considering leaving their public sector jobs in pursuit of better paying jobs in the private sector. Most of them (87%) noted that the salaries offered by public health institutions were not competitive and it was difficult to live on the salary they were currently receiving (Table 7.4), hence it was necessary for public health sector professionals to do two or more jobs to make ends meet. Focus group participants noted that 'nurses in the public

*Table 7.4* Employment Benefits and Working Conditions

| Do You Agree with the Following Statements? | Yes (%) |
|---|---|
| **Employment benefits: public versus private sector** | |
| The public health sector does not offer competitive salaries to health workers in this country | 87 |
| If I received a better salary, I would be happy to stay in my present position | 87 |
| I worry that I will have not be adequately provided for when I retire | 81 |
| If you work in the public health service, it is necessary to do two (or more) jobs to make ends meet | 79 |
| The private sector offer better fringe benefits to health workers in this country than the public sector | 78 |
| I am considering moving to the private sector because I will receive a better salary | 68 |
| I find it difficult to live on the salary I receive | 68 |
| **Work conditions: rural and urban areas** | |
| Working in a rural area means that I will have to live in poor housing | 54 |
| There are positive incentives for working in a rural area in my country | 16 |

N = 231

sector are engaging in a lot of part-time work in private clinics. By the time they come for their normal duties, they will be too tired to work. That is why we get poor service when we visit the clinic.' The health professionals also expressed fears over their social security in old age, with 81% fearing they would not be adequately provided for when they retired. What is encouraging is that 81% of the professionals wanted to continue working in the public health institutions but would want their levels of remuneration reviewed.

Besides public to private sector movement of health professionals, a second migration stream was rural to urban migration. Rural areas in Zimbabwe are poorly developed, lack economic opportunities and have poorly developed infrastructure. Such conditions make them unattractive destinations for skilled health professionals. More than half the professionals (54%) believed they would have poor accommodation if they were posted to rural locations. Health professionals who opt to work in rural areas in Zimbabwe are entitled to a number of fringe benefits, but only 16% of the surveyed professionals regarded these incentives as being adequate. Developing rural infrastructure should be a national priority area to ensure the retention, or better still, the attraction of skilled health professionals to such areas.

As many as 68% of the health professionals were considering leaving the country in the near future. For nurses, the proportion was higher at 71%. The most likely destination was the United Kingdom (29%), but a sizeable proportion (22%) preferred destinations within Africa (mostly South Africa followed by Botswana). Other fairly popular intended destinations included Australia (6%), the United States (5%), New Zealand (2%) and Canada (2%). Even though intentions do not automatically translate into action, the extent of dissatisfaction in the health sector is clearly massive.

The major reasons for intending to migrate were primarily economic (Table 7.5). Most professionals wished to emigrate to receive better remuneration (55%), or wanted to save money quickly in order to buy a car or pay off a home loan (54%). Still others intended to emigrate for better living conditions (47%), were discouraged by the lack of resources and facilities within the health care system of Zimbabwe (45%), saw no future in Zimbabwe (45%), or were frustrated by the declining health care services in the country (43%). A low but significant number of health professionals wanted to move because of safety concerns for their children (25%) while others were contemplating leaving the country because of high levels of violence and crime (23%)

Economic factors were the critical influence on the migration decisions of health professionals, especially because Zimbabwe's economic fortunes have been on a downward trend since the adoption of the controversial land reform programme in the late 1990s and the violent campaigns that accompanied the 2000 parliamentary and 2002 presidential elections. Violence was greatest in rural areas leading to the departure of a significant number of professionals from there. Other health professionals migrated because of professional factors, reflecting the poor economic conditions prevailing in the country, and the continuing decline of health services. Those who had already emigrated confirmed the factors that influenced still resident workers. Economic factors cited by emigrant professionals included low remuneration (56%) and the general decline of the national economy (40%). Political factors included high levels of crime and violence (48%) and that they saw no future in the country (48%). Among the professional factors, the dominant ones cited were the general decline in health services (44%), linked to their poor management (36%) and the need to gain experience abroad (24%). Social factors included the need to find better living conditions (48%) alongside family influences (12%).

The major factors that would influence health professionals to remain in Zimbabwe (Table 7.6) were better salaries (76.6%), better fringe benefits

*Table 7.5* Reason for Intention to Move

| Reason | Percentage (%) |
|---|---|
| Because I will receive better remuneration in another country | 55 |
| Because of a general decline in the economic situation in this country | 55 |
| To save money quickly in order to buy a car, pay off a home loan, or for a similar reason | 54 |
| In order to find better living conditions | 47 |
| Because I see no future in this country | 45 |
| Because of a lack of resources and facilities within the health care system of this country | 45 |
| Because there is a general decline in the health care services of this country | 43 |
| Because the workload in the health services of this country is too heavy | 39 |
| Because of insufficient opportunities for promotion and self-improvement | 32 |
| To gain experience abroad | 32 |
| Because the value systems in this country have declined to such an extent that I can no longer see my way clear to remain here | 32 |
| To ensure a safer environment for my children | 25 |
| Because of the high levels of violence and crime in this country | 23 |
| N = 231 | |

Note: Question is multiple response

(71.4%), a more pleasant working environment (69.3%), improved facilities and resources in the care system (63.3%) and a reasonable workload (59.7%). Other significant factors included the presence of a more peaceful social environment (51.5%) and more accessible education and training opportunities (50.6%).

## HIV/AIDS and Migration

With the deadly virus said to have infected 25–30% of its sexually active population, Zimbabwe is one of several sub-Saharan African countries badly affected by the HIV/AIDS pandemic (UNAIDS 2002). HIV/AIDS

Table 7.6 Factors Motivating Retention of Health Workers in Zimbabwe

| Factor | Percentage (%) |
|---|---|
| Better salaries | 76.6 |
| Better fringe benefits | 71.4 |
| A more pleasant and caring working environment | 69.3 |
| Improved facilities and resources in the health services of the country | 63.6 |
| A more reasonable work load | 59.7 |
| A more peaceful social environment in the country | 51.5 |
| More accessible education and training opportunities | 50.6 |
| Better working relationships in the public health sector | 48.9 |
| Better quality education and training in my professional field | 45.9 |
| The provision of adequate day care facilities for children of employees | 43.7 |
| Better leadership in the health sector | 43.3 |
| The appointment of more competent health service managers | 42.4 |
| Innovative training opportunities such as Distance Education | 34.6 |

N = 231

has increased the workload of the few remaining health staff, while many are said to have migrated from the country due to lack of preventive measures, which exposes them to the risk of contracting the disease. Exposure to HIV/AIDS has created a stressful environment in which workers become frightened at the thought of contracting the disease. More than half of the health professionals interviewed (61%) reported that their health institutions took adequate precautions against HIV infection, however 57% were constantly worried that they would get infected from an accident at work. Health workers at some institutions reported a shortage of gloves, which increased their risk of contracting the disease, especially when conducting deliveries. Some nurses suggested that a risk allowance be introduced and paid to them. The disease has increased their workload and 58.4% indicated that they found caring for HIV/AIDS patients stressful, a factor that might result in patients getting poor quality care. More positively, 76% were glad to use their professional skills even though they found caring for patients with HIV/AIDS demanding.

## EFFECTS OF MIGRATION OF
## SKILLED HEALTH PERSONNEL

The migration of skilled health workers from the country has adversely affected the quality of health care offered in the health institutions, including falling standards of care, which include 'uncaring and abusive' attitudes toward patients (Mutizwa-Mangiza 1998). This is largely attributed to low morale resulting from an excessive workload associated with the stress of dealing with so many dying patients. Some focus group participants reported that some patients were being turned away from busy clinics so that they could be attended to by the same medical doctors at their private clinics. This has an obvious effect on equity of access to health care for the poorest.

The decline in the number of skilled health professionals in the public sector has resulted in significant changes in the quality of care provided. The shortage of skilled health professionals has added to the workloads of staff who chose not to migrate (Republic of Zimbabwe 1999). The Ministry estimates the current doctor/patient ratio as one doctor to 6,000 patients, but this is not common at all levels of health care. Data on workloads showed that doctors employed in district hospitals have heavier workloads than those in provincial and central hospitals (Table 7.7). While the out-patient attendance per doctor at Gweru Provincial Hospital was 1:18,653 in 1999, at Kadoma District Hospital it was 1:28,087. Doctors posted in less developed areas have a much heavier workload than those employed in more developed city areas.

In Zimbabwe, nurses form the backbone of the country's health delivery system and run most of the health centres situated in the economically disadvantaged areas. Nurses working in rural areas have over the years functioned in an increasingly expanded role, taking on the responsibilities of pharmacist, doctor, physiotherapist and so forth (Chasokela 2001). According to the Ministry estimates, the current nurse/patient ratio is one nurse to 700 patients. Nurses employed at provincial health institutions have nurse-to-patient ratios that are lower than the national average (Table 7.7). For instance, in 2000 the nurse-to-patient ratios for Mutare and Gweru Provincial Hospitals were 1:592 and 1:100 respectively. This is considerably lower than the ratios of 1:3,023 and 1:1,388 at Nyanga and Kadoma district hospitals respectively. The situation is even worse for nurses employed at the health centres where doctors' visits are rare. For instance, in 2000 the nurse-to-patient attendance ratio at Waverly Clinic (Kadoma) stood at 1:7,500 and at 1:10,500 for Epworth Poly Clinic. The pattern that emerges from these data is that the workload of nurses becomes significantly lighter as they move from health centres to district and provincial health institutions. The heavy workload the nurses endured at these institutions is one of the main reasons for their movement from health centres to district and provincial health care centres, which has made it necessary for less qualified

*Table 7.7* Client Attendance at Selected Health Institutions in Zimbabwe

| | *Doctors* | | | |
|---|---|---|---|---|
| | *Variable* | *1998* | *1999* | *2000* |
| Gweru Provincial Hospital | Number of out-patients | 145 220 | 149 221 | 51 001 |
| | Number at Post | 7 | 8 | 8 |
| | Out-patient Attendance/Doctor | 20 746 | 18 653 | 8 650 |
| Kadoma District Hospital | Number of out-patients | 171 372 | 168 522 | 155 462 |
| | Number at Post | 7 | 6 | 6 |
| | Out-patient Attendance/Doctor | 24 482 | 28 087 | 25 910 |
| | *Nurses* | | | |
| | *Variable* | *1998* | *1999* | *2000* |
| Gweru Provincial Hospital | Number of out-patients | 23 110 | 23 177 | 23 428 |
| | Number at Post | 238 | 232 | 235 |
| | Out-patient Attendance/Nurse | 97 | 100 | 100 |
| Kadoma District Hospital | Number of out-patients | 171 372 | 168 522 | 155 462 |
| | Number at Post | 105 | 113 | 112 |
| | Out-patient Attendance/Nurse | 1 632 | 1 491 | 1 388 |
| Epworth Poly Clinic | Number of out-patients | 22 440 | 38 000 | 42 000 |
| | Number at Post | 5 | 5 | 4 |
| | Out-patient Attendance/Nurse | 4 488 | 7 600 | 10 500 |

staff (namely nurse aides) to carry out nursing duties owing to the shortage of qualified professionals.

Migration has led to understaffing of health institutions, which means that patients have to wait longer before they receive medical attention; indeed, some patients die from otherwise curable conditions. Experienced personnel have been lost from the system, the quality of care has fallen and the health system of the country has virtually collapsed. Marginal and disadvantaged areas, such as rural districts, have been the worst affected because skilled workers tend to shun such places. Better trained and experienced professionals have been lost from the public health sector as the economic crisis has worsened. The burden of taking care of public health system users has fallen on inexperienced junior doctors, and less qualified nurses, so compromising the quality of care. While most have performed reasonably well in the prevailing circumstances, service delivery in major hospitals has sometimes ground to a halt, especially when skilled workers engaged in industrial action to press for better salaries and conditions of service. Private health institutions benefited from the disgruntlement of public sector health professionals, many of whom they recruited by offering attractive packages and better working conditions. Unfortunately, the poor remain unable to access private health services as they charged exorbitant fees.

Training schools have also been affected by migration as they have lost experienced teaching staff. The few remaining lecturers have to cope with heavy workloads. The University of Zimbabwe's School of Medicine, currently the only institution in Zimbabwe which trains doctors, had a vacancy rate of 60% in November 2006, with only 127 out of 324 teaching positions filled (*The Herald*, 16/11/2006). This obviously affects the quality of training which medical students receive and enrolment rates are likely to fall in future if the medical school continues losing lecturers.

## The Role of Traditional and Faith-Based Healers

The role of traditional healers in contemporary society substantially declined with the introduction of modern allopathic medicine. However, due to the collapse of the formal health care system in recent years, traditional healers have begun to play an increasingly important role in the health care system. The Zimbabwe National Traditional Healers Association (ZINATHA), an organisation that represents 50,000 traditional healers and herbalists, has been actively promoting the use of traditional medicine and has embarked on a large-scale project of processing herbal medicines. Some traditional healers also claim to cure HIV/AIDS, a claim that has generated brisk business in the face of a growing HIV/AIDS crisis in the country. The traditional healers charge a low fee for the services they offer and have become popular with a significant proportion of the country's population, most of whom are poor. Even wealthy clients sometimes visit the traditional healers. However, the proposal by ZINATHA to have some of its members operating in the underused hospital structures has not received support from the government (*The Herald* 8/11/2006). Another major development, especially in the last ten years, has been the growth in importance of faith-based healers, again largely attributable to the problems facing the formal health care system. They have become popular, particularly in the country's major cities where they enjoy a large following.

## Policy Responses

The Zimbabwean government has introduced numerous policies and strategies in a bid to reduce the impacts of health professionals' migration on service delivery and to encourage the retention of skilled health personnel in the public sector. These efforts have met varying levels of success. Foreign health professionals have been recruited to ease staffing shortages particularly in economically disadvantaged rural areas. The Zimbabwean government has an agreement with the Cuban government and in 2005 there were 350 Cuban doctors practicing in the country (Hernandez et al. 2005). The doctors have largely been deployed to the rural areas ignored by local doctors. The Cuban government pays the salaries of the doctors and the Zimbabwean government provides them with an allowance to meet their day-to-day expenses. There have been complaints by the Cuban doctors that the allowances they are getting are not enough to meet their daily needs (*The Daily Mirror* 28/03/2006). Without doubt, the Cuban doctors have helped ease staffing shortages and improved the quality of care, particularly in the disadvantaged rural areas, though their overall contribution was hampered by language problems as they were Spanish speaking. Even though they were offered English language courses to help them communicate with the local people, some rural people do not speak English and literacy levels are generally poor.

A number of strategies have been put in place by the government in order to ensure the retention of skilled health personnel in the public sector, including the provision of housing and a transport allowance, call and stand-by allowances, a performance management system, salary reviews, fellowship and scholarship programmes, advanced training programmes, and bonding of newly-trained graduates. Fellowship and scholarship programmes, together with advanced training programmes, are meant to enhance the capacity of the health professionals in the discharge of their services and are also meant to reduce the migration of health professionals while furthering their studies. Salary reviews were introduced to match the cost of living in an environment of hyperinflation, and call allowances allow professionals to work extra hours due to staff shortages. Currently, there are better call allowances in rural than urban areas. However, the government's policy that call allowances should not exceed the salary of the health professionals has generated antagonism from members of the health team whose extra hours exceed their normal working hours. Bonding has been introduced to reduce the loss of newly qualified professionals.

These measures have yielded mixed results. Bonding, for instance, was introduced as a way of making sure that newly qualified health staff worked in the public sector for a certain number of years before being allowed to move to either the private sector or overseas. All newly qualified health professionals are required to serve in the public sector for a number of years, equivalent to the duration of their professional training, to be issued with a certificate of good standing. Most countries require health professionals to have a certificate of good standing issued by the country of origin before they can register for professional practice. Health professionals are willing to serve the period of their bond but either move to the private sector or overseas thereafter, hence bonding has not been an effective measure of retaining health professionals in Zimbabwe, only delaying the inevitable departure of the professionals from the public sector. The salary gap between the private and public sector is huge and growing. Salary adjustments are always being eroded by ever increasing inflation and health professionals frequently go on strike to press for higher wages. This shows the weaknesses of most institutional responses as they address the effects and not the root causes of the problem. Serious efforts to improve the welfare of the workers need to look at ways of addressing the country's economic and political problems; any other measure only yields short term results.

## CONCLUSION

Zimbabwe's health sector is faced with a severe human resource crisis and this has resulted in adverse impacts on the quality of health service delivery. Most of the country's health institutions are understaffed and operate with skeleton staffs reeling under heavy workloads. The shortage of health professionals is most critical in rural areas, where most health centres are served by under-qualified health staff, but better in urban areas, where there are alternative sources of medical care. Besides offering better health care services, albeit at higher fees, the private sector also provides an escape route for disgruntled public health sector professionals. The migration of health professionals to the private sector has been a major factor in the decline in the quality of public health care services. HIV/AIDS has added to the strain experienced by health workers and some professionals alleged that their health institutions were taking inadequate measures to protect them from the risk of contracting the disease. Economic factors were key to the migration of health workers from the public sector. Public sector salaries are far below those in the private sector, and this mismatch has been critical. Public to private sector migration closely follows the rural–urban migration of skilled health professionals. For many reasons, health professionals have found conditions in the rural areas unattractive. Once professionals have moved from the public to the private sector, it is easier for them to engage in overseas migration.

The migration of skilled health workers from Zimbabwe needs to be addressed as a matter of urgency because it has reached critical levels. The government must be sensitive to the welfare of the health professionals and should desist from its heavy handed approach when health professionals express their grievances. Arresting the current brain drain from the country, in general and from public health institutions in particular, should be a major national goal. A healthy health sector is a prerequisite for economic growth and sustainable development because it ensures the availability of a healthy workforce, hence adopting and implementing an integrated policy that will retain skilled health professionals in the country would benefit all users of public health systems, but especially the poor. Since this study was undertaken before the economic crisis in Zimbabwe worsened it is unfortunately unlikely that new directions will be adopted in the near future.

## ACKNOWLEDGMENTS

Funding for this study was provided by the Division of Health Systems and Services Development (DSD) of the World Health Organisation's AFRO Region. I gratefully acknowledge the technical assistance of Professor Jane Mutambirwa in conducting the field research.

## REFERENCES

Adepoju, A (1995) Migration in Africa: An overview, in J Baker and T Aina (Eds), *The migration experience in Africa*, Uppsala: Nordiska Afrikainstitutet, pp. 87–108.

Awases, M, Gbary, A, Nyoni, J and Chatora, R (2004) *Migration of health professionals in six countries: A synthesis report*, Brazzaville: WHO Regional Office for Africa.

Central Statistical Office (2007) *Statistics at a glance*, http://www.zimstat.co.zw/index.html accessed 18 March 2007.

Chasokela, C (2001) Policy challenges for the nursing profession, *Africa Policy Development Review*, 1(1), 1–6.

Chikanda, A (2005) Nurse migration from Zimbabwe: Analysis of recent trends and impacts, *Nursing Inquiry*, 12, 162–174.

Chikanda, A (2006) Skilled health professionals' migration and its impact on health delivery in Zimbabwe, *Journal of Ethnic and Migration Studies*, 32, 667–680.

Clemens, M and Petterson, G (2005) *A new database for health professional emigration from Africa*, Washington: Centre for Global Development.

Dovlo, D, (2003) *The brain drain and retention of health professionals in Africa*, Regional Training Conference on Improving Tertiary Education in sub-Saharan Africa: Things That Work! September 23–25, 2003, Accra, http://www.world bank.org/afr/teia/conf_0903/final.pdf, accessed 16 November 2005.

Dzirutwe, F (2002) Brain drain hits health sector, *Sunday Mail*, 10 June, 12.

Gaidzanwa, R (1999) *Voting with their feet: Migrant Zimbabwean nurses and doctors in the era of structural adjustment*, Uppsala: Nordiska Afrikainstitutet, Research Report No. 111.

Gould, W (1988) Government policies and international migration of skilled workers in sub-Saharan Africa, *Geoforum*, 19, 433–435.

Hernandez, A, Maurer, B and Elpern, D (2005) Noma: An elegy to innocence and youth, *International Journal of Dermatology*, 44, 661–663.

House of Commons (2004) Written answers to questions, *House of Commons Hansard*, Volume 418, No. 542, Columns 251W–262W.

Huddart, J, Picazo, O and Duale, S (2003) *The health sector human resource crisis in Africa: An issues paper*, Washington DC Support for Analysis and Research in Africa (SARA)—Academy for Educational Development.

Kirigia, J, Gbary, A, Nyoni, J, Seddoh, A and Muthuri, L (2006) The cost of health related brain drain to the WHO African Region, *African Journal of Health Sciences*,13, 1–12.

Leise, B (2004) *The state of the health workforce in sub-Saharan Africa: Evidence of crisis and analysis of contributing factors*, Washington: The World Bank, Africa Region Human Development Working Paper Series 32804.

Lowell, B L and Findlay, A (2001) *Migration of highly skilled persons from developing countries: Impact and policy responses*, Geneva: ILO, International Migration Paper No. 44.

Meyer, J-B and Brown, M (1999) *Scientific diasporas: A new approach to the brain drain*, Budapest: Paper prepared for the World Conference on Science, UNESCO-ICSU, 26 June–1 July.

Mutizwa-Mangiza D (1998) *The impact of health sector reform on public sector health worker motivation in Zimbabwe*, Bethesda, Maryland: Abt Associates (Major Applied Research 5, Working Paper No. 4).

Oyowe, A (1996) Brain drain colossal loss of investment for developing countries, *The Courier*, 159, 59–60.

Republic of Zimbabwe (1999) *Commission of review into the health sector: Key messages report*, Harare: Government of Zimbabwe.

Russell, S S (1993) International migration, in K Foote, K Hill and L Martin (Eds), *Demographic change in sub-Saharan Africa*, Washington: National Academy Press, pp. 297–349.

UNAIDS (2002) *HIV/AIDS in Zimbabwe*, USAID Brief, The Synergy Project, HIV/AIDS Technical Assistance Department, July.

Wadda, R (2000) *Brain drain and capacity building in Africa: The Gambian experience*, Paper to the Regional Conference on Brain Drain and Capacity Building in Africa, 22–24 January, Addis Ababa, Ethiopia.

World Health Organization (2006) *World health statistics 2006*, World Health Organization: Geneva, available at http://www.who.int/.pdf accessed 17 March 2007.

# 8 Migrant Nurses and the Experience of Skill
## South African Nurses in the UK Health Care Sector

*Colleen McNeil-Walsh*

South African nurses migrate to work in health care settings in the United Kingdom and elsewhere for a multiplicity of reasons. The desire to further their careers, earn higher salaries and escape poor working environments emerge strongly from the narratives of these nurses. Given the importance placed on professional reasons for migration, it is evident that South African nurses aim to utilise their nursing skill to maximum effect once working in the United Kingdom. The importance of skill is recognised throughout the world, since the skills of the workforce affect the quality of nursing care and even 'determine the performance of health systems' (Global Health Care Trust 2003:2). However, South African nurses and migrant nurses as a generic group find that, once in their country of destination, they are unable in some instances, to fully utilise their existing skills. In this way, migration becomes strongly associated with deskilling (Allan and Aggergard Larsen 2003).

This chapter addresses skills and nurse migration through a case study of South African nurses working in the United Kingdom. This group of skilled migrants have, in recent years, become key participants in labour migration flows out of South Africa and into the global migration arena. The experience of these nurses is multi-faceted. The maintenance or severance of ties to South Africa, their experiences of nursing in the United Kingdom, their ethnic origin, and their specific family circumstances, all serve to shape migration trajectories. The chapter focuses on the experiences that South African nurses have of the U.K. nursing profession specifically in relation to the experience of deskilling. Migration creates a complex context in which the interplay of regulatory frameworks and institutional policy shapes the work experience of South African nurses in very specific ways and it is within this broad context that skill is defined, perceived, recognised and transferred. Skill in any context is both multivalent and complex (Gallie 1994), and migration enhances this complexity.

The complexity of the relationship between skills and migration can be disentangled through developing a framework adapted from the work of

Brown (2001). The concept of skill in relation to migrant nurses embodies three dimensions, which provide the basis for a broad analytical framework to be constructed, to address the complexity of skill and migration and understand how this shapes the work experience of South African nurses. The first dimension that makes up this analysis is that skill is a contested concept (it is assessed in different ways, it is variously defined and skills are ordered hierarchically). The second dimension is that skill is socially constructed (it is shaped and determined by the social, economic and cultural context in which work takes place). The third dimension is that skill embodies a political element and is significant to the agendas of governments and regulatory bodies. In this way, the skills of nursing and nurses are appropriated at a societal level.

The following section of this chapter examines the migratory flows of nurses out of South Africa to the United Kingdom. Migrant nurse narratives are then drawn upon to illustrate the analytical framework on skill in more detail. Finally consideration is paid to the issues inherent in return migration of nurses to South Africa and the future of nurse migration.

## MEASURING MIGRATION

Although South Africa shares some of the experiences and concerns faced by other countries whose nurses are participants in migration flows, South Africa's specific political and socio-economic make-up and its historical links to the United Kingdom, place it in a distinctive situation in relation to nurse migration. Its history of skilled worker migration, its position as a receiver and supplier of health professionals, and that it faces significant healthcare challenges, are some of the factors that make the South African case 'exemplary' (OECD 2004:117).

Furthermore, that the United Kingdom has been the most favoured destination for South African nurses in recent years, adds to the significance of the South African case in terms of nurse migration. In the last eight years, South Africa has been in the top five countries from which nurses have been admitted to the United Kingdom Nursing and Midwifery Council (NMC) register. The significance of this is examined by, firstly, locating nurse migration within the wider debates on the feminisation of migration and, secondly, considering the extent and the nature of nurse migration flows to the United Kingdom.

Not only has overall migration from South Africa increased significantly in the recent past (Van Rooyen 2000), but the composition of these flows has also changed in that the increased migration of nurses reflects a feminisation of migration, an increased participation of women. The study of migration has, historically, paid little attention to the participation of women. As Kofman et al. argue, 'Most studies appear to be gender-neutral while utilising models of migration based on the experiences of men' (2000:3). But women the world over have a history of migration—they have migrated as internal and external migrants, as dependents of spouses and as migrants in their own right. In South Africa, albeit to differing extents, the participation of women in migration has historically exhibited all these patterns, dispelling 'the myth that migration is synonymous with men' (Dobson 2000:21).

Historically, South African women have been largely active within internal migration flows, characterised by the movement of African women from the 'independent homelands'—self-governing regions that surrounded South Africa during Apartheid rule and which served to supply South Africa with largely unskilled African labour (Davenport and Saunders 2000). This largely involved migration as domestic servants into South Africa, and their incorporation into the waged economy (Cock 1984). South Africa's history of female migration has therefore been significant but has been characterised by flows of a specific nature—largely internal migration and predominantly unskilled. The country has a culture of migration that reflects the racial and political character of its past.

In the context of South Africa's changing political nature and the broader dynamics of globalisation, an 'extension' of internal migration trends has become evident in the increasing migration of nurses. On a global scale, as noted by the World Health Assembly, 'highly trained and skilled health personnel from the developing countries continue to emigrate at an increasing rate to certain countries' (World Health Assembly 2004:1). Nurses exemplify the increased participation of women in the flows of skilled workers (Hawthorne 2001:213)

In the last eight years, South Africa has been a significant provider of nurses to the United Kingdom. Figure 8.1 below shows the number of nurses who have migrated to the United Kingdom since 1998–1999 and indicates that South Africa has usually been amongst the main sources (alongside India, Philippines, Australia, and Nigeria). The number of South African nurses applying for registration to the United Kingdom NMC in the last decade has followed an upward trend, but applications have dipped in the last three years from a peak of over 2,100 in 2001–2002 to just 378 in 2005–2006.

Finally, applications by South African nurses to the South African Nursing council (SANC) for verification of qualifications (Figure 8.2) show that the United Kingdom has been the favoured destination for South African nurses by a significant margin.

In 2003 it was estimated that if the migration of nurses from South Africa continued to follow the rising trend, nurses would have been lost to South Africa at between 1% and 2% per year (Hall and Erasmus 2003:542). In numerical terms this is not in itself significant, and the rate is presently falling. However, because the nurse–patient ratio is already lower than in other countries such as the United Kingdom (but higher than in other African countries), the loss in real terms is significant. The World Health Report (WHO 2006:196) shows that in 2004 the density of nurses (excluding

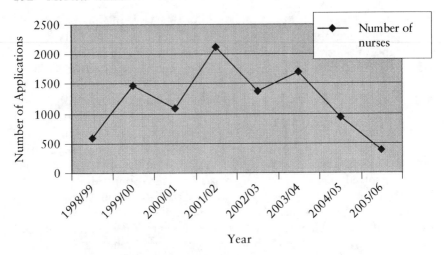

*Figure 8.1* Applications for registration to the UK NMC by South African nurses, 1998–2006.

*Source:* Compiled from the UK NMC Statistical analysis of the register for 2004/2005 and 2005/06.

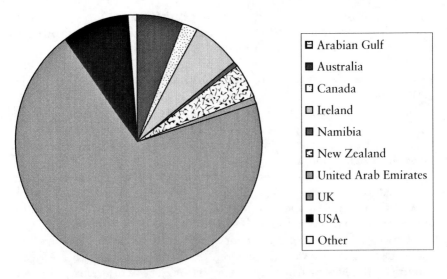

*Figure 8.2* Number of applications to the SANC for verification, 2001–2005.

midwives) per 1,000 population in South Africa was 4.1. Given the many other pressures facing South Africa's health care system through the loss of nurses to retirement and the movement of nurses from the overcrowded public health care sector to the private health care sector (Hall and Erasmus 2003), migration represents a considerable drain on South Africa's nursing workforce.

The SANC regulates the nursing profession in South Africa. The SANC figures refer to the number of nurses who have requested verification of their qualifications from this body, representing the first step in the migration process. Although these figures only provide a general picture of the extent to which nurses are considering migration, they show changing trends in the number of applications, providing an indication of the probable extent of migration rather than an accurate record since there is no evidence that migration has actually taken place. Once a nurse's qualifications have been verified, an application to the body that regulates the nursing profession in the United Kingdom, the United Kingdom NMC, can be made. As with the SANC figures, registration with the NMC is an expression of intent to work in the United Kingdom but migration might not actually take place or the process simply be delayed.

Two further factors complicate the analysis of nurse migration flows. Firstly the increasingly porous nature of South Africa's borders, since the abolition of Apartheid rule in 1994, and the strength of South Africa's economy relative to most other African countries (OECD 2004) have altered the sources and extent of migration flows into South Africa particularly from other sub-Saharan countries like Nigeria, Senegal, Sierra Leone, Zaire, Kenya and Uganda (Adepoju 2000). Although historically women migrated from other parts of Southern Africa to train as nurses in South Africa (Mashaba 1995) the post-apartheid government opened up opportunities for nurses who had already trained in other African countries to work in South Africa's health care sector. The outcome of this is that applications to the SANC and the NMC include both those who have trained in South Africa and some who have trained in another African country. Secondly, however, the NMC and SANC data do not provide information on the composition of migrant flows by ethnic origin, age or branch of nursing that a nurse has registered for. It is therefore difficult to gain a detailed overall profile of migrant nurses, and thus important to consider the individual experiences of migrant nurses in order to understand migration as a process that involves more than the measurement of flows, but has very real consequences for individual migrants and their communities.

## NARRATIVES OF SOUTH AFRICAN NURSES

The discussion thus far has outlined the issues and trends evident in the migration of nurses from South Africa to the United Kingdom. This section draws on narratives collected through interviews with South African nurses presently working in the United Kingdom. These narratives provide insight and understanding into the ways in which individuals experience nursing as migrants and as nurses who have trained in the specific social and institutional context of South Africa. The eight nurses whose narratives are drawn on below had all been working in the United Kingdom for at least five years in a range of settings (three worked in private care homes, four worked in private mental hospitals, one worked in the NHS). Two were male and six female, and all came to the United Kingdom as experienced nurses with qualifications in excess of the basic, three year professional nurse qualification.

Their life stories and work experiences are considered within the analytical framework referred to at the beginning of the chapter—that skill is contested, socially constructed and embodies a political dimension. Each is discussed in turn.

## Skill as a Contested Concept

Three interrelated aspects make skill a contested concept. The first is that skill is assessed and in different ways. Beechey (1982) considers the assessment of skill in quantifiable terms where skill is measurable on two levels. At the objective level, it is the competency of the individual that is being measured: competency encompasses technical knowledge, skills and behaviour. At the subjective level, it is the control and status associated with the job, that is the degree of control over the labour process that the skill engenders and the status that is accorded to the skill by others. This is further complicated by the fact that any one job might encompass and involve a range of skills but not all those skills will be necessary to carry out the job. Arguably, it is possible to measure the skills required to perform a task (the technical competencies) but additional skills, or key skills (Brown 2001), are more difficult to build into the assessment process. Such skills might be advantageous in performing the required task (such as a more positive overall work experience and making a task easier to execute) but would not actually be necessary to perform the task.

An example of how additional or key skills are assessed in the case of migrant nurses is seen in the English proficiency test that all internationally qualified nurses who registered with in the United Kingdom after September 2005 must pass before their application to the NMC can be processed. Previously, South African-trained nurses were not required to take an English proficiency test but are now required to do so under the new Overseas Nurses Programme, since the test must be taken by all internationally qualified nurses, even if their first language in English. Nurses from the European Union wishing to work in the United Kingdom are however exempt from the test even though the language differences may be greater between most European Union countries and the United Kingdom, than for nurses from many non-European Union countries (Likupe 2006). Hence to understand which skill is being assessed it is crucial to consider how skill is being assessed and in what broader social context this takes place.

The second aspect that contributes to the contested nature of skill is that skill is defined in different ways. The status assigned to particular work at the outset (work may be defined as skilled or unskilled for instance) determines what skills are measured in any assessment process. Skill has been 'variously defined as the expertise, ability or competence to undertake specific activities often acquired through formal instruction or work experience' (Brown 2001:23). The basis of any definition of what constitutes 'skill' may therefore be arrived at from very different starting points—from the competency level required to undertake a task to the level of skill appropriate to the status of 'expert.'

Likewise, there is debate around the definition of deskilling. The classical interpretation of deskilling is located within Braverman's 'deskilling thesis' which argues that work in modern society has become increasingly mechanical and the work process increasingly segmented, and hence the planning (conception) of tasks has become separated from their implementation (execution). Jobs have increasingly become devoid of skill and workers have subsequently lost control over the work that they do (Braverman 1974). That deskilling is synonymous with loss of control can to some extent be applied to the experience of South African migrant nurses in the United Kingdom. South Africa follows a comprehensive training model whereby on completion of their training, nurses are able to work in different branches of nursing: qualification as a 'professional nurse' allows a nurse to work in general nursing, midwifery, and psychiatric nursing (Mashaba 1995). This breadth of training gives nurses a range of experiences and opportunities for skill development. A South African nurse applying for registration to the NMC, pays a fee for each branch of nursing being registered for, so South African nurses will, in the first instance, choose one area of their nursing experience to register on the application.

The direct outcome of this is that migrant nurses temporarily or permanently stop using nursing skills specific to the branches of nursing they have not registered for. A nurse will also lose (temporarily or permanently), the skill required to administer clinical procedures that, in the United Kingdom, require a separate qualification certificate. As a general nurse in South Africa, nurses are trained to perform clinical procedures such as suturing and prescribing but, in the United Kingdom, are required to do a certificate course in order to perform those procedures. Whether or not they take that course depends on the branch of nursing registered for—so not all nurses will need to do the certificate course because certain clinical procedures are not essential to the work they do. Significantly it is a change in nursing context (i.e., country) rather than a change of job that results in the experience of deskilling. Gallie (1994:55) argues that 'deskilling in so far as it occurs, is very rarely experienced by people that remain in the same job; rather it is connected to changes between jobs.' The process of migration itself, in which institutional and regulatory procedures are embedded, creates the conditions for deskilling.

The nature of the registration process outlined above is a crucial source of discontent for South African nurses and their narratives suggest that this results in a subjective and objective experience of deskilling.

> I'm only using my mental health qualifications, which makes me feel like I'm losing out on my general skills that I qualified with. I didn't know that the work I started here was registered with the NMC as just mental health nursing. I didn't know. Because you know what it's like—you don't understand that there are two different forms and you registered for one—you didn't register for general and so on.

> From South Africa when I came to this country—I was a chief professional nurse there—and now, coming here I am a senior staff nurse and you don't sort of understand it—staff nurse. In South Africa a staff nurse is an enrolled nurse. Here, a staff nurse is someone who is registered.

> There, I was trained to put up the drip, to do the emergencies like resuscitating the patient and to take the blood and obviously giving medication, and prescribing medication for minor ailments. But when you come here, you can't prescribe, you can't take blood because you are not taught to work as a phlebotomist. And you can't put up a drip because you must first be taught and get a certificate like the other jobs. And then there is the issue of physical ailment. You are in a position in the hospital where there is supposed to be a doctor or a GP who must come and look at the physical side of the patient—so even if they say 'Oh, here's a dressing,' you have to say, 'Oh, I don't know how to do a dressing!' So the job then was like one quarter of a job which I was doing in South Africa.

> (Black male nurse)

A second nurse similarly emphasised:

> Doctors are doing things that we used to do: putting up the drip, intravenous medication, taking blood. I've thought about that a lot. One of the reasons is for safety, prevention of accidents and unsafe practice—if you have got the certificate to prove the course you have the cover from the institution and the NMC if there's a mistake. So I suppose from a safe practice point of view it's important but I found it difficult as you have the certificate [from South Africa]. That pin in the UK [the certificate] gives that person a sort of status. I don't know if it's about

creating jobs—if nurses can do everything it also prevents more specific jobs being created.

(White female nurse)

Others have reflected on the indirect transferability of skills acquired in South Africa:

I haven't used my midwifery training after those first few years. I can't use it here. Nobody has asked me about my experience in South Africa. You have to really work hard to show yourself—you have to push hard. People are not interested in what you can do. It feels that as long as you can do what they want you to do, that's fine. I think moving to England has made me worse off financially. Where would I have been had I stayed in management where my skills and experience were accumulated? Here people say, So what? Here I'm multi-skilled but I'm not specialised. But there is an advantage to being multi-skilled. In mental health, I see a patient from a community perspective and a workplace perspective. For me it's an advantage to be multi-skilled but it reality it's not good for my career.

(White female nurse)

The General training was good when I was a student. It was very broad. You got a broad experience. It provides a good basis. I think it gave me a good grounding. All the midwifery stuff I don't do now because I do general nursing.

(White female nurse)

The narratives below suggest that both positive and negative experiences are evident amongst South African nurses:

The only thing about it is when you start—I mean when I started at this hospital I had been in nursing 14 years but the way I was treated—it was like I was a newly qualified nurse. At some point I was thinking, What is this about? You are treated like a nursing assistant really.

(Black female nurse)

What I would say is that coming from South Africa our training is different. It's like we are over-qualified. So we come here with the type of qualifications we've got—like I'm a mental health nurse, I'm a general nurse, I'm a midwife. . . . I used to work like a doctor. So when you mix with the nurses who trained here they don't accept you well with the type of qualifications and experience you have.

(Black female nurse)

Apart from people commenting on my accent, people have been nice and accepting. Nobody worried that my skills came from another country.

(White female nurse)

Finally, skill is important to migrant nurses on a personal level:

It's just to prove myself, to prove that I am able and capable. It's like a mission—I want to do a good job but it's important for it to be recognised—those skills and experience. So it's not just about financial reward but a professional recognition that my work is important and I'm doing a good job and to be seen as a professional person. The advantage of extra work (additional work in other health care settings) is that it's good for the money—my salary is not good enough but I also realise that it's nice to keep your hand in the acute field—there is a kind of obsession to keep your skills alive.

(White female nurse)

It is clear that the traditional definition of deskilling cannot be applied with complete ease to the context of nurse migration because the process and the experience of work within that context is dynamic and multifaceted—new work contexts present opportunities for nurses to develop new skills, even if opportunities are limited and new skills developed are not directly assessed. Migration provides opportunities, even by default, for skill development. For those South African nurses for whom English is their second language, migration to the United Kingdom offers an environment in which to further their English language proficiency. For any migrant, the personal skills developed, as new environments are constantly negotiated, means that skills development, though not directly assessed, takes place. Hence, although skills are lost temporarily or permanently and nurses experience deskilling through a loss of control over their own labour, new skills may also be acquired in a tacit or concrete way through qualifications or continual professional development. Skills development as well as deskilling can therefore take place simultaneously.

Central to the opportunities provided for skills development and the contested nature of skill on a general level, is that skill is intrinsically gendered. Defining skill is therefore problematic as it may be defined on the basis of demand (skills in short supply are given a higher status), on the basis of experience and also on the basis of gender (Kofman and Raghuram 2005). Thus jobs requiring significant use of information technology occupy higher positions on the skill hierarchy than those within the caring and education field. Likewise, health professionals are classified as skilled (nurses) and highly skilled (doctors). This distinction is important since it influences ease of movement and the benefits accrued by global migration. Highly skilled workers, rather than skilled workers, attract the benefits accrued to the Highly Skilled Migration Programme, in which no prior offer of employment is required and the individual worker is not tied to a post that is associated with one employer (Clarke and Salt 2003:572). Likewise nurses (skilled workers) rather than doctors (highly skilled professionals) remain on the Skills Shortage Occupation List.

Skill is also hierarchical—the third dimension that makes skill a contested concept. Skill is accorded different values at different times, and this dynamic aspect of skill means that any consideration of skill formation must 'always include an analysis of the historical, institutional, cultural, political and economic context' (Brown 2001:25). Hence skills acquired in a nurse's country of origin risk being granted a lower status on the skill hierarchy because the context in which professional qualifications and experience are acquired creates differences in the way that skills of migrant nurses are perceived by others.

## Skill as a Social Construct

The claim made above, that the skills of South African nurses are more likely to be placed lower down on the skills hierarchy within the United Kingdom, highlights the argument that skills formation within specific health care settings is shaped by the dynamics inherent in broader social and cultural contexts (Winkelmann-Gleed 2005). Skills are valued because they contribute to needs in particular contexts. South Africa's history of violent conflict has created a very particular experience of nursing, shaped by the location of health care settings (in terms of socio-economic status and the size of the population that they serve). Some health care settings require the use and development of very specific nursing skills, often in situations where human and physical resources are limited. The specificity of each health care setting must be taken into account when considering how nursing skills develop: 'By examining a unit's culture, one can reveal codes of practice that influence performance and learning of practical skill' (Bjork 1999: 45).

Hence, skill development in health care settings characterised by poor resources, high levels of critical care and relatively high levels of autonomy, will result in the accumulation of skill that is in some ways universal, but in other contexts will be very context specific. This is evident in tasks specific to and embodied in the ethos and ethics of a particular health care setting, such as where the personal care of patients is carried out by qualified nurses in the United Kingdom but by care assistants and relatives in other countries (Winkelman-Gleed 2005). This specificity of health care settings is also evident in the training and regulations that govern nursing practice in each context. Thus, as indicated earlier, South Africa follows a 'comprehensive' training model in which student nurses cover three branches of nursing (general, midwifery and psychiatric nursing) and qualify to practice in them all. For South African nurses, the acquisition and development of skills either in the home country or in the United Kingdom, is determined by the specific national nursing training and regulatory procedures and the broader social and cultural context.

This is illustrated in the highly gendered nature of nursing in the United Kingdom and South Africa. Nursing in the United Kingdom remains predominantly a female profession. In the year ending March 2006, men made up 11% of the nursing workforce and women 89%, though in South Africa the overall percentage of males as at the end of 2006 was only a little lower (7%). Gender segregation is evident not only in this objective, numerical form but also in a subjective form—a perception that nursing is 'women's work' and a career that is 'appropriate for women' (Hardill and MacDonald 2000). In the South African context this is powerfully illustrated in the experience related in the narrative below:

> I think with midwifery, I just loved it. I felt joy the second I see the baby and the mother is okay. But midwifery especially for a male person, is difficult, especially in a black culture. Women are used to male doctors, not male nurses. When a woman is in pain during delivery she will call, 'Come here boy!' I think we are better midwives because we shout less and are more patient and understanding. But some used to call me doctor. Somehow you got that respect—I can trust my doctor.

> (Black male nurse)

Nursing in both countries is also shaped by the dynamics of race and ethnicity. In South Africa, this is illustrated in the significant shift in the racial composition of the nursing workforce since the end of the Apartheid regime in 1994 and the changing political climate. Nurse training has become more accessible to all races and the racial composition of the nursing sector and better reflects the overall demography of South Africa. In 1980 the public sector was made up of 52% White, 39% African and the remaining 9% Coloured and Indian nurses. By 2001 this had altered dramatically, with African nurses making up the majority of nurses in the public health sector (78%), Coloured and Indian nurses made up 15% and Whites 7% (Hall and Erasmus 2003:539).

The following narratives illustrate the significance of race and ethnicity to the work experiences of South African nurses in the United Kingdom:

When you come here maybe the majority of people who are working under you—they are white. And in South Africa, we were not used to giving orders to white people because originally they were like our bosses even if it didn't matter if they didn't know what they were doing!

(Black male nurse)

It's like the way you are treated by colleagues. They just want to frustrate you. In my previous job it was fine—I was happy there but not where I am now. Most of our people are complaining about the treatment they get from white people and management.

(Black female nurse)

Ethnic differences thus complicate the acquisition, recognition and transmission of skill and experience.

## Skill as a Political Concept

The third element linking migrant nurses and skill is that skill is influenced by the broader political context in which migrant nurses are located. The composition of the nursing workforce has always been directly shaped by the policies of South African governments, most evident in the ethnic composition of the workforce, noted above.

Return migration is also an intensely political issue, linked closely to the notion of national identity. WHO has stated that: 'If health workers return, they bring significant skills and expertise back to their home countries' (2006:101). Calls for nurses to return to South Africa on a permanent or temporary basis to help address skill and workforce shortages in the health care sector have been made at a governmental and organisational level.

The migration trajectories of nurses are shaped by the broad contexts outlined thus far but are also shaped by very personal and individual considerations. Regardless of efforts to encourage return migration at the institutional or political level, nurses do not always return to South Africa in the long term, and if they do, entry back into the nursing profession or into the public sector is not guaranteed. The following narratives illustrate this:

You know, to be honest it just feels like . . . I'm just not comfortable being in another country. The first thing is it's too far from your family. The second is it doesn't feel like home and when you are here, and I realise that most of the time when I go home I ask myself, Why did I do it? But how can you sustain yourself and your future? I've had enough of nursing and I'm hoping, it is my dream, to go back home. I don't want to be a nurse in South Africa. I've got some business plans. I want to get started on this before I go because then I know everything will be okay.

I don't want to find myself back in nursing. I feel happy helping people but I just think that I've had enough. I think it's just the way people are treating nurses—the public and the government and it's just the same here as it is in South Africa. You do your best and nobody cares. So you end up losing that passion—you think, it's just a job now—I'm going to work and I'm going home. You don't get anything really . . . you know when I started my training I really loved it. Now you know. . . .

(Black female nurse)

Now that I will have permanent residence status soon, I don't have to ask employers to sort out work permits. Now the door will be open to work here, go back or go somewhere else in Europe. The problem is, where will I be able to use my skills? If I go to South Africa now, it will be a dilemma because I've been out of management and they don't do the type of psycho-social nursing I do here. I feel stuck, therefore. I seem to be on a life-long mission! I would like to go back and do it differently. What I've learnt here can be transferred into the medical model there. People need to know how to deal with post-traumatic stress and there needs to be someone to help nurses. Here there's no 'How are you? How are you coping?' That's what I've learnt here—you have to make space to talk as an interdisciplinary team and that would be an exciting thing to try in South Africa. . . . When I think back to what I've enjoyed most in my work history—I love the interpersonal work and with this experience of working with personality disorders I would love to transfer this to a position where I help staff to enjoy their work.

(White female nurse)

We had planned before to be here for five years and then go back home. But when you are here with your family, it is not so easy to save money. You pay for everything that you use so saving is out of the question. . . . You do overtime but there's more tax. It's frustrating at times and I think, 'Am I going to spend the rest of my life here'? Then one day am I going to win the lottery?! We wish to go in 2010 to stay for a while but not for good. But we've got used to living here—perhaps we will go home and visit here.

(Black male nurse)

I will stay in nursing. It's what I know; it's what I like. I can't see myself doing anything else.

(White female nurse—This woman had U.K. citizenship and intended to settle permanently in the United Kingdom)

Entry into the public health care sector, where nursing shortage is most acute, is also not guaranteed when return migration does take place. Despite the oversupply of nurses in the private sector, nurses who return to South Africa do not necessarily return to the understaffed public sector as illustrated here:

> My family is back home. I must go home. I won't work full-time but part-time because the hospitals are very bad. They have deteriorated so much and I don't think I could cope with that. White women back home work in private hospitals. No matter how educated you are, you are undermined because you're a Black nurse. But I will go into a private hospital and stay in nursing. That's my life. But my family also has a business. . . .
>
> (Black female nurse)

Although skill operates on an individual level (the nurse) and embodies subjective and objective meaning, nursing skill is also important to society as a whole. The very nature of nursing, a profession which embodies a 'duty of care,' means that those skills are valued on a societal level and considered to be crucial to a society's wellbeing and ability to operate effectively. The migration of health professionals from less developed countries threatens the ability of governments to provide adequate health care to their citizens. 'When a country has a fragile health system, the loss of its workforce can bring the whole system close to collapse and the consequences can be measured in lives lost' (WHO 2006:101). Hence, nurse migration is often couched through a discourse of ethics, the basis of which is that in addressing the skills shortage in the United Kingdom through the recruitment of migrant nurses, the capacity of the nursing workforce elsewhere is depleted. Consequently, the ability of countries like South Africa to provide adequate health care is jeopardised.

In 1997, Nelson Mandela urged the U.K. government to halt its direct recruitment of nurses from South Africa as the country was itself experiencing a shortage of nurses (Kingma 2006:126). The outcome was that in 2001 (amended in 2003) the U.K. Department of Health introduced an ethical Code of Recruitment that stated that NHS hospitals can no longer recruit nurses from South Africa (and 153 other countries) through agencies actively recruiting there (see Crush and Rogerson, this book). The routes through which nurses can migrate to the United Kingdom became limited to family reunion, direct applications to the NHS, or applying directly for jobs in the independent sector. However, the extent to which the code can be fully effective is questionable. Work permits continued to be issued to nurses from countries on the 'prohibited list' after the ban was implemented (Kingma 2006). Three reasons have been suggested for this: ethical codes of recruitment are in reality 'soft law' in that sanctions are not imposed on employers who breach the code; recruitment agencies advertise positions on the Internet and nurses are free to access such information; and nurses from countries on the banned list are entitled to seek work in countries other than the United Kingdom (Dumont and Meyer 2004:139).

That skill also embodies a political dimension is also illustrated by the bilateral agreement signed in 2003 between South Africa and the United Kingdom, which aims to facilitate the exchange of information and expertise between the countries (WHO 2006). This involves workforce and strategic planning, professional regulation, public health and primary care, public–private partnership, revitalisation of hospitals, twinning of hospitals to share best practice, and training in health care management. Although this bilateral agreement is about nursing and nurses, it is an agreement between countries occupying different economic and political positions within the global arena, and the agreement is explicitly political. What the policy illustrates is that skills, particularly when in short supply, are a precious commodity to be bargained for at the highest level.

## CONCLUSION

This chapter has highlighted the complexity inherent in the notion of skill in the context of South African nurses and migration. In every country from which nurses migrate, each nurse interacts in some way with regulatory and institutional mechanisms that require skills to be assessed and ordered. Within the generic group 'migrant nurse' there is both homogeneity and difference, borne out of the specific contexts from which nurses originate and to which they migrate. For South African nurses, the experience of nursing in the United Kingdom is shaped by the specific history, culture and political context of their origins and the institutional and social fabric of the United Kingdom as a whole and the nursing profession specifically. Opportunities and barriers emerge from such contexts. The three elements on which this analysis of skills rests (contestation, social construction and politics) are evident in all source countries but the specificity of South Africa's political, social and economic context raises particular questions in a study of nurse migration.

In the past three years, the number of South African nurses applying for registration to the United Kingdom NMC has decreased. At its peak in 2001–2002, some 2,114 nurses applied for registration, but in 2005–2006 just 378 nurses applied to the NMC. Has the migration of South African nurses in the last decade merely been a passing trend simply serving as 'a reserve army of labour, a temporary stop gap to fill labour shortages'? (Hardill and MacDonald 2000:690). It is possible that the U.K. Ethical Code of Recruitment is making migration to the United Kingdom more difficult for South African nurses, but more probable that, as is the case for migrant nurses from other countries, South African nurses are unable to find vacant posts in the United Kingdom because 'the active international recruitment policy followed by the Department of Health in England since the beginning of the decade has been phased down' (Buchan and Seccombe 2006:83). How long the downward trend in the migration of South African nurses will be sustained is an open question. Data are lacking on the number of such nurses working in private care homes but it is unlikely that this alternative route will be sealed off from South African nurses when registration with the NMC is not a requirement of such employment. In the long term, it is unlikely that nurse migration from South Africa to the United Kingdom will end given the dynamic nature of migration flows and the needs and changing capacity of health care sectors. Skills will continue to be negotiated, dissolved and reconstituted.

## REFERENCES

Adepoju, A (2000) Issues and recent trends in international migration in sub-Saharan Africa, *International Social Science Journal*, 165, 383–394.

Allan, H and Aggergard Larsen, J (2003) *"We need respect": Experiences of internationally recruited nurses in the UK*, London: Royal College of Nursing.

Beechey, V (1982) The sexual division of labour and the labour process: A critical assessment of Braverman, in S Wood (Ed), *The degradation of work: Skill, deskilling and the labour process*, London: Hutchinson, pp. 54–73.

Bjork, I (1999) Practical skills development in new nurses, *Nursing Inquiry* 6(1), 34–47.

Braverman, H (1974) *Labour and monopoly capital: The degradation of work in the twentieth century*, New York: Monthly Review Press.

Brown, P (2001) Skill formation in the 21st century, in P Brown, A Green and H Lauder (Eds), *High skills: Globalization, competitiveness and skill formation*, Oxford: Oxford University Press, pp.1–52.

Buchan, J and Seccombe, I (2006) *Worlds apart? The UK and international nurses*, London: Royal College of Nursing.

Clarke, J and Salt, J (2003) Work permits and foreign labour in the UK: A statistical review, *Labour Market Trends*, 111(11), 563–574.

Cock, J (1984) *Maids and madams: A study of the politics of exploitation*, Johannesburg: Raven Press.

Davenport, R and Saunders, C (2000) *South Africa: A modern history*, London: Macmillan.

Dobson, B (2000) Women on the move: Gender and cross-border migration to South Africa from Lesotho, Mozambique and Zimbabwe, in D McDonald (Ed), *On borders: Perspectives on international migration in Southern Africa*, Toronto: Southern African Migration Project, pp. 119–150.

Dumont, J and Meyer, J (2004) The international mobility of health professionals: An evaluation and analysis based on the case of South Africa, in OECD (Ed), *Trends in international migration*, Paris: OECD, pp. 150–205.

Gallie, D (1994) Patterns of skill change: Upskilling, deskilling, or polarization?, in R Penn, M Rose and J Rubery (Eds), *Skill and occupational change*, Oxford: Oxford University Press, pp. 41–76.

Global Health Care Trust (2003) Human resources for health and development, www.globalhealthtrust.org, accessed 26 January 2006.

Hall, E and Erasmus J (2003) Medical practitioners and nurses, in HSRC, *Human resources development review 2003*, Pretoria: Human Sciences Research Centre, pp. 523–553.

Hardill, I and MacDonald, S (2000) Skilled international migration: The experience of nurses in the UK, *Regional Studies*, 34, 681–692.

Hawthorne, L (2001) The globalisation of the nursing workforce: Barriers confronting overseas qualified nurses in Australia, *Nursing Inquiry*, 8, 213–229.

Kingma, M (2006) *Nurses on the move*, Ithaca: Cornell University Press.

Kofman, E, Phizacklea, A, Raghuram, P and Sales, R (2000) *Gender and international migration in Europe: Employment, welfare and politics*, London: Routledge.

Kofman, E and Raghuram, P (2005) Gender and skilled migrants: Into and beyond the work place, *Geoforum*, 36, 149–154.

Likupe, G (2006) Experiences of African nurses in the UK National Health Service: A literature review, *Issues in Clinical Nursing*, 15, 1213–1220.

Mashaba, T (1995) *Rising to the challenge of change: A history of Black nursing in South Africa*, Kenwyn: Junta.

Nursing and Midwifery Council: Statistical analysis of the register, 1 April 2004 to 31 March 2005, published August 2005, www.nmc.ac.uk, accessed 20 November 2006.

Nursing and Midwifery Council: Statistical analysis of the register, 1 April 2005 to 31 March 2006, www.nmc.ac.uk, accessed 29 April 2007.

Van Rooyen, J (2000) *The new great trek: The story of South Africa's White exodus*, Pretoria: Unisa Press.

Winkelmann-Gleed, A (2005) *Migrant nurses: Motivation, integration and contribution*, Oxford: Radcliffe Publishing.

World Health Assembly (2004) International Migration of Health Personnel: a challenge for health systems in developing countries, WHA 57.19 Geneva: World Health Organisation.

World Health Organization (2006) *Working together for health*, Geneva: WHO.

# 9 Chinese Nurses in Australia
## Migration, Work, and Identity

*Christina Ho*

Compared to most female migrants to Australia, nurses tend to find work relatively easily after arrival, reflecting the shortage of nursing skills in the national workforce. However, their jobs in Australia are usually of lower status than those they left behind, leading to downward social mobility. This has long been a common experience in Australia for migrants from non-English speaking backgrounds, particularly women. This chapter documents this downward mobility among migrant nurses, and explores how it is subjectively experienced. It focuses on one group of migrant nurses in Australia—those who have migrated from Hong Kong over the last two decades. In many ways, these Chinese nurses' experiences typify those of skilled migrants in Australia. However, their relative ease of entry into the Australian workforce enhances the range of choices open to them in shaping their new lives, allowing a detailed exploration of the impact of international migration on migrants' identities and lifestyles, which indicates a profound ambivalence in Chinese nurses' evaluation of their lives in Australia. While migration means a fall in social status, both at work and in society more generally, it also enables a higher degree of freedom and autonomy, both within and outside the workplace. Chinese nurses therefore often experience migration to Australia as deeply contradictory.

The chapter uses a combination of qualitative and quantitative methods to explore Chinese nurses' experiences in Australia. To provide a background to these experiences, it uses census data and the Longitudinal Survey of Immigrants to Australia (LSIA), a large-scale survey which tracks the settlement outcomes of migrants during their initial years in Australia. Commissioned by the Department of Immigration and Multicultural Affairs (DIMA), the LSIA surveyed 5,192 primary applicants (the person upon whom the approval to migrate was based) entering Australia between September 1993 and August 1995, and interviewed them three times: six months (wave 1), 18 months (wave 2) and three and a half years (wave 3) after arrival (DIMA 2005). The LSIA included 78 nurses, that is migrants who reported that their last job prior to migration was in nursing, who form a distinct group relative to the total migrant intake.

To explore how migration and settlement are experienced by nurses, I draw on the life histories of eight nurses from Hong Kong, who had lived in Australia for between 7 and 21 years, were interviewed between 2002 and 2005, and were recruited using snowball sampling. Most were interviewed as part of a larger study of Chinese migrant women's experiences (Ho 2006a), but as nurses, their experiences are distinctive. All lived and worked in Sydney, and all but one (who had moved into counselling) were working as nurses, mostly in public hospitals or nursing homes. These life histories provide the complexity, subjective experiences and personal reflections that lie behind the large scale quantitative data.

## NURSING: A GLOBALISED PROFESSION

While nursing has historically offered a high level of geographic mobility, the last few decades have seen a 'rapid globalisation' of the profession (Hawthorne 2001:213), and the Australian government now views nursing as an 'international commodity' (DEST 2001). Like many other Western nations, Australia has become increasingly dependent on overseas qualified nurses to meet a chronic domestic skill shortage, caused by the growth in demand for healthcare from an aging population, coupled with the continued exodus of Australian nurses from a profession perceived to involve increasingly heavy workloads and poor remuneration. A 2006 government report estimated that by 2010, there would be a national shortage of up to 40,000 nurses (NSW Audit Office 2006:5).

Nursing is therefore perennially found on the Department of Immigration's list of 'occupations in demand,' and nurses attract the maximum number of points in the 'points test' determining eligibility for entry as a skilled migrant to Australia (DIMA 2006a). Doctors and nurses feature prominently on the Immigration Department's website for the skilled migration program (in fact, they are the only professions specifically named on the skilled migration front page), which offers the extra incentive that 'most visa applications for nurses receive priority processing' (DIMA 2006b). This active recruitment of nurses has been reasonably effective. For example, in New South Wales alone, of the almost 7,000 nurses employed between 2002 and 2006, more than 15% were recruited from overseas (NSW Audit Office 2006:2).

While nursing is losing popularity among the Australian born, the profession increasingly facilitates the migration of the overseas-trained. In many ways, nurses typify the growing global mobility of skilled female migrants. As Hawthorne (2001:213) notes, the globalisation of nursing reflects not only skill shortages in Western countries, but also the 'growing agency and participation of women in skilled migration, their desire for improved quality of life, enhanced professional opportunity and remuneration, family reunion and adventure.' While traditionally seen as 'trailing spouses,' female migrants are increasingly acknowledged as active agents in global movements of skilled professionals (Kofman 2000, 2004), reflecting increasing levels of education among women, and the growth of opportunities in industries employing women.

## Chinese Nurses on the Move

In the last two decades, Hong Kong has been a significant source of skilled migrants to the West. In the 1980s and early 1990s, countries like Canada, the United States and Australia experienced a mass influx of Hong Kong professionals, anxious about the 1997 handover of Hong Kong sovereignty to China, particularly after the 1991 Tiananmen Square massacre. The Hong Kong government estimated that the level of emigration increased from an average of approximately 20,000 per year between 1980 and 1986, to around 60,000 in the early 1990s, peaking at 66,000 in 1992 (Skeldon 1995).

In Australia, the 2001 Census recorded 67,122 Hong Kong-born persons residing in the country. These migrants tend to be relatively skilled, with 42% holding post-secondary qualifications, compared to 35% for the total Australian population (Australian Bureau of Statistics, unpublished 2001 Census figures). Recent migrants from Hong Kong usually arrived through the skilled migration program. For example, among those arriving between 1993 and 1995, 61% of men and 44% of women came as skilled or business migrants (unpublished data from LSIA, wave 1). Women from Hong Kong make up a substantial proportion of migrant nurses currently working in Australia today.

For some Chinese nurses, the possibility of working internationally was a factor in the initial decision to study nursing, and international travel and migration are relatively commonplace. Many displayed a remarkably cosmopolitan outlook. When Elise, aged 47 at the time of interview, was asked why she chose a career in nursing, she replied, 'You can go anywhere.' After her training in Hong Kong, Elise worked in Glasgow for a year, before deciding to migrate to Australia. Similarly, Cheryl, 53, stated that many young nurses viewed travelling to the United Kingdom as a 'pilgrimage,' or, as Carolyn, 45, put it, it was 'trendy' to do further study and obtain registration in the United Kingdom.

Another respondent, Su-lin, 49, also chose the profession for its portability, saying that although she had no definite plans to go anywhere, she knew that nursing would be 'useful worldwide.' After her training in Hong Kong, Su-lin worked and studied in London for 12 months, so that when she migrated to Australia in the late 1980s, she was able to obtain immediate registration. Su-lin typified the cosmopolitan outlook common among the Hong Kong middle class. Years before she made any decisions about her career, her father insisted that she attend an English language school, believing that English proficiency would ensure 'a better future.' Su-lin's trip to London was a vindication of this decision, as she was selected and sponsored by her employer to go overseas because of her good English skills.

As noted earlier, this outward orientation among the Hong Kong middle class was dramatically amplified in the lead up to the 1997 handover, when emigration was common among the Hong Kong professionals, including nurses. As Carolyn remarked:

> Well in nursing, people often feel it's good to travel to get experience and training. . . . With all the 1997 stuff, every person is doing it. . . . Most of my friends were migrating already. It was a very natural thing to do. Everyone in the hospital was doing it, and lots of professional people. . . . When you go to work, everyone's talking about it. So I went to get it, too.

The prospect of the 1997 handover was a catalyst for the emigration of substantial numbers of Hong Kong nurses, who tended to be already predisposed to international mobility, particularly for purposes of education and employment.

## MIGRANT NURSES IN THE AUSTRALIAN WORKFORCE

As a result of growing skilled migration to Australia, the last decade has seen a 'dramatic ethnic diversification' of Australian nursing (Hawthorne 2001:213), with unprecedented numbers of nurses arriving from non-Western countries. Census figures from 2001 show that more than a quarter (27%) of all nursing professionals in Australia were born overseas (see Table 9.1). Europeans comprised nearly half of all migrant nurses (and more than half the Europeans were born in England), followed by Asian born nurses, with Hong Kong being the third largest Asian source country, after Malaysia and the Philippines.

What have been the experiences of recently arrived nurses in Australia? This section uses data from the LSIA to build a profile of migrant nurse employment and settlement in Australia. One significant factor shaping nurses' experiences is obviously gender. Reflecting the international female domination of nursing, the vast majority of migrating nurses (91%) surveyed in the LSIA were female. This contrasts with the overall intake, where women comprised only 43% of all primary applicants. Nursing is therefore one of the few female-dominated professions represented in the skilled migration program.

Consequently nurses took a distinctive path in migrating to Australia. While women normally migrate to Australia via the family reunion program, a substantial proportion of female nurses (41%) migrated on the basis of their occupational qualifications, through the Independent–Skilled category. This was almost four times the proportion for all female primary applicants

Table 9.1 Nursing Professionals
by Birthplace, 2001

| Birthplace | Percent |
|---|---|
| Australia | 73.3 |
| Overseas | 26.7 |
| Europe | 48.4 |
| Asia | 22.6 |
| Pacific | 14.6 |
| Other | 14.4 |
| Total | 100.0 |

N=171,592
Source: unpublished 2001 Census figures, Australian Bureau of Statistics

(11%), reflecting the Australian government's active recruitment of over-seas-trained nurses. Accordingly, while only 17% of all female migrants had sought qualifications assessment (either before or after arrival), 60% of female nurses had done so.

The high demand for their skills is also reflected in migrant nurses' high employment rates relative to female migrants more generally. After 6 months in Australia, more than half (60%) of the nurses surveyed in the LSIA were employed, compared to only a quarter (25%) of all female migrants. More-over, while migration often disrupts careers, forcing migrants (at least ini-tially) to take up jobs in unrelated fields, this was generally not the case for nurses: six months after arrival, 85% of those who were employed were working as registered nurses. Their higher employment rate put female nurses in a better financial position than other migrants, with only 19% report-ing that they earned no income, compared to 34% of all female migrants. Overall, nurses clearly experience a much smoother transition into a new labour force relative to other migrants, particularly female migrants, who frequently find themselves out of employment or working in areas unrelated to their occupational skills.

While the LSIA data paint a relatively positive picture of migrant nurses' employment experiences, nurses can have dramatically different experiences depending on where they migrated from. Those from English-speaking backgrounds and Commonwealth countries tended to have a much easier transition than other migrants. To work as a registered nurse in New South Wales, for example, nurses need to pass an English test and demonstrate competency standards devised by the Australian Nursing and Midwifery

Council (ANMC). Most overseas-trained nurses undertake a Competency Based Assessment Program, although this may be waived for nurses from English speaking countries, as well as those from Hong Kong and Singapore (ANMC 2005). The region of origin can have a major impact on the length of time taken to secure registration (Hawthorne 2001). While nurses from an English speaking background (ESB) or a Commonwealth Asian country secure it in a couple of months, other Asians, along with continental Europeans, typically wait 1 to 2 years. ESB nurses usually pass 'seamlessly' into employment, while nurses from non-English speaking backgrounds (NESB) have to overcome major hurdles to re-establish their careers (Hawthorne 2001:213).

As a result, many NESB nurses migrating to Australia withdraw from the labour market, at least initially, or accept sub-professional employment (Hawthorne 2001:218). This mirrors Birrell and Hawthorne's (1997) earlier analysis of 1991 census data, which showed that while the unemployment rate for migrant nurses was only 3%, a further 28% were not in the labour force, often reflecting unsuccessful job searching. Those NESB nurses who do find employment are often concentrated in lower status jobs, such as Assistants in Nursing (AIN), or in less desirable sectors of the industry, such as nursing homes or public hospitals. In comparison, ESB nurses are significantly more likely to be employed in professionally prized private sector hospitals (DEST 2001, Hawthorne 2001:224).

Hong Kong nurses, migrating from what was then a Commonwealth country, generally had few problems transferring their skills to the Australian workforce. Many reported that getting a job was a matter of simply going to a hospital and asking, or ringing up and enquiring about vacancies. This was all that was required to secure an interview. In the words of Katie, who migrated to Australia in 1985, 'It was easy to find a job. You just have to go to [a] hospital and ask, or ring up and go in.' However, although securing a job was easy, it was difficult to find employment in more desirable workplaces. Almost all the nurses were employed in lower-status sectors of nursing homes or public hospitals (the only exceptions were one respondent who was employed in a private hospital, and one who was working as a counsellor for a community organisation). Many also noted that there was a definite hierarchy in nursing based on ethnicity. In particular, respondents noticed that low-paid AINs were invariably newcomers. As Cheryl commented, young Australians were not attracted to AIN work: 'You can get more money in Franklins [a supermarket chain]. . . . And it's quite strenuous work.' Therefore, she said, 'only the migrants' worked as AINs, 'even though they may be highly educated in their own country.' Elise also explained:

> Before Tiananmen Square, there were lots of Chinese in AIN. Now it's more Filipinos and now African people, in my nursing home anyway. It's always the newcomers that do the work, and then after they've been

here for a while, they move on. That's why it used to be Chinese and then the Filipinos and now the Africans. The White Australians don't do this work.

These patterns of segmentation have prompted the Australian government to question whether the process of recognising overseas-gained qualifications can be made more flexible for NESB nurses. In its 2001 National Review of Nursing Education, the Department of Education, Science and Training argued that the overseas-qualified nurse was 'essentially an untapped resource in nursing' because the process for the recruitment and regulation of overseas-qualified nurses was 'exceptionally underdeveloped' (DEST 2001). For example, nurses who failed any of the set competency standards were given little or no opportunity to pursue other options in their practice of nursing, when it may be useful to offer an 'intern' year or even provisional registration as enrolled nurses. 'This would allow various clinical or cultural competencies to be developed or resolved within a supported environment' (DEST 2001).

## MIGRANT NURSES' WORKPLACE EXPERIENCES

Australia's nursing shortage in large part reflects the cost control managerialism, intensification and under-remuneration of nursing work that have been noted for at least a decade. Ongoing budget cuts and reforms to the management of nursing have increased workloads while reducing staff numbers and other resources. Australian hospitals' shift to a 'cost control' approach has resulted in increased patient through-put and increased acuity of patients serviced (Buchanan and Considine 2002, DEST 2002).

These Australian changes are part of an international trend in the restructuring of health services, guided by principles of 'scientific management' and economic efficiency, which have increased nurses' workloads as fewer staff care for larger numbers of more dependent patients (see Adams et al. 2000, Aiken et al. 2001, Brannon 1994, Cooke 2006, Wigens 1997). Thus Australia's nursing shortage and the widespread discontent in the profession are mirrored in many other First World nations. For example, in their study of hospital nurses in five Western countries, Aiken et al. (2001) found that up to 40% of surveyed registered nurses were dissatisfied with their jobs, and only 30 to 40% reported that there were enough nurses to provide high-quality care.

The Chinese nurses also testified to the deteriorating working conditions encountered by nursing professionals in Australia. Many spoke bitterly about the excessive workloads they encountered, the continuing shortage of staff in their workplaces, and the lack of resources available, sometimes including basic items such as bandages and gloves (particularly in nursing homes). Cheryl's comment is typical:

> When I first joined the nursing home [8 years ago], they were relatively well staffed, but they cut and cut. Now we have to look after 40 residents whereas before we only had 20. . . . They're very demanding. It's ridiculous sometimes. . . . We don't have enough nurses to work.

One noticeable recurring theme was the stress generated by high staff turnover and the casualisation of nursing, with hospitals and nursing homes increasingly relying on 'agency' staff. In New South Wales in 2005–2006, the public health sector used overtime and agency nurses to provide the equivalent of 1,217 full-time nurses, an increase of 21% from 2001–2002 (NSW Audit Office 2006:3). This practice particularly intensified the work of nurses responsible for supervising a growing proportion of staff who were unfamiliar with the workplace and patients. Katie, a clinical nurse specialist in a pathology department of a public hospital, complained about having to constantly train staff who stayed for only short periods of time: 'It's quite stressful, worse than before. Before we had enough staff and the workload is not that heavy. [Now] people leave all the time. . . . They train and then they leave.' Carolyn noted that budget cuts at her nursing home had meant that more AINs were being employed instead of RNs, which simply increased the workload of the remaining RNs: 'The workload has increased and it's not very satisfactory. The AINs are not qualified to do dressing, which means I have to do all the dressing. [When it's my shift, I have to do] seven days worth of dressing. It's very frustrating.'

This dissatisfaction felt by migrant nurses raises questions about whether importing nursing professionals from overseas is an effective or sustainable solution to the labour shortage. As they integrate into the local workforce, migrant nurses are subject to the same frustrations that are causing locally-trained nurses to leave the profession, suggesting that addressing the nursing shortage cannot avoid the urgent need to improve working conditions.

While most respondents were unambiguous in their criticism of budget cuts in their workplaces, their overall evaluation of their working lives in Australia was more complex and often ambivalent. In particular, there was frustration at a perceived process of deskilling. Many respondents argued that while nursing was considered a highly skilled professional job in Hong Kong, they felt that nursing was a less valued occupation in Australia, and noted that much of their daily work was consumed with basic patient care. However, these basic tasks were also part of a 'holistic care' model of nursing, which many respondents encountered for the first time in Australia, and which was a source of new satisfaction in the job. This paradox informs the overall ambivalence that nurses often had about their working lives in Australia. The very processes that undermined their professional status also allowed them to develop new ways of approaching their work, which could be enormously rewarding. This paradox in the workplace parallels nurses' experiences with migration more generally, as will be explained below.

The expansion of 'basic care' in nursing can in part be traced back to cost control managerialism. As patient throughput and acuity increase, it is no surprise that nurses are forced to perform more basic care for more dependent patients. This is borne out in international research. In every country included in Aitken et al.'s study (2001:49), nurses reported spending time on tasks that did not call upon their professional training, such as cleaning rooms or transporting food trays, while care activities requiring their skills, such as those relating to oral hygiene and skin care were often left undone. In Cooke's U.K. study, nurses spoke at length about the expansion in their 'hands on' care, denoting routine, low status work (2006:231). Jackson (1995:33) also found that migrant nurses in Australia often felt strongly that 'basic care' should not be the domain of the registered nurse, because it was a 'waste of knowledge.' Echoing these reports, the Chinese nurses often complained about having to perform functions that did not make use of their knowledge. Many contrasted Australian nursing's approach to patient care with the more hierarchical approach adopted in Hong Kong, where registered nurses performed higher level tasks, leaving 'basic care,' like bathing and toileting, to junior nursing staff. As Katie stated, 'Before in Hong Kong, you just follow the doctors in their rounds and tell the student nurses what to do, what medication to give. It was more supervisory. . . . Here you do everything.'

However, even as the nurses complained about the basic nature of many of their daily tasks, many also saw these functions as part of the holistic care that they were able to give in Australian settings, from which they derived a great deal of job satisfaction. Holistic care or 'total patient care' is part of the 'new nursing,' which moves away from the bio-medical model focusing on disease, to holistic frameworks that view patients as individuals, whose overall social circumstances are important in shaping their well being (Hau 2004, Wigens 1997). The ability to develop relationships with patients is a key concept in holistic care, with psychological and social care aspects playing a key role alongside physical care (Wigens 1997).

The nurses argued that although the work was heavier and more basic, holistic 'total patient care' allowed them to get to know patients, something that was rare in Hong Kong. As Katie said, 'You get to know the patients more here, their emotions, their family. Total patient care is better.' Su-lin commented, 'I do everything for all the patients, so I have a better relationship with patients. Hong Kong has a more conservative culture. You don't have time to spend with patients. . . . The job is more satisfying here.' Similarly, Carolyn explained that although she was surprised at having to do so much 'frontline work,' she had come to appreciate this model, where 'whether you're a fresh graduate or senior staff, it's holistic care for each patient.'

These positive expressions of nursing work contrast with mainstream commentaries that emphasise the undermining effect that new managerial practices have on nurses' ability to provide holistic care (Buchanan and Considine 2002, Cooke 2006, DEST 2002, Hau 2004, Wigens 1997). The ideology of holistic, individualised care conflicts with managerial practices whose aim is to increase productivity and efficiency, pushing nurses toward a 'production line' style of caring. Because of increasing workloads, nurses often only have time to address patients' immediate physical needs, and can become discouraged at neglecting their psycho-social needs. Moreover, attempting to reconcile the two competing priorities, for example, by trying to disguise the number of patients a nurse is responsible for, can be highly emotionally draining, and leave nurses feeling guilty about their insincerity (Wigens 1997:1120).

In the eyes of Chinese nurses however, in spite of these reforms, the Australian system still allowed nurses more scope for holistic care than did hospitals in Hong Kong. Most noted that, despite their complaints, working conditions were still far superior in Australia. As Su-lin commented, 'Nurses here are always whingeing but compared to what I came from—there were so many people in Hong Kong, it was always rushed.' Many also commented that, having come from such hectic working environments, they often found Australian-trained nurses to be inefficient and even 'lazy.' As Carolyn stated, 'The most hard working ward are all Asians.'

Respondents' ability to build relationships with patients and residents was mirrored in staff relations, as the nurses expressed their appreciation of Australia's more egalitarian workplace culture. As Michelle explained, in Hong Kong, doctors dominated the workplace and continually asserted their superiority, while in Australia, she felt doctor–nurse relations were less hierarchical. In the words of Su-lin, nurse training in Hong Kong was 'like military training,' with extremely hierarchical staff structures:

> When I was a student nurse, anyone just one day senior than you is your supervisor. In the lift, everyone had to go in before me. You have to say thank you if you are told off by the supervisor. Here, you call the manager by their name, and you can say if you think something is unreasonable.

Chinese nurses' experiences of working in Australia were thus full of paradoxes. While they felt that their professional status was reduced in Australia, in part because of the prevalence of relatively low skill tasks in their daily work, these very tasks were what allowed them to take a more holistic approach to their caring work, which ultimately was a source of pleasure. The relative lack of hierarchy among nurses, paralleled in nurse–doctor relationships, while leading to a perceived deskilling, also introduced Chinese nurses to new and better ways of doing their jobs. This paradox is present in a strikingly similar way in how the Chinese nurses experienced their lives more generally in Australia, as the next section shows.

## NURSES' EXPERIENCES OF AUSTRALIAN LIFESTYLES

Not only do Chinese migrant nurses find nursing to be less professionally valued in Australia, but even within the profession, there are few opportunities for career advancement. As Hawthorne's study shows (2001:223), NESB nurses are significantly less likely than ESB nurses to progress beyond baseline registered nursing employment. Very few are to be found in higher managerial or nurse supervisor positions. Likewise, the migrant nurses Jackson interviewed saw nursing as a 'dead end job' with little or no room for advancement. These nurses knew that promotion required higher qualifications, and believed that NESB women were disadvantaged when seeking to gain such qualifications (Jackson 1996:123).

All but one of the Chinese nurses were employed as registered nurses (with the exception of Katie, who was working as a clinical nurse specialist), despite the fact that many had had managerial roles in Hong Kong. Apart from learning how to use new technology at work, most stated that they had not had opportunities for further professional training, therefore few believed they would be promoted in Australia. This blocked mobility was felt all the more strongly when the nurses compared their experiences with those of their peers who stayed in Hong Kong. Most were confident that, had they not migrated, they would have enjoyed considerable career progression, as their former colleagues had done. For example, when I asked Katie what she thought she would be doing if she had stayed in Hong Kong, she replied, 'I would be a NUM [Nursing Unit Manager] by now. All my classmates, most are NUM already. In Australia I never applied, or I miss[ed] the chance.'

Yet paradoxically, despite this lack of career advancement, many respondents stated that they preferred life in Australia, where they felt they had more time and autonomy to shape their lifecourse. In fact, the opportunity to have a less work-oriented life was valued by many nurses. As Carolyn explained:

> Before, I was a ward manager, so I would have had a good career development. . . . [But] in Hong Kong, I would just be working very hard. . . . I very much pity that sort of life. The feeling in Hong Kong is you have to [work]—it's very rare for a housewife not to work, if you are educated. If you are deliberately not working, it looks like you are very foolish. You can't find a group of mothers not working. People in Hong Kong are facing different pressures. You just can't see a good view of your whole life. You don't have perspective. It's only about getting more money.

Elise also appreciated the freedom afforded to women in Australia to be 'more family oriented.' At the time of interview, she had worked part-time in the same nursing home for more than 15 years, and had never been interested in seeking promotion. She preferred to have the extra time to devote to her family. In comparison, she said that Hong Kong women were more aggressive and competitive, and Hong Kong nurses were preoccupied with getting more experience to gain promotions. She recalled her surprise at working in Scotland and discovering that it was not unusual for married women to give up their jobs:

> When I was in Scotland, the nurses there [said to me] 'if I get married, I won't work.' That was quite shocking to hear that. . . . In Hong Kong, it's an industrial city so it needs every bit of manpower, and men are not enough, so women have to work.

The availability of part-time jobs in Australia was valued by most of the nurses, and many said that the best aspect of nursing in Australia was its flexible hours. Part-time work is a prominent feature of the nursing work-force in Australia. In 2001, a majority of nursing professionals (with the exception of directors of nursing and nurse managers) worked less than 35 hours per week, and the proportion working part-time had grown over the previous 14 years (Shah and Burke 2001). Nursing is therefore an exception to the general Australian trend of increasing working hours.

Australian nursing also stands in stark contrast to the Hong Kong labour market, where part-time work is virtually non-existent. As Elise said,

> Well the thing is, in Hong Kong, there's no part-time jobs. Everyone has to work full-time . . . but in Australia, for women it's good because you can have [a] part-time job, so you can look after your kids. You can choose your shifts.

Similarly, Carolyn said that because there was no culture of part-time work in Hong Kong, working mothers just had to keep 'rolling on.' However working mothers in Hong Kong are often supported by relatively low-cost live-in domestic workers. This has been a common practice among professional families since the 1970s, when the Hong Kong government allowed foreign nationals, mostly from the Philippines and other Southeast Asian countries, to enter the colony to work as 'helpers' (Constable 1997:29). In 2003, there were approximately 250,000 foreign domestic helpers in Hong Kong, more than half of whom were Filipinos (Torres 2003). This enabled women to continue working full-time after they had children.

While many Chinese women had difficulty initially adjusting to domestic life without hired help in Australia (Ho 2006a), many gradually came to enjoy their expanded domestic role, and the time to spend with their families. Many stated that, given the choice, they would rather take part-time jobs or shift work so they could look after their children. Carolyn said she chose to work two part-time jobs, one in a nursing home, where she worked short shifts to coincide with her child's school day, and the other in a public hospital, where she was 'the Saturday morning girl' for more than 10 years. 'Nursing is good for working part-time to look after your family,' she stated. These shifts in work/family roles reflect and contribute to deeper changes in Chinese women's values and identities.

## Reorienting Values and Identities

In some cases, migration to Australia can deeply change women's priorities and values. Hong Kong women often find themselves increasingly questioning their previously work-oriented, materialistic lifestyles. In particular, the culture of having children raised by domestic workers appears increasingly unsatisfactory after settling in a country where it is rare. Some nurses explained that they had never given much thought to something that was so common in Hong Kong, yet in Australia it seemed a strange and less than ideal arrangement. Therefore, despite downward mobility, most said that they did not regret coming to Australia, because Australian life, while not necessarily supportive of their careers, did open up new spaces of personal identity not connected with employment. While previously their lives had been overwhelmingly work-oriented, the Australian lifestyle provided more time with the family, more autonomy and scope for self-development, and ultimately allowed the women to gain a new independence and sense of self.

For example, Wendy, a former nurse who migrated to Australia in 1990 with her husband and two children, took 2 years out of the workforce to assist her family adjust to a new country, and to study counselling, which she had always been interested in. She worked part-time as a counsellor. While migration meant a financial sacrifice, Wendy enjoyed Australians' less materialistic and more relaxed lifestyle. While in Hong Kong, she had never taken a family holiday: 'We're more into the Australian style of having holidays a few times a year, you know. But we are still hard working! [laughs]. But we're aware that we have to enjoy life as well.' Working less also allowed Wendy to pursue personal interests, such as studying. Consequently, she had noticed a change in herself, such that she was now more concerned with 'quality of life.' Su-lin was also grateful to be freed from the careerism that she said dominated working women's lives in Hong Kong. In Australia, she said, there was no expectation that one had to 'climb the corporate ladder.' In fact, she enjoyed the reduction in responsibility at work, going from a unit manager in Hong Kong to a registered nurse in Australia. Even the reduction in her salary was something positive, as it relieved her of her previous burden as the family's main breadwinner.

These nurses' narratives show that ironically, although admitted to Australia for their economic attributes, migration can sometimes lead skilled women toward a much less market-based orientation in their lives. While Chinese nurses face downward social mobility in Australia, this very experience can result in much more profound changes in how they come to see themselves. Over time, they identify less and less as 'career women' and come to develop other aspects of their identity in their pursuit of 'quality of life' in a new country (Ho 2006b). Of course, it is impossible to determine to what extent these stated changes in priorities and values are simply efforts to rationalise less than ideal employment experiences, to put a 'positive spin' on sub-optimal outcomes. However, migrants from Hong Kong generally have the capacity to return there should the need arise, and in fact, thousands around the world have repatriated, indicating that those who stayed in Australia are likely to have made a choice to do so.

## CONCLUSION

Migrant nurses form a distinct group among Australia's skilled migrants. Unlike many educated migrants whose careers are dramatically disrupted by migration, the chronic shortage of nurses in Australia generally allows migrant nurses a relatively smooth transition to the local workforce. However, this transition can vary greatly depending on migrants' country of origin, with those from English-speaking and Commonwealth countries faring much better than others. This chapter has examined the experiences of a group of nurses who, coming from a (former) Commonwealth country, Hong Kong, usually have few problems obtaining registration and employment in the Australian healthcare sector. However, although they are able to successfully transfer their qualifications across borders, they generally do not advance in their careers, but rather experience downward mobility in terms of occupational seniority and overall financial status in Australia. There were clear hierarchies based on ethnicity within Australian nursing, and it was difficult for nurses from non-English speaking backgrounds to rise to positions of seniority.

How migrant nurses experience this downward mobility is complex. Many expressed frustration at their perceived deskilling in Australia, against a backdrop of dissatisfaction at ongoing work intensification occurring across the profession. However, processes of deskilling were also catalysts for reworking nurses' approaches to both their jobs and life more generally. At work, deskilling, in the form of having to undertake much more basic, low skill tasks, was part of a more holistic approach to care that allowed nurses to develop relationships with their patients, something that was rare in Hong Kong. Outside work, they found themselves reorienting their energies away from the world of careers and materialistic concerns toward 'quality of life.' Ultimately, migration to Australia opened new opportunities for living life differently and for shaping a new sense of self.

What are the implications of these findings for the role of migration in the Australian healthcare sector? Although the Australian government, like many other Western governments, has become increasingly reliant on recruiting overseas-trained nurses to meet the skills shortage, this study poses some questions about the long-term viability of this strategy. As we have seen, one aspect of nursing work particularly appreciated by Chinese nurses was the opportunity to provide holistic care, which historically has been a key draw-card for nurses generally. However, this model of individualised care is being undermined by the rationalisation of healthcare provision in Australia, with its emphasis on economic efficiency. Although Australian working conditions are still felt to be superior to those in Hong Kong, as Chinese nurses integrate into the Australian workforce, many of their frustrations come to echo those of locally-trained nurses, suggesting that the factors pushing nurses away from the profession are also likely to be felt by migrant nurses. At the core of the nursing shortage is the deterioration of working conditions in the profession over many years. Importing foreign nurses can only be a temporary solution in the absence of serious efforts to address issues of workload and remuneration.

On the other hand, the experiences of the migrant nurses outlined here show vividly that migration is not simply an economic affair. Although nurses are admitted for their occupational skills, this economic framework does not capture the complexity of the experiences of many skilled migrants. While migrant nurses clearly contribute economically to Australia, they also add to the richness of Australia's modern multicultural society, and this, perhaps, is of more lasting value. In addition, migration provides the opportunity for newcomers to be introduced to different ways of approaching work and life. These social outcomes have always been part of the more immeasurable value of migration and cultural diversity, and represent a more solid, holistic framework for underpinning a sustainable migration policy.

## REFERENCES

Adams, A, Lugsden, E, Chase, J, Arber, S and Bond, S (2000) Skill-mix changes and work intensification in nursing, *Work, Employment and Society*, 14, 541–555.

Aiken, L, Clarke, S, Sloanne, D, Sochalski, J, et al. (2001) Nurses' reports on hospital care in five countries, *Health Affairs*, 20(3), 43–53.

ANMC (Australian Nursing and Midwifery Council) (2005) International Section, http://www.anmc.org.au, accessed: 3 June 2006.

Australian Bureau of Statistics (2002) *2001 census of population and housing*, Cat. No. 2015.0.

Birrell, R and Hawthorne, L (1997) *Immigrants and the professions in Australia*, Melbourne: Centre for Population and Urban Research, Monash University.

Brannon, R (1994) Professionalisation and work intensification: Nursing in the cost containment era, *Work and Occupations*, 2, 157–178.

Buchanan, J and Considine, G (2002) *"Stop telling us to cope": NSW nurses explain why they are leaving the profession. A report for the NSW Nurses Association*, Sydney: Australian Centre for Industrial Relations Research and Training, University of Sydney.

Constable, N (1997) *Maid to order in Hong Kong: Stories of Filipina workers*, Ithaca: Cornell University Press.

Cooke, H (2006) Seagull management and the control of nursing work, *Work, Employment and Society*, 20, 223–243.

DEST (Department of Education, Science and Training) (2001) *National Review of Nursing Education*, http://www.dest.gov.au, accessed: 15 June 2006.

DEST (Department of Education, Science and Training) (2002) *Our duty of care*, National Review of Nursing Education 2002, http://www.dest.gov.au/highered/programmes/nursing, accessed: 5 December 2006.

DIMA (Department of Immigration and Multicultural Affairs) (2005) The Longitudinal Survey of Immigrants to Australia, http://www.immi.gov.au/research/lsia/index.htm, updated 8 April 2005.

DIMA (Department of Immigration and Multicultural Affairs) (2006a) Skilled Occupation List, http://www.immi.gov.au/allforms/pdf/1121i.pdf, accessed 5 June 2006.

DIMA (Department of Immigration and Multicultural Affairs) (2006b) Working in Australia as a nurse, http://www.immi.gov.au/skilled/medical-practitioners/nurses.htm, accessed 6 December 2006.

Hau, W (2004) Caring holistically within new managerialism, *Nursing Inquiry*, 11(1), 2–13.

Hawthorne, L (2001) The globalisation of the nursing workforce: Barriers confronting overseas qualified nurses in Australia, *Nursing Inquiry*, 8(4), 213–229.

Ho, C (2006a) Migration as feminisation? Chinese women's experiences of work and family in Australia, *Journal of Ethnic and Migration Studies*, 32, 497–514.

Ho, C (2006b) Women Crossing Borders: The changing identities of professional Chinese migrant women in Australia, *PORTAL Journal of Multidisciplinary International Studies*, 3(2), http://epress.lib.uts.edu.au/ojs/index.php/portal accessed 10 June 2006.

Jackson, D (1995) Constructing nursing practice: Country of origin, culture and competency, *International Journal of Nursing Practice*, 1, 32–36.

Jackson, D (1996) The multicultural workplace: Comfort, safety, and migrant nurses, *Contemporary Nurse*, 5(3), 120–126.

Kofman, E (2000) The invisibility of skilled female migrants and gender relations in studies of skilled migration in Europe, *International Journal of Population Geography*, 6, 45–59.

Kofman, E (2004) Gendered global migrations: Diversity and stratification, *International Feminist Journal of Politics*, 6, 643–665.

NSW Audit Office (2006) *Performance audit: Attracting, retaining and managing nurses in hospitals: NSW Health*, Sydney: NSW Audit Office.

Shah, C and Burke, G (2001) *Job growth and replacement in nursing occupations*, Canberra: DEST National Review of Nursing Education.

Skeldon, R (1995) Emigration from Hong Kong: 1945–1994: The demographic lead-up to 1997, in R Skeldon (Ed), *Emigration from Hong Kong*, Hong Kong: The Chinese University Press, pp. 51–77.

Torres, M A (2003) GMA bans HK deployment for Pinays, *The Manila Times*, March 6.

Wigens, L (1997) The conflict between "new nursing" and "scientific management" as perceived by surgical nurses, *Journal of Advanced Nursing*, 25, 1116–1122.

# 10  The Impact of the Outmigration of Female Care Workers on Informal Family Care in Nigeria and Bulgaria

*Sarah Harper, Isabella Aboderin and Iva Ruchieva*

The aging of societies has led to an increase in labour migration, particularly to Europe and other industrialised nations (OECD 2005, Salt et al 2004). A particular focus has emerged on the rising numbers of mostly female health and social care workers migrating from poorer developing world or Eastern European countries. This migration responds to increasing care needs and labour shortages in destination countries, fuelled by the progressive aging of their populations. This is predicated increasingly to occur within the health and social care market, as low-mortality/low-fertility results in an increase in the number and percentage of older adults requiring health and social care at the very time that that the number of young workers entering this sector is falling (Buchan 2002, Buchan and Sochalski 2004).

In African contexts formal health care workers such as nurses or doctors, especially from sub-Saharan Africa, move to nations such as the United Kingdom, the United States or Australia, alleviating care (especially eldercare) staff shortfalls in the destination countries (Buchan 2002, Mensah et al. 2005). Parallel to this, an emergent concern has focused on the migration of mainly female informal care workers from poorer eastern European countries to provide urgently needed domestic eldercare in richer European Union nations such as Italy or Greece (Da Roit 2004; Bettio et al. 2003, 2004a, 2004b; Mestheneos and Triantafillou 2005).

Most studies to date have focused on formal sector migrants and have explored macro migration flows, structural drivers or 'push' and 'pull' factors for migration and personal migration motives, the impact on health systems in source countries (e.g., Chikanda, this book; Eastwood et al. 2005; Mensah et al. 2005) and the migrants' work experiences in host countries (e.g., Allan and Larsen 2003). The little research so far conducted on informal sector migrants has begun to examine migrant labour patterns and flows (Bettio et al. 2004a, 2004b), migrants' work conditions and experiences (Da Roit 2004, Bettio et al. 2004b) and impacts on host families in receiving countries (Da Roit 2004). To date, little attention has been given to the impact on social care, primarily family care in source countries, which has been disrupted by the removal of key females from these systems.

This chapter will describe part of a larger cross-national exploratory study on migrant care workers. Two groups of female eldercare labour migrants were studied: Nigerian nurses employed in the independent nursing home sector in the United Kingdom and Bulgarian migrant women providing informal eldercare in the domestic setting in Greece. Some sixty in-depth interviews were undertaken in four field sites.

The United Kingdom is globally one of the major 'recipients' of migrant nursing labour and Nigeria is one of its most significant supplier countries of trained nurses. It is the fourth largest developing world 'provider' of nurses after India, the Philippines and South Africa, and numbers of Nigerians on the U.K. nursing register have risen sharply since 1998 (Buchan and Sochalski 2004). Moreover, due to its large population (133 million), Nigeria is critical to the achievement of the Millennium Development Goals and thus central to debates on the impact of health care migration in sub-Saharan Africa. Greece is one of the major, though hitherto relatively understudied, southern European states relying on informal migrant labour to provide care for its older population (Mestheneos and Triantafillou 2005). Within Greece, Bulgarians are the immigrant group most strongly represented in the in informal eldercare sector (Markova and Sarris 1997).

## METHODS

In depth interviews were carried out in the United Kingdom and Nigeria, in two phases. Phase One comprised in-depth interviews with twenty five Nigerian (mainly Yoruba) nurses working for a large independent eldercare provider in England. Interviews explored nurses' 'sending' circumstances, migration rationales and adaptations, transition experiences, family impacts and future plans. Supplementary information was gathered in informal contextual interviews with care home managers and non-migrant Nigerian nurses. Phase Two, conducted in Ibadan, a major city in Nigeria's South Western Yoruba region, explored the perspectives and experiences of nurses and nursing tutors in the Nigerian health system, returnee migrant nurses and family members of migrated nurses: a further fourteen in-depth interviews. Supplementary information was gathered through informal contextual interviews with several key informants.

The second investigation was conducted in Greece and Bulgaria, again in two phases. The first took place in Athens and involved in-depth interviews and participant observation among a sample of 18 female Bulgarian migrants in Greece, who were either currently employed, or have been employed in the recent past, as informal carers. The second phase was conducted in various sites in Bulgaria and entailed in-depth interviews with return migrants who had previously been employed in the informal care sector in Greece, and adult children of migrants, left behind in the source country as their mothers migrated to Greece, resulting in eight in-depth interviews.

Interviews in both studies typically lasted 1–2 hours and broad topic guides were used to ensure a measure of consistency across interviews, and provide publicly available documentation, however questioning was kept as open as possible, rather than simply seeking confirmation of prior expectations. Data analysis, typical for qualitative research, did not follow a fixed protocol but evolved during the study. The process began during fieldwork, accompanying data collection and continued after return from the field. Concurrent systematic comparison between themes in the United Kingdom/Nigeria and Greece/Bulgaria studies generated further insights into contrasts and similarities and the structural and contextual factors shaping these.

## THE IMPACT OF MIGRATION

In both the Nigerian and Bulgarian cases, almost all migrants were mid- to older-age women and many were part of an extended vertical family with at least one grandparent still alive. In both settings no older person or spouse had moved to join the female care worker, though in the Nigerian case several nurses had brought their children. This reflects the restrictive immigration conditions applied in both source countries by the host nations, the restrictive work/living conditions in Greece for care workers, and in both source countries older persons' preferences for remaining 'at home' in old age. The differential immigration of children of the care workers reflects the longer stay of the Nigerian nurses, versus a more temporary transient stay of the Bulgarians, and the fact that one rationale for the Nigerian migration was to provide their children with a British education. Of particular interest was the differential decision making behind the two sets of migrations (Harper et al. 2006). Both groups laid heavy emphasis on their position within their family structure when taking the decision to migrate. While the Nigerian nurses saw the presence of children as a crucial factor, often migrating for or with the children in order to enhance their education and other well-being, the Bulgarians migrated because they were the family 'spare women,' with little or no family obligations, including that of dependent children. The presence of this family based decision making is key here and is not found in literature on male migrants. This chapter will explore the differential impact of this migration on the two generational groups in the two cultural contexts.

## Children, Older Parents, Eldercare and Emotional Support

Younger children remaining in Nigeria are primarily cared for by their father and/or grandmother, typically the maternal grandparent. This can raise problems especially for children and husband, and at times for the grandparent. The main problem identified for the husbands is the difficulty coping with the absence of wife and child care, particularly the lack of a sexual partner, and a woman to do household chores, give advice, and act as primary reference person for children and intermediary between father and children. The problems identified for the children include difficulties in coping with mother's absence, such as being unsure how to relate to and confide in the new adult caregiver. However, on the whole the maternal grandmother in particular had less concerns as they were usually willing to take on increased child care responsibility, as this met cultural role expectations, and they typically experienced a sense of joy in seeing and being around their grandchildren more, thus emphasising typical Yoruba family dynamics. The Bulgarian evidence was mixed for, as indicated above, most of the care workers had no young children, and for this reason had been 'selected' to migrate.

Both in Nigeria and Bulgaria, grandparents crucially facilitated migration by caring for migrants' children who remained in the source country either temporarily (until they joined the mother) or permanently. In both countries the care provided by grandmothers is seen by the migrants and the grandmothers as part of a 'natural task' for grandmothers. Indeed, in many cases it is simply an extension of the child care that grandmothers provided even before migration, while the migrant was at work. In both source countries, the migration of the daughter and the ensuing adaptations in care arrangements had various impacts on the support and well-being of grandparents. Firstly, the child-care role can, on the one hand, be positive for grandparents: a sense of fulfilment in supporting grandchildren—underpinned by the cultural importance attached to conceptions of grandparents' roles, their ability to contribute to grandchildren's socialisation and future; and simply company and 'something to do.' On the other hand, however, child care provision for some grandparents could be physically straining. In some cases it meant relocation (e.g., from home village to town) and grandparents having to give up prior social and economic engagement. Generally, it was viewed as something to be 'endured' for the sake of their adult children and their grandchildren.

A second key impact was on the routine care-giving for frail or functionally impaired older parents. In Nigeria, there are presently no alternatives to family care-giving as no formal care provision exists. None of the migrants were engaged in such care-giving prior to migration. Only one grandparent actually needed care for functional impairments at the time the nurse migrated—which was provided by a sibling of the migrant nurse. In only two cases had a need for care-giving arisen after migration, and this was provided by migrants' siblings, another relative or by a hired carer. In terms of the actual quantity of available care givers, the nurses' absence does not create shortages or lack of potential care-givers since generally large family sizes in Nigeria enable some flexibility. With a Total Fertility Rate in Nigeria from the 1950s to 1980s of 6.9, most migrant women have a large number of siblings who can step into any vacuum.

In Bulgaria, none of the older generation needed care-giving for functional impairments at the time the female carers migrated. If such a need were to arise, however, there would be far fewer family members to draw on, hence the migrant's absence potentially creates a shortage of potential caregivers. This is a function of much smaller family sizes compared to Nigeria. Given the TFR in Bulgaria from 1950s to 1980s of 2.48–2.0, most migrants have only one or no siblings, and more limited extended family ties. However, the Bulgarian migrants—aware of their filial obligation—would not have left if a care need had existed prior to their migration, or they anticipated one, with no other potential caregivers. If such care requirement suddenly arise in their absence, return would be possible given the transient nature of much of their work, to avoid a real care gap.

While the quantity of available caregivers in Nigeria might not be an issue, the quality of the care presents a different picture. In Nigeria, the health system is such that necessary health care is not easily accessible unless one is close to 'gatekeepers' with connections; nurses, prior to migration, play such a crucial gatekeeper role for older relatives, and other family members, due to their professional knowledge and contacts. Their absence can mean a serious reduction in older adults' access to adequate routine or critical health care when needed—with sometimes fatal consequences. Nurses expressed a sense of guilt and responsibility for not having been there to help improve their parents' (or other relatives') health or even prevent their deaths.

In Bulgaria, migrants' absences do not limit access of older adults to critical health care. Few of these women have had formal health care training or hold gatekeeper positions in the health care services. Rather, migrants perceive it to cause an absence of critical emotional support when the older relative needs it. Some, with a sense of what a good daughter 'should' do, expressed guilt over a relative's death in their absence, and for not having been there when they were needed.

In Nigeria, the migrant's (and her children's) absence can also have a significant impact on company and emotional well-being or 'support' for the older generation. This can create a 'vacuum,' especially if prior contact was regular, emphasising the importance accorded to being around one's children and grandchildren in old age. In Bulgaria, a similar emotional 'vacuum' was created by migrants' absences, creating a strong fear of not seeing the migrant before death, made more acute because of smaller family sizes and lack of alternative emotional givers.

By contrast, in Nigeria, older parents clearly experience a rise in status and a sense of pride as a result of their daughter being 'abroad' in the

United Kingdom (which partly compensates for the loss of company). This perceived status rise is linked to assumptions that being in the United Kingdom denotes economic betterment, compared to remaining in Nigeria; conceptions of 'success' in life, and being in the United Kingdom (and other Western countries) represent an 'advanced' state in economy, knowledge and progress. This has its roots in the historical colonial relationship, but also in people's awareness of the very real divergence between Western and Nigerian development and living standards and development. In Bulgaria, in contrast, there was no such sense of raised status or pride accompanying a daughter's migration to Greece. This reflects conceptions of Greece (like other European Union states but in contrast to the United States) not representing an 'upgrade' or advanced state compared to Bulgaria, combined with historically rooted animosity toward it. As a result, parents whose daughters had migrated to work in Greece tended to experience a sense of humiliation or deflation in status.

## Economic Support

In Nigeria, all older parents expected and received material support (in cash or kind) from nurses (more than they provided before migration)—reflecting common norms and migrants' acute sense of their filial obligation, though the amount given depended on the parallel resource needs of the migrants and their accompanying children, who are given priority. For some older parents, economic support has a critical, substantial positive impact on livelihood given the absence of formal old age economic security provision in Nigeria. For others, who have enough resources of their own, in contrast, it represents merely a 'token gesture,' enabling them to fulfill 'wants' or give to other, more needy family members or contribute more generously to family affairs (such as weddings and funerals).

In Bulgaria, all older parents received material support from migrant daughters though this was often part of a general transfer to the household. Many did not need these remittances to survive, due to their house ownership and receipt of a state pension. However, material support enabled them to fulfill more 'wants' and live more comfortably.

## CONCLUSION

Key parallels and contrasts exist in the structural and cultural contexts and outcomes of the Nigerian and Bulgarian cases, which link in to emerging debates on female health and social care migration, ageing and migration in the developing world, and transnational family practices. Despite their hitherto relative invisibility in research on the impacts of female or health and social care migration, older generation family members, although they do not feature centrally in the envisaged economic aims of the migration, are often directly and sometimes critically impacted upon by the migration. This involves various positive and negative impacts, resulting from the absence of daughters, which influence not only their economic, but also their social, emotional and physical well-being—and thus their quality of life as they age.

In both countries negative and positive impacts occur in cultural contexts which clearly emphasise filial obligation—reflected in migrant daughters' acute awareness of their obligations toward the parental generation, including the importance of being with family as a key determinant of a good old age, and the role of grandmothers in providing child care for grandchildren when needed—which underpins grandmothers' central role in facilitating migration through provision of care for children remaining in the source country. Such a child care function of the grandparents' generation has also been noted (though not yet much explored) in literature on migrant transnational family practices (Da 2003, Plaza 2000)

Despite the very similar cultural underpinnings in terms of intergenerational obligations and conceptions of the importance of family in old age, the nature and intensity (though in most cases not the basic direction) of migration on the older generation varies between the two countries. This is a function of the disparate professional background (the fact that Nigerian migrants are qualified (health) care professionals while the Bulgarian migrants are not), and the radically different structural contexts in source countries, particularly the very different economic situation, reflecting economic strain, poverty and living standards. There are also differences in family structures, particularly family size, as well as the degree to which links and exchanges exist between more extended family members. The contrasting public social and health service system, in particular the ease of access to, and affordability of, appropriate health care, and the presence or absence of a formal system of old age economic security provision (e.g., pension) is also a factor. Finally, there are very different historical links, and present differences in level of economic development, between source and destination country.

In both countries, the migration can cause a potential drain of 'critical care or support.' The notion of a care-drain has been raised in connection with female informal migrants to the West (nannies and maids) who leave their children behind, depriving them of at least one important dimension of maternal love, care and nurturing, which might (though it does not inevitably) affect their well-being and development (Parrenas 2001, 2002; Hochschild 2002). In Nigeria particularly, a similar 'care-drain' can affect older adults as a result of their daughter's migration, because daughters are nurses, resulting in possible lack of access to acute, critical or adequate chronic health care when needed. As a result of the existing health delivery system and their professional qualifications, nurses (prior to migration) are key (and not easily replaceable) health care resources for their families. In Bulgaria, while access to health care is no problem, given the status of the health system and the fact that the migrant daughters are not health care professionals, their absence, because of the small family size and the absence of other siblings (and sources of formally provided support) can lead to a lack of emotional and practical support, with equally serious consequences. Due to small household sizes, daughters are key, and not easily replaceable, emotional and practical care resources.

In contrast to a potentially critical 'care-drain,' migration—and the daughter's greater earnings—results in the enhanced economic well-being of the older generation—as remittances are sent in cash or kind, regularly or sporadically. Economic security is a critical factor determining well-being in old age. Although a positive impact is evident, and enables many recipients to live 'comfortably,' it is not necessarily sufficient to meet older people's needs, or sustain their livelihoods. This depends on the comparative (and priority) level of need for the limited resources that the middle-aged migrant and her offspring have to secure their 'future' and on the older person's level of income from other sources such as assets, savings or pensions. Both crucially depend on public social service systems in the home country—in particular the 'costs' of good education and the presence or absence of formal old age economic security provision such as pensions.

International health and social care migration to provide eldercare in destination countries can clearly have important, potentially critical, impacts on the well-being of the migrants' families left behind. Against a context of rapid population aging in source countries, these impacts need to be considered in international debates on the consequences of health and social care migration from developing or emerging economies and the necessary policy responses.

# REFERENCES

Allan, H and Aggergard Larsen, J (2003) *"We need respect": Experiences of internationally recruited nurses in the UK*, London: Royal College of Nursing.

Bettio, F, D'Amato, M and Mazzotta, F (2003) *Long term care for the elderly in Italy: Is extended family still important?* mimeo.

Bettio, F, Mazzato, F and Solinas, G (2004a) *Long term care in Italy. Survey results: Gender analysis and long term care of the elderly*, Rome: European Commission and Fondazione Brodolini.

Bettio, F, Simonazzi, A, Solinas, G and Villa, P (2004b) *Female migrants in the Italian elderly care system*, Paper presented to 25th Conference of the International Working Party on Labour Market Segmentation, Intergenerational Issues, the Welfare State and the Labour Market, Brisbane, 22–24 July.

Buchan, J (2002) *Here to stay? International nurses in the UK*, London: RCN.

Buchan, J and Sochalski, J (2004) The migration of nurses: Trends and policies, *Bulletin of the World Health Organization*, 82, 587–594.

Da, W (2003) Transnational grandparenting: child care arrangements among migrants from the People's Republic of China to Australia, *Journal of International Migration and Integration*, 4, 79–103.

Da Roit, B (2004) *Changing intergenerational solidarities in a Mediterranean welfare state*, Paper presented to International Sociological Association RC-11 Sociology of Ageing, Inter-Congress Conference, 7–9 September, Roehampton University, London.

Eastwood, J, Conroy, R, Naicker, S, West, P, Tutt, R, Plange-Rhule, J (2005) Loss of health professionals from sub-Saharan Africa: The pivotal role of the UK, *The Lancet*, 365, 1893–1900.

Harper, S, Aboderin, I and Ruchieva, I (2006) *Understanding the decisions of female migrant health and social care workers: A family justification model*, Working Paper Oxford Institute of Aging.

Hochschild, A R (2002) Love and gold, in B Ehrenreich and A R Hochschild (Eds), *Global Woman*, London: Granta, pp. 15–30.

Markova, E and Sarris, A H, (1997) The performance of Bulgarian illegal immigrants in the Greek labour market, *South European Society and Politics*, 2(2), 57–77.

Mensah, K, Mackintosh, M and Henry, L W (2005) *The skills drain of health professionals from the developing world: A framework for policy formation*, London: Medact.

Mestheneos, E and Triantafillou, M (2005) *Pan European background report on EUROFAMCARE*, Hamburg: EUROFAMCARE Consortium.

OECD (2005) *Trends in international migration*, Paris: OECD.

Parrenas, R (2001) Mothering from a distance: Emotions, gender and inter-generational relations in Filipino transnational families, *Feminist Studies*, 27, 361–391.

Parrenas, R (2002) The care crisis in the Philippines: Children and transnational families in the new global economy, in B Ehrenreich and A R Hochschild (Eds), *Global Woman*, London: Granta, pp. 39–54.

Plaza, D (2000) Transnational grannies: The changing family responsibilities of elderly African Caribbean-born women resident in Britain, *Social Indicators Research*, 51, 75–105.

Salt, J, Clarke, J and Wanner, P (2004) *International labour migration*, Paris: Population Studies No. 44, Council of Europe.

# 11 Transient Greener Pastures in Managed, Temporary Labour Migration in the Pacific
## Fiji Nurses in the Marshall Islands

*Avelina Rokoduru*

Fiji is a small island state of about 800,000 people in the South Pacific. Rather more than half the population are indigenous Fijians and most of the remainder are Indo-Fijians, the descendants of migrant labourers brought to work in the sugar cane plantations from the late nineteenth century. Fiji has a fragile economy, centered on tourism, sugar and clothing manufacture, but evolving global trade patterns have reduced the viability of both agriculture and textiles. One outcome has been a growing incidence of international migration and a rise in remittances. Labour migration from Fiji only began around the 1960s and its rapid rise is a phenomenon of the past decade. With the permanent migration of mostly skilled Indo-Fijians to Canada, United Kingdom, United States and neighbouring Australia and New Zealand, a drain of skilled human resources has become significant. Currently, apart from such 'standard' skilled migrants as teachers, doctors, lawyers, pilots, engineers and technicians, migration has diversified to include defence personnel and security guards, skilled sportspeople, unskilled and semi-skilled personnel to work as domestic workers, care givers and fruit pickers.

Nurses have been one substantial migrant group. This chapter examines one particular group of migrant nurses, from a 2002 study, who migrated to work in the Ebeye Health Clinic, on the island of Ebeye (Kwajalein atoll), and the central Majuro Hospital, located on the main island of Majuro, the capital of the much smaller Pacific island state: the Republic of the Marshall Islands (RMI). It examines the profile of the nurses, their recruitment, their reasons for migration, their contracts and work conditions, their salaries and remittances, and their various experiences as a migrant community away from home. The Marshall Islands, in the northern Pacific, formerly a U.S. administered territory, has a limited economy, highly dependent on U.S. aid, and with wage levels substantially above those in most of the south Pacific. The Marshall Islands is highly urbanised with more than two thirds of the population living at high densities in either Ebeye or Majuro, the two centres of the eastern and western groups of islands.

Migration of nurses from Fiji has primarily had an economic base. Lewe-niqila et al. (2000) examined the reasons why 'the nightingales' have been leaving Fiji and concluded that nurses migrated due to poor work conditions, a very low salary scale and poor nursing management. In the twenty-first century the resignation of nurses has continued both for migration and further studies at local or overseas institutions. At the same time, Fijian doctors were migrating to New Zealand because of poor working conditions in Fiji's public hospitals, political instability, low salaries, inadequate facilities, poor administration in the Ministry of Health, and limited scope for postgraduate medical training in Fiji. The mean age of emigrant doctors was 34 years; most were employed in public hospitals and both Indo-Fijian and Fijian doctors were leaving (Naidu 1997). Whether the same reasons influenced the nurses in the Marshall Islands is discussed below.

## FIJIAN NURSES IN THE MARSHALL ISLANDS

Fifteen Fijian nurses who worked and lived in different parts of the RMI were involved in this study. One was a Fijian male who lived and worked on an outer island, 2 worked in the central Majuro Hospital and 12 worked on Ebeye island. All the nurses were Christians and of Fijian ethnicity. Their ages ranged from 25–45 years, and while the male and one female nurse were single, the remainder were married, with 10 having one or more children. Only 2 lived with their families in RMI, the others being separated from their families in Fiji. All the nurses had nursing certificates and diplomas while 2 had progressed to acquiring nursing degrees through correspondence with the Central Queensland University (CQU), Australia. The majority (11) had worked and acquired nursing experience in Fiji for between 6 and 18 years and the remaining 4 nurses had worked for at least 2 to 3 years in Fiji prior to their move to RMI. While all the nurses had been staff nurses in Fiji prior to their move, their status changed slightly in RMI, where one nurse became Head Nurse, another became a Nursing Sister, yet another became a Mid-wife, while 12 continued staff nurse work but at a better salary level for a lower work load, as discussed below.

All the nurses were privately recruited from Fiji, where none of Fiji's Ministry of Labour and Industrial Relations, Ministry of Foreign Affairs (Department of Immigration) or the Ministry of Health (Nursing Division) were formally engaged or informed in the process of recruitment. Contracts were not therefore examined by those institutions prior to migration. The three main recruitment agents were Fijian nurses already working in RMI, Suva-based RMI embassy officials working in Fiji and RMI's Department of Health officials who travelled to Suva in search of recruits. Consequently, all the nurses were hired on merit and experience, given the demand for the high level nursing skills in RMI. Most had many years experience and had worked at the Colonial War Memorial Hospital (the biggest hospital) in Fiji's capital, Suva, though all had received training to work alone or as part of a group (District Nurses) in remote rural areas of Fiji, and this work experience proved invaluable overseas (Rokoduru 2002:46). In RMI most worked at the Ebeye Health Center where they made up a third of the 38 nurses. A further third of the nurses there were from the RMI and the remainder were evenly divided between Filipinos and migrants from the nearby Federated States of Micronesia.

For most of the nurses, the decision to leave Fiji and take up nursing employment in RMI was a personal decision that excluded their spouses. This was partly due to existing marital differences and tensions in Fiji. The temporary nature of the migration, the close proximity of Fiji, so that the migrants could tackle personal issues at home, and the fear and possibility of failure, coupled with recrimination from their families, friends and workmates complicated this decision. The general sentiment was that if the movement was a failure, only a few people would know. If the migration had been to a metropolitan country, such as Australia or New Zealand, and more permanent in nature, there would have been wider consultations with friends and kin beforehand.

The reasons for migration were mainly economic and to some extent were a reaction against poor administration and management in the health sector and especially in the Nursing Division. Apart from very attractive salary packages, the other factors considered by the nurses included the fact that RMI was relatively accessible, and they were going to a job with similar workloads but with a higher salary package. The opportunity to save money away from Fiji, with its related social and cultural obligations, was also considered early in the migration process. 'We have less number of patients, less responsibilities and we do less work compared to working in Fiji where work load is very heavy and we are paid less [than in the Marshall Islands]' (Staff Nurse, July, 2002). The main attraction was the salary package paid in U.S. currency. While the nurses were receiving an annual salary of around FJ$14,000 (US$8750) to FJ$18,000 (US$11,235) before migration (and most nurses had been in these salary ranges for up to 16 years of their employment) the RMI salary often at least doubled that amount, especially when linked to additional contractual provisions and benefits. Staff nurses in Fiji begin on a salary of F$10,920 which gradually increases to F$15,409 (US$9620) if the nurses chose to make nursing a life career and by then had worked 12 years as a staff nurse (Fiji Nursing Association 2002:62). All of the nurses who moved to the Marshall Islands were qualified registered staff nurses from Fiji and their salary levels began at US$18,000, an equivalent of about F$30,000, roughly twice what could be earned in Fiji. This was a huge increase for the nurses, especially while still working as staff nurses and with lower work loads. Nurses were thus migrating to the RMI due to poor work conditions, a very low salary scale and poor nursing management, broadly the same reasons that applied more generally (Leweniqila et al. 2000).

The nurses were hired as expatriates with employment contracts generally for 3-year terms, which were annually renewable after the successful completion of the first term. Along with the attractive salaries, the nurses' contracts also included fares and cargo charges in both directions, the costs of reunification of family members in RMI, and free or subsidised transport costs to work and return. Nurses living on Kwajalein were provided daily ferry and taxi tickets to and from the Ebeye Hospital where they worked, while the nurses on Majuro received subsidised transport to and from the hospital. Travel and meal allowances were paid for night shifts, which also involved a special pay rate. Nurses were members of a superannuation scheme, had paid annual and sick leaves, and received free medical treatment (excluding illnesses that needed special medical attention) as part of their package. Such medical needs were paid by their employers in conjunction with the health insurance schemes to which individual nurses were affiliated. They also received either a housing allowance or partly or fully-furnished accommodation for the duration of the contract. Costs for housing renovations and furniture needs and maintenance were fully paid. Finally, other bills for water, electricity, telephone, gas, and maintenance were either fully met or subsidised.

This was a far cry from a nurse's standard contract in Fiji. Apart from a low salary, leave periods, superannuation and medical treatment, accommodation for nurses in Fiji was only provided for those working in rural nursing stations and a select few who lived within the compound of the urban hospitals. The majority of nurses in Fiji lived in their own accommodation, paid their own amenity bills and met the costs of their own daily transport to and from work. Contracts in RMI were far more attractive, though superannuation in RMI was actually a deterrent according to the Fiji migrant nurses; even though regular periodic payments were made, money saved as superannuation could not be immediately accessed at the completion of their contract in RMI. Superannuation funds were only released on two conditions: that a worker turned 55 years old and was physically present to receive the superannuation funds. Most nurses had no plans to stay and work until the age of retirement and returning to RMI to receive the superannuation would probably be uneconomic.

## BENEFITS OF MIGRATION

Remittances are an important part of Pacific Island migration, but until recently it was assumed that they were significant primarily in the smaller Polynesian islands. Although remittances have played a role in Fiji for many years (Stanwix and Connell 1995), in the context of skilled migration, they have not played a major part in Fiji's economy until this century, alongside the increased migration of Fiji soldiers and security workers for peacekeeping duties in the Middle East in the present century, and the migration of nurses.

An active exchange of remittances (in cash and kind) existed between the Fijian nurses in RMI, and their families and friends. Remittances were not only sent because of kinship ties and traditional obligations but also on a needs basis on both sides of the remittance transactions. All the nurses sent something home: money, gifts of Marshallese traditional artifacts, canned foodstuffs (especially U.S.-packed jars of peanut butter and candy), and clothing items went to their families and friends. By comparison, Fijians living in Sydney sent direct money transfers, and money for plane fares and goods, including secondhand and new clothes, food and housing materials (Stanwix and Connell 1995). The differences in goods sent by Fijians from Sydney and the nurses from RMI can be attributed to the contrasting socio-economic status of the host countries and therefore what was available locally.

Every fortnight, nurses sent home money, mainly through the Western Union offices in Majuro and Ebeye. The 7 Ebeye nurses who responded, collectively remitted cash to a value of US$3,200 fortnightly, which represented a significant proportion of their incomes, and also sent clothes and other gifts. Cash remittances were sent to parents and/or spouses in order to pay for general family subsistence, for the welfare of their children and to meet telephone, water, electricity, and gas bills, home, car and other property loans, school and medical fees and certain traditional obligations. Money was the main component of remittances from Ebeye. In return the nurses received foods such as peas, spices, curry powder, Fiji-made noodles, canned tuna and meat. Fiji-made beauty oils, baby products, crochet threads and needles, CDs and DVDs of Fijian music and dubbed broadcasts of international rugby matches were also sent. These goods were usually taken by Fiji nationals travelling to the Marshall Islands on business. Remittances thus maintained social ties between migrants and those back in the islands, as well as acting as 'insurance premiums' for the migrants. They paid off debts, financed migration moves for kin, and enabled the purchase of consumer goods, including houses (Connell and Brown 1995). Remittances thus often reinforced a traditional set of values and thus tended to reinforce the social hierarchy. Nurses also sent money on request and for special occasions, such as birthdays, and to assist the family on the death of a relative. The high frequency and volume of remittances that were sent were facilitated by the readily available internet and telephone services that enabled frequent contact between the migrants and their families and friends in Fiji. Networks were well established between the migrants, their relatives, friends, coworkers and especially the contacts who regularly travelled the region working for regional institutions, private businesses or non-governmental organisations. These contacts facilitated more remittance flows and became messengers and couriers between the migrants and Fiji. Cash and goods were sent primarily to relatives, but also to church groups, academic institutions and organizations such as the Fiji Housing Authority, Fiji Electricity Authority, Home Finance and Carpenters Motors (Fiji), life insurance institutions and Telecom Fiji, for telephone bills.

Aside from the obvious economic benefits of skilled labour migration, other benefits were more abstract. Migration and new employment meant empowerment and character-building that enriched their lives and made them more meaningful away from Fiji. Experiences in the host country gave nurses additional skills, promoted individual freedom, strengthened social and personal values and provided a higher degree of self-esteem and confidence. At least 3 Fiji nurses were up-skilling themselves by taking correspondence courses in nursing with the Central Queensland University. These courses would provide them with degrees in nursing, and expanded opportunities to fulfill their personal and professional ambitions. Likewise, at least 3 other nurses were awarded new positions as senior nurses, which gave them higher incomes, new administrative duties and management skills, while another actively involved herself in youth programs on Ebeye to further her Christian calling.

For more than half the nurses, time away from Fiji represented peace and safety from troubled marriages fraught with regular confrontations that were stressful and sometimes embarrassing (Rokoduru, 2002:46). From a safe distance, they were able to re-evaluate their marriages and work out probable solutions and compromises for themselves and their spouses in Fiji. Most of the nurses acknowledged working, learning and living within a new Pacific cultural environment as beneficial, and that the experiences gained had contributed to their personal development and appreciation for other Pacific places and cultural environments beyond their own.

The Fijian nurses were able to share their work skills with the local nurses. The practical nurses (most of whom were local Marshallese with no formal training in nursing) were trained in nursing care on site, and were placed under the supervision of the Fijian nurses for instruction and training. The Fijian nurses imparted skills and knowledge in the correct handling of various equipment, proper methods and procedures and patient treatment as well as record keeping. The impact of these exchanges between the Fijian nurses and their local counterparts were neither immediately evident nor quantifiable, but gave the Fijians new pride and confidence and even brought peace and contentment to their lives. Both in financial terms and in a more abstract social sense migration had proved rewarding.


## THE RIGHTS OF NURSES

As temporary migrant workers Fijian nurses had limited civil, political and social rights in the Marshall Islands. The majority had no wide-ranging labour rights as they were considered 'aliens' in the Marshalls. While they were generally compensated through paid sick leave and Medicare for injuries and illnesses suffered at work, they noted a degree of laxity in Occupational Health and Safety Standards in and around the hospital and health centre they worked in: there were no Health Inspectors for their workplaces and a conspicuous absence of health masks to protect them from contracting tuberculosis, a lung infection that was rampant in the Marshalls.

The alien status of the nurses prohibited them from changing jobs without work permits. They were issued temporary work permits for a particular job category and their visas were processed on the strength of these permits. They were not eligible to attend training sessions to advance their own academic status or employment productivity. Training and attending conferences and seminars were left entirely to local staff and were only given to the Fijian nurses when no local people were available to attend or where they were inadequately qualified to attend. Moreover, when Fijian nurses had been granted opportunities for further training, they had to fulfil criteria such as completion of an allocated number of contractual terms, and/or surrendering their passports, and/or being the most qualified person to attend training workshops, seminars and conferences. The Marshallese government's denial of open work permits, and differential treatment between the local citizens and the Fijian migrants, emphasised that skilled nurse migration from Fiji to RMI was essentially temporary. Only as long as there was need, until local people could fill these positions, would Fijian nurses be considered for vacancies. Necessarily this discouraged migrants from remaining and developing roots in the Marshall Islands.

Moreover, such industrial rights as being able to belong to a trade union, participate in elections for office bearers of a trade union, or go on strike, were categorically denied them, as explicitly stated in their contracts. Indeed, there are no trade unions in RMI to facilitate the address of work-related issues and complaints the nurses might have. 'E Tabu! According to our contract, we are not to join any such association. We have a nurses association here but this is only for social parties' (Senior Nurse, August 2002).

However, most of the nurses were satisfied with this arrangement as industrial rights and taking industrial action against the government were not priorities in their lives. What was more important were the attractive salary packages and the contracts and benefits that came with that.

The Fijian nurses did have full social and civil rights, including access to education for themselves and their families, access to their own and their family's health care, access to a superannuation scheme (despite the difficulty of gaining access to its benefits), and freedom of expression, movement and religion. By contrast rights of political association were denied them through their contractual terms and conditions. Generally, the nurses had little interest in local political issues and no interest in voting. They acknowledged their alien status and were unwilling to compromise their employment contract for the sake of participating in political activities (Rokoduru 2004:221).

The Fijian nurses enjoyed the majority of human rights with the exception of their industrial and political rights. As temporary migrants, they had signed their contracts well aware of this and had willingly surrendered these rights for socio-economic gains. The rights accorded to them in their contracts facilitated a comfortable lifestyle away from home yet prohibited them from creating or participating in any industrial or political activity that might have resulted in any instability. They were generally aware of and accepted these legal limitations to their rights. The opportunity to earn a higher level of income, in a given time span, complete with benefits and on a temporary work permit was too attractive a package to challenge.

## NURSES AS A MINORITY GROUP

All of the nurses in the Marshall Islands voluntarily bonded amongst themselves to form a minority migrant community away from home. The community was mainly forged on the bases of common occupations, ethnic and cultural identity, and Christianity, alongside friendship and kinship ties amongst the migrants. There was, therefore, some degree of collective consciousness (or feeling of being a community) based on shared language, traditions, religion, history and experiences. There was no evidence in their daily interaction with the local people that the small Fijian community was being marginalised in any way and thus created in adversity. The majority of the nurses indicated that they had not experienced racial, economic or political tensions with the local people. By contrast they valued cross-cultural experiences, doing good and being kind to each other, sharing similar Pacific cultures, and experiencing the friendliness of the local people.

As a community the nurses helped each other in various ways. Individually or as a group, they assisted each other in cash, food or in other ways. This was especially so when new migrant nurses from Fiji arrived in RMI, where they received assistance from the Fiji nursing community until they established themselves in the new environment. In both Ebeye and Majuro, there were active weekly Christian meetings for bible studies and worship, which helped to strengthen ties amongst the members of this community as well as to provide spiritual support. When an individual nurse needed to finance obligatory traditional practices for kin in Fiji (such as funerals, weddings, and annual church conferences) the other members of the community would offer financial assistance and goods to that particular nurse. The community collectively celebrated Fiji Day with much feasting and dancing and annually commemorated Fiji's Independence by performing well-received Fiji cultural performances in public concerts for the local people. Gatherings for kava drinking, fishing trips and meetings over common concerns continuously brought the migrants together. Community support maintained social cohesion and safety away from home; social and religious ties and obligations united the nurses.

On a personal level, at least two nurses had experienced work-related disagreements and confrontations and infringement of work contracts with the local nurses and a health official respectively. In those instances, the nurses had used traditional diplomatic gestures or existing professional channels of communication to ease tensions and address work problems, as illustrated here:

> I have problems with practical nurses when they won't follow instructions telling me that I should do it by myself as I am paid to do it. I just explain things to the practical nurses and if they still don't follow that, I take it up with the senior nurses to come and attend to that task. As a group, I call a meeting and we discuss things through.

(Senior Nurse, July, 2002)

Some of the nurses had integrated well with local families, and participated in local cultural rituals and ceremonies, such as wedding and birthday celebrations, death rituals, construction of new houses, churches and fences. Some had joined local religious groups and participated in their gatherings. Overall, the nurses in the Marshall Islands had adapted well to their new living environment.

While the Fijian nurses were all in the RMI on a temporary basis, many had become well-established in Ebeye and Majuro. The attractive work contracts and conditions together with the relative proximity of the Marshall Islands to Fiji, and several similar cultural attributes, made migration an economically sound choice for the nurses, and one that enabled social harmony, personal fulfillment and some degree of upward social mobility. Remittances and new work experiences were significant, despite living conditions and arrangements conveying a sense of transience: an obvious example of managed migration. For these nurses, the grass—or perhaps the taro—was indeed greener in the Marshall Islands, and migration continues from Fiji to RMI. Some of the nurses who were there in the early years of this century have either returned to Fiji, at the end of their contracts, or migrated to other Pacific Islands such as the Northern Marianas, Hawaii or even mainland United States. At least a third of the nurses intended to move on to the United States when they could and the majority wished to remain in the RMI. For all of them, the Marshall Islands sojourn has been a valuable and important endpoint or a stepping stone.

## REFERENCES

Connell, J and Brown, P (1995) Migration and remittances in the South Pacific: Towards New Perspectives, *Asian and Pacific Migration Journal*, 4, 1–33.
Fiji Nursing Association (2002) *45th annual general meeting report*, Tanoa International Hotel, Nadi, 23 March.
Leweniqila, M, Camaivuna, L and Dokoni, F (2000) Why the nightingales are flying away, *Nursing Research News*, mimeo, Suva.
Naidu, L (1997) *Contemporary professional emigration from Fiji: The case of medical doctors and the efficacy of the Ministry of Health*, unpublished M.A. Thesis, University of the South Pacific, Suva.

Rokoduru, A (2002) The contemporary migration of skilled labour from Fiji to other Pacific Island Countries (PICs), in K Lyon and C Voigt-Graf (Eds), *5th International APMRN Conference Selected Papers*, APMRN Working Paper No.12, Wollongong, pp. 43–48.

Rokoduru, A (2004) Fiji's women migrant workers and human rights—the case of nurses and teachers in the Republic of Marshall Islands, *Journal of Pacific Studies*, 27, 205–227.

Stanwix, C and Connell, J (1995) To The Islands: The Remittances of Fijians in Sydney, *Asian and Pacific Migration Journal*, 4, 69–87.

# 12 Reconceptualising UK's Transnational Medical Labour Market

*Parvati Raghuram*

The last few years have seen a range of theoretical insights that link people's activities and engagements across different places (Vertovec 2004). Much of this literature can be included within the broad rubric of transnationalism, a mode of understanding that highlights the extent to which migration is not a simple or singular process but is marked by continued affiliations, networks and redistributions of resources and goods across space (Levitt 2001, Levitt et al. 2003). The framework of 'transnationalism' offers a way of understanding how the links between two or more places are maintained and of emphasising the agency of migrants who maintain these relations across space (Vertovec 2004). However, much of the current literature on transnational migration has been 'agency-heavy' and 'structure-light' (Bailey 2001:421, but see Margheritis 2007). Migrants' movements 'occur within a larger geopolitical context and global economy' (Hyndman and Walton-Roberts 2000:247) with both state and non-state actors playing a key role in organising migration, resulting in complex interactions and hybridised forms between global processes and the nation-state. In seeking to map out interrelationships that transcend states, researchers have focused their attention on familial and kinship relations and networks (Hondagneu-Sotelo and Avila 1997, Yeoh et al. 2002). Yet, there is little work that looks at the role played by migration regulations and labour markets in shaping this continuous engagement across place. British medical labour markets, steeped as they are in imperial history, provide one site where this continuous and constitutive relationship between different places may be explored.

This chapter highlights some of the linkages and interdependencies that have shaped medical labour migration to the United Kingdom and traces the tensions that become evident when this relationality is ignored or forgotten. The chapter is divided into four parts. The first section outlines some of the reasons why transnational theorising has not been applied in exploring the interdependencies of medical labour markets. The second section explores the history and nature of these interdependencies as they were established particularly through the second half of the twentieth century. The third section lays out some of the ways in which these historical linkages have been disentangled through the enactment of new immigration regulations, and the final section suggests some of the implications of these moves for rethinking medical labour migration.

## NATIONAL HEALTH, TRANSNATIONAL CONNECTIONS

Transnationalism offers a way of thinking about migration at scales other than that of the nation-state. One of the explicit aims of much of this literature has been to bring out an understanding of migration at local scales and to decentre the state, which has for long been the primary level at which migration has been analysed. Its ability to unsettle the methodological nationalism that dogged much migration studies has meant that it has become a valuable tool for analysing migrant behaviour and experiences (Vertovec 2004).

The tensions between these modes of analysing migration that recognise the mobilities of individuals and the multiplicities of their affiliations comes undone when faced with nationally based discourses around migration of health professionals. Unlike discourses of brain circulation that have been used to analytically capture the hypermobility of migrants in the IT (Saxenian 2000) and financial sectors (Beaverstock 1994) of globalizing industry, migration of health workers usually assumes and privileges a methodological nationalism and a commitment to nationally bounded populations (Lowell et al. 2004, Ray et al. 2006). One reason for this is that both the state and nationally organised professional bodies have considerable investment in provision of health training and delivery because provision of health is a central tenet of a welfare state. The frequent geographical conflation of nation state and welfare state in analysis of welfare (Clarke 2005), alongside the constitutive nature of welfare provision to the identities of some nation states, has meant that there is often slippage between health, welfare and nation. Secondly, the analytical significance of the nation in counting inequality has meant that most comparative datasets are produced by and within national boundaries so that the effects of health worker migration too are counted at and become accountable at the level of the nation state. This is despite the effects of such migration being much more spatially variable across regions, urban/rural and class and gender divides. Moreover, the many globalising forces that influence health provision such as health tourism, commercialisation and entry of multi-national providers to health provision, amongst others, are also rarely brought into discussions of medical migration.

As a result of the overwhelming focus on the nation state for understanding health worker migration, this is also the scale at which discussions of optimum migration (Commander et al. 2004), ethical policy (Department of Health 2001) and surrounding debates around their efficacy (Martineau and Willetts 2006) and notions of development (Buchan and Dovlo 2004) are mobilised. The attachments to the multiple places through which doctors and nurses move and their transnational affiliations within a historically constituted transnational medical labour market and training provision are rarely recognised (but see Decker 2001, McNeil-Walsh 2004). The range of other places and processes that are implicated in the production of many aspects of this welfare are either ignored or forgotten.

One example of this is that in writing a narrative of health provision in the United Kingdom, it is easy to construct a national story because it is the singular example of a national health provision system that is comprehensive— from the cradle to the grave as Aneurin Bevan famously said—and also free at the point of delivery. For many, the NHS is therefore an exemplary outcome of the welfare state. If the then Chancellor of the Exchequer Gordon Brown is to be believed, it is not simply a health provider but a very British institution. In a speech to the Fabian Society in January 2006, 'A modern view of Britishness founded on responsibility, liberty and fairness,' he called NHS 'one of the great British institutions—what 90% of British people think portrays a positive symbol of the real Britain—founded on the core value of fairness that all should have access to health care founded on need not ability to pay.' As Kyriakides and Virdee (2003:284) say, 'the status of the NHS doctor largely reflects the importance of the British medical establishment as a guarantor of the moral order and the ideological resonance which "humanitarianism" affords in the preservation of that order.' The NHS is thus a significant site where the 'best of Britishness' is mobilised.

Yet, many other sites and spaces are required to produce this very British institution. Ever since its inception in 1948, a significant part of the workforce has been drawn from outside the country:

> migrant doctors from specific geographical locations have historically played a fundamental, but paradoxical role in the maintenance of the NHS: they are integral to its running but are not awarded the status that such a position would seemingly confer. The reception and occupational location of this crucial source of labour have reflected both the negative portrayal of migrants in wider British society and the specific institutional function that the NHS plays in safeguarding ideological identification through a sense of 'Greatness' from which the 'non-British' are excluded.
>
> (Kyriakides and Virdee 2003:283–284)

For the last quarter of a century migrants have made up a quarter to a third of all doctors in the United Kingdom. They have played a huge part in the less prestigious and lucrative parts of the health service such as geriatric medicine and mental health (Bornat 2004). Since many United Kingdom medical graduates too travel abroad for work experience, for elective options in international health during their studies and as part of international exchange programmes (Thomson et al. 2005), it is not enough to see this as a one-way flow. Medical training and practice in many different places are implicated in the provision of training and labour in the NHS. The following section traces some of the ways in which these interlinkages have been embedded.

## THE BRITISH MEDICAL LABOUR MARKET AS A TRANSNATIONAL FIELD

In the United Kingdom the most significant change to the Health Service came through the introduction of the National Health Service in 1948 (Rivett 1998). In creating a unified national health service, there was a struggle to ensure that doctors who trained in the United Kingdom would not only have access to jobs in the NHS but would also not suffer unduly from loss of private incomes within the private sector due to the nationalisation of much of the health provision. Thus, limits were placed on the number of doctors who were annually trained in the United Kingdom and a close relationship between undergraduate medical training and medical 'manpower' was established. The pyramidal structure of medical training meant that medical staff requirements in lower grades were however greater than for those who could achieve upward mobility into full-scale career posts. This service requirement was met through the deployment of migrant doctors who, it was deemed, would come to the United Kingdom to obtain training but would then return to their own countries. Like other trainees they were to be solely employed in the national health provision and in doing so would help to fill labour market shortages, especially in the lower rungs of the health service (Decker 2001).

This dependence on migrant health workers was also facilitated by the historical links that Commonwealth countries and their education systems had with the British health system (Pati and Harrison 2001, Forbes 2005). As far back as 1849, four medical students were brought from India to study medicine in the United Kingdom. One such student, Chuckerbutty, completed his course and the Bengal government was asked to provide him with a post in Calcutta Medical College commensurate with his education 'so that he could have an opportunity of communicating to his countrymen the scientific knowledge and practical acquirements attained by him in this country' (Fisher 2004:373). Migrant trainee doctors have a long history.

However, the 1886 Medical Act first permitted migrant doctors to register to work in the United Kingdom (Kyriakides and Virdee 2003). Through the end of the nineteenth century and into the beginning of the twentieth a number of colonial subjects came to the United Kingdom to obtain medical education as there were few centres for such education in the colonies. In India, for instance, there were only four medical colleges until 1900; two were established in the 1830s and two in the 1840s in an early flush of educational investment.

Postgraduate medical training opportunities were non-existent in the colonies and were slow to mushroom in many parts of the postcolonial world. This lacuna meant that the former imperial centre could continue to recruit a range of ambitious doctors who wanted to use mobility as a route to furthering their training. Moreover, the mark of medical educational achievement in the British Commonwealth remained (and still at least in part remains) the qualifications offered by the Royal Colleges of the various specialisms and obtaining these qualifications required doctors to come to the United Kingdom to train. They provided accreditation that had an international reach for doctors. An award of a Fellowship of the Royal College of Surgeons or a Membership of the Royal College of Physicians continued to act as a passport to further mobility. Socio-economically, these degrees were not only a mark of human capital, of accredited skills and knowledge, but also held cultural capital arising from the weight of the authority of hundreds of years of historical privilege. Geographically, these degrees helped doctors who obtained them to move to other countries, particularly within the Commonwealth. The Gulf countries rewarded doctors who stopped on the way back from the United Kingdom with financial rewards several times that which they gave to migrant doctors who came directly from their home countries, without the stamp of approval that United Kingdom training provided.

Through the decades a range of provisions have been introduced to ease, and more recently regulate, the mobility of doctors who moved through the U.K. medical sector and the forms of regulation have varied within the overall framework of wider acceptance of immigration and the needs of the health service. The 1962 Commonwealth Immigration Act, the 1971 Immigration Act and the 1981 Nationality Act all resulted in limiting the range and scope of immigration of doctors, particularly from the new Commonwealth. The introduction of further stipulations on the maximum period that migrant doctors would be allowed to stay and practice in the United Kingdom (5 years) firmly pushed medical workers into the role of transient labour providers. At the same time the inclusion of the United Kingdom in the European labour market also helped to provide a vast new source of potential labour for the National Health Service.

Medical institutions and regulatory bodies too participated in the culture of suspicion of overseas-qualified doctors that came to be adopted through the 1970s. Under the garb of protecting the U.K. population from 'less competent' overseas doctors a range of measures were introduced to ensure that migrant doctors had equivalent competencies and skills to those who were U.K. qualified. Doctors from the old Commonwealth were however excluded from these regulations in consonance with the racial filtering that marked much legislation in the 1970s. This led to the withdrawal of recognition of degrees obtained from particular institutions and subsequently from all medical training institutions in countries such as India and served to limit the migration of doctors from the new Commonwealth in particular.

Medical regulatory organisations established new sets of examinations to assess the medical and linguistic competence of doctors migrating from outside the European Union. On the other hand, the growing facilitation of equivalence procedures for European doctors' qualifications and new regulations to smooth the mobility of European workers increased the role that they played in the health service. The link between the possibility of replacing migrant doctors from the new Commonwealth with those from Europe was explicitly laid out in the Merrison Committee report of 1975 (Kyriakides and Virdee 2003).

Despite this, there has been a steady growth of overseas doctors working in the United Kingdom. Major increases occurred largely from 1953 when the number of medical posts were expanded but were followed by a cut in medical student intakes due to errors in 'manpower planning.' Emigration continued but with particular peaks between 1957–1960 and again a decade later (Decker 2001). Overseas doctors, therefore, play a paradoxical role in the maintenance of the NHS: they are integral to its running but were never awarded the status that such a position would seemingly confer. They played a crucial role in setting up new specialisms such as geriatrics (Bornat 2004). Moreover, as Kyriakides and Virdee (2003) have argued in their theorisation of the racially stratified National Health Service, migrant doctors also played a crucial role in shaping British postcolonial identity.

The legacy of these layers of regulations—immigration and labour market—was that until early 2006 the conditions of medical migrants' entry into the country and into the labour force varied depending on country of birth, country of qualification and educational institution from which the qualifications were obtained (Department of Health 2005). For career purposes, migrant doctors were usually defined not by their country of origin or their right to residence but by their country of qualification. Regulatory bodies within the medical profession emphasised the place of qualification in their determination of who constitutes an overseas doctor. The NHS census thus differentiates between those who are U.K. qualified, European Economic Area (other EEA) qualified and overseas doctors (i.e. those who qualified outside the EEA, as the European Union is now usually called). Those who qualified outside the EEA are classified as 'other overseas' or International Medical Graduates or IMGs. These terms are used interchangeably here. For example, the large numbers of medical students who come from countries such as Malaysia to study medicine in the United Kingdom were not considered to be overseas doctors.

These differences in classification and data collection reflected the differences between doctors in terms of rights of settlement and the recognition of their previous employment. Doctors who have qualified in the EEA have rights to enter and remain in the United Kingdom and their qualifications are accredited in line with regulations that have harmonised European qualifications. Doctors from non-EEA countries, on the other hand, have much more limited rights either to work or settle. Recognition of qualifications varies along a number of vectors, but primarily reflects the country in which medical qualifications were obtained. However, even applicants from the same country may find that their experience and qualifications are differently recognised based on the medical colleges from which they graduated or the hospitals in which they worked. Moreover, this recognition will also depend on the extent of labour market shortages in their speciality. As a result, for most non-EEA doctors the route to working in the United Kingdom is quite convoluted and complex.

The primary mode of entry for overseas doctors was through a permit-free training system that allowed doctors who had passed an English language exam as well as the exam conducted by the Professional and Linguistics Assessment Board (PLAB) to enter and stay in the United Kingdom (Raghuram and Kofman 2002). The period of stay varied with the nature of training sought from a minimum period of 12 months for pre-registration House Officers through to a maximum period of 4 years for doctors working in other training grades, although applications for extensions were sometimes considered.

Some doctors entered through the International Fellowship Scheme and the Managed Placement Scheme, which recruited high level employees, usually consultants. The former was offered for a fixed period, usually 2 years, and was available only in specialities that had severe shortages, while the latter posts, although initially offered on a temporary basis, could develop into full-time permanent posts. Entry of doctors through both schemes was still relatively small. Recruitment through these schemes was more likely to be influenced by the Government's guidelines for ethical recruiting, which restricted the countries from which the U.K. government was permitted to actively recruit (Department of Health 2001). In particular, active recruitment from developing countries was not encouraged unless the government of the country had specifically permitted the United Kingdom to undertake a recruitment programme.

After entry, many doctors moved on to clinical attachments (unpaid observer posts) before they would be considered for training posts. Subsequent career pathways depended on whether they obtained training or non-training posts, and the level and nature of both training and non-training posts occupied (see Table 12.1). Doctors who completed their permit-free training period often moved on to Work Permits if they were appointed to career grade posts (consultant and /or non-consultant career grade doctors such as Staff Grade and Associate Specialities (SAS) doctors). Some doctors moved to the Highly Skilled Migrant Programme (HSMP) based on their eligibility. The former was utilised only for non-training posts while the latter has been more differentially used.

Between 1979 and 2001, overseas doctors without a right of residence in the United Kingdom were not allowed to enter General Practice and these restrictions were extended to assistant and locum posts in 1985. Furthermore, General Practice trainees were not allowed to enter under the

*Table 12.1* Immigration Regulations and Career Pathways

| Grade | Immigration Regulation |
|---|---|
| Pre-Registration House Officer | Permit free for 12 months. Extension of stay for not more than 12 months |
| House Officer | Permit free for up to 3 years |
| Senior House Officer | Permit free for up to 3 years |
| | Extension of up to three years as long as not more than 3 years is spent at this or equivalent grade |
| Registrar | Permit free for 3 years with extensions, each of up to 3 years |
| Sub-consultant grade | Work-permit |
| Consultant | Work-permit |

Source: This table was created from information provided in the Guide to Immigration and Employment of Overseas Medical and Dental Students, Doctors and Dentists in the UK.

permit-free training scheme so those aspiring to enter General Practice had to meet the requirements of other business people wishing to obtain a permit to work in the United Kingdom, including evidence of their ability to invest 200,000 pounds into their practice (MWSAC 1997). This meant that there had been little intake of new migrants into this part of the medical work-force. However, these rules were altered in November 2001 and overseas doctors are increasingly entering General Practice training schemes. Trainee General Practitioners sit the qualifying examination to enter the Vocational Training Scheme (VTS) and undergo 3 years of training, also usually on permit-free immigration regulations. General Practitioners are considered as career grade doctors and are therefore either on a Work Permit scheme or on the HSMP.

Notwithstanding these differential conditions of entry/stay for overseas doctors, the proportion of overseas doctors increased from 23 to 26% between 1995 and 2000. These were largely doctors who had qualified in countries of the Third World, particularly in the new Commonwealth, and who had long dominated medical migration (Mejía 1978). India was the largest source country for doctors in the 1970s (Mejía 1978) and continues to be important even today (Mullan 2005, 2006; Robinson and Carey 2000).

The result of these migrations is evident in Tables 12.2 and 12.3. Based on analysis of the annual census of doctors in England taken in September of each year, the tables outline the large and continuing significance of International Medical Graduates (IMGs), and the increasing feminisation of all

Table 12.2 Overseas Born International Medical Graduates 1992–2004

| Ethnic Group | Overseas Qualified Female Doctors 1992 | | Overseas Qualified Male Doctors 1992 | | Overseas Qualified Female Doctors 2004 | | Overseas Qualified Male Doctors 2004 | |
|---|---|---|---|---|---|---|---|---|
| | Numbers | Percent of Total Overseas Qualified Female | Numbers | Percent of Total Overseas Qualified Male | Numbers | Percent of Total Overseas Qualified Female | Numbers | Percent of Total Overseas Qualified Male |
| Any other ethnic group | 577 | 20% | 1795 | 19% | 573 | 8% | 2110 | 11% |
| Asian or Asian British (All groups with Asian in them) | 1093 | 37% | 3714 | 39% | 4304 | 60% | 11481 | 62% |
| Black or Black British | 259 | 9% | 1034 | 11% | 572 | 8% | 1555 | 8% |
| Chinese | | | | | 85 | 1% | 137 | 0.7% |
| Mixed | | | | | 152 | 2% | 391 | 3% |
| Not stated | 594 | 20% | 1848 | 20% | 264 | 4% | 633 | 3.4% |
| White | 405 | 14% | 1052 | 11% | 1214 | 17% | 2205 | 12% |
| Total | 2928 | 100% | 9443 | 100% | 7164 | 100% | 18512 | 100% |

Table 12.3 Doctors by Region of Qualification and Gender, 1992–2004

Doctors by Country of Qualification and Gender—England, 2004 by Numbers

| | EEA Qualified | | Other Overseas Qualified | | UK Qualified | | |
|---|---|---|---|---|---|---|---|
| | M | F | M | F | M | F | Total |
| 1992 | 1723 | 969 | 9443 | 2928 | 26886 | 13374 | 55323 |
| 1998 | 2487 | 1568 | 11809 | 4094 | 28256 | 16634 | 64848 |
| 2004 | 2887 | 1961 | 18512 | 7164 | 31646 | 20974 | 83144 |

Doctors by Country of Qualification and Gender—England, 2004 by Percent of Total Doctors

| | EEA Qualified | | Other Overseas Qualified | | UK Qualified | | Total |
|---|---|---|---|---|---|---|---|
| | M | F | M | F | M | F | 100% |
| 1992 | 3.11% | 1.75% | 17.06% | 5.29% | 48.60% | 24.17% | 100% |
| 1998 | 3.84% | 2.42% | 18.21% | 6.31% | 43.57% | 25.65% | 100% |
| 2004 | 3.47% | 2.36% | 22.26% | 8.62% | 38.06% | 25.23% | 100% |

hospital doctors. The tables highlight the large and increasing proportions of doctors working in England who had their initial training outside the United Kingdom. They thus bear witness to the embeddedness of the British NHS labour market in transnational medical training fields. However, this picture was radically altered in 2006 with new regulations limiting the entry and circulation of doctors who were citizens from outside the EEA, resulting in a new landscape of medical recruitment in the United Kingdom. The next section outlines these recent shifts and the impact of the bid for autonomy on IMGs in the United Kingdom.

## RETHINKING THE LINKAGES

On 7 March 2006, the Immigration and Nationality Department announced a series of changes to immigration regulations summarised in the document 'A point-based system: Making migration work for Britain.' The new regulations, based around a point system, were open to consultation (HMSO 2006). Alongside this much-publicised set of changes, new regulations on the entry of doctors were also announced. They came into effect without much public consultation less than a month after they were first announced and have altered the face of health provision in the United Kingdom.

The new regulations involved bringing doctors into the 5-tier points-based system and the peremptory abolition of the permit-free training category through which most IMGs worked in the United Kingdom. Transitional arrangements were to be provided for those already in training posts in the United Kingdom, posts which would come to an end when the current training programmes on which they are enrolled finish.

The implication of these regulation changes arise from their content, the ways in which they have been introduced and the ways in which they are implemented. The short notice and the lack of consultation meant that thousands of IMGs were suddenly faced with uncertainty and often unemployment. Those who had taken the PLAB exam and not yet entered a permit free training scheme were no longer eligible for jobs as they would not meet the requirements of the new points based system. Their investment in the exam (involving fees of £145 for each attempt at PLAB 1, and £430 for each PLAB 2 sitting) and costs of travelling to the United Kingdom to undertake the second part of the exam were wasted. The losses incurred by the many doctors who were in unpaid clinical attachment posts while waiting for their first paid job were even greater. This represented a huge unrecoverable loss of resources for many IMGs, as these amounts represented very large sums of money compared to the salaries they were likely to earn in their home countries (Attili 2006). It may take doctors many years simply to pay back debts incurred in coming to sit these examinations in the United Kingdom. The British Association of Physicians of Indian Origin (BAPIO) estimated that several thousand Indian doctors were affected in this way.

For doctors who were already in post, the retrospective application of regulations meant that they had to negotiate a system to which they had never signed up. Those in training posts were no longer able to complete their training according to the regulations of the system that they joined, or complete their training in the United Kingdom. They were also not eligible to sit the membership examinations set by the Royal Colleges as they would not have the years of experience in the United Kingdom that were required. The new regulations meant that investments in time and money made by IMGs from relatively poor countries to come to the United Kingdom resulted in their acquiring no transferable skills or qualifications.

The sudden shift from regulations that had been in place for decades meant that those applying the rules had little understanding of how to negotiate the changes. Doctors applying for posts that might entail applying for work permits found that the transitional arrangements had not yet been specified. Doctors who had switched to the Highly Skilled Migrant Programme were subjected to different interpretations of rules by different deaneries (Narayan 2006). In particular, the shift from country of qualification to residency/citizenship rights as a filter for jobs led to considerable confusion. For instance, some deaneries issued a notice that they would no longer shortlist non-EEA graduates, while others excluded non-EEA citizens. HSMP candidates who applied for jobs and who had signed a commitment to remain in the United Kingdom and to seek work in that country now found that many deaneries were treating them as equivalent to Tier 2 applicants on the basis that they were non-EEA citizens. Moreover, foreign students who had graduated from British medical schools also found that they were no longer eligible to complete their specialist training in the United Kingdom (Tee 2006). Other forms of discrimination occurred, too. Some deaneries failed to provide results for exams sat (such as among General Practitioners who sat the examinations to enter the Vocational Training Scheme) on the basis that applicants would not be allowed to take up a job later. In the shift to a market-based economy, as suggested by the new regulations, applicants who had paid fees and sat an examination should have been eligible to know their results.

Dismantling the permit-free training system that had been in place for over 20 years involved an emphatic disassociation from a commitment to facilitating the training of IMGs through special immigration regulations. The historical linkages around training provision are elided in the message put out by the Minister for Health in March 2006. He announced: 'We recognise that international doctors have made a huge contribution to the NHS since it was founded in 1948 and there will still be opportunities for overseas staff to come to the United Kingdom. We will continue to need small numbers of specialist doctors, who can bring their skills and experience to the NHS. However, increasingly the NHS will be less reliant on international medical recruitment' (Department of Health 2006). The earlier system, based on a reciprocal relation between training and labour, was forgotten in these new regulations. The points-based system does not have the flexibility to incorporate the relation between work and training that underpinned doctors' migration. And, these regulations were justified through a narrative of self-sufficiency and through evoking a picture of national labour markets.

The impetus for these changes came from a number of other changes in medical labour markets. The growth in number of doctors was part of the NHS Plan drawn up in July 2000. Some 7,500 more hospital consultants and 2,000 more GPs were to be recruited by 2004 of which it was recognised that a number would be recruited from overseas (Department of Health 2000). However, this was to be supplemented by 1000 extra undergraduates or a 31% increase in home entrants to medical college between 2000 and 2005. Together these produced a rapid increase in the number of local graduates. At the same time the European Union expanded to include 10 new member states and the United Kingdom decided to give migrants from these countries access to the U.K. labour market increasing the pool of labour available for filling medical training and career posts in the United Kingdom.

This increase in numbers happened at the same time that there was increasing pressure on hospitals to reduce expenditure so that staffing increases came to be increasingly scrutinised. Alongside these changes were a raft of changes to both medical training and service provision. Under the banner of Modernising Medical Careers the nature and structure of the medical workforce is being reorganised. The new regulations reduce the number of training posts and also tie these posts into a structured training programme. Ultimately, they aim to reduce the pyramidal base of the training structure so that the number of specialist posts available will roughly match the number of entrants into training. The two exceptions to this will be a small number of fixed term specialist training posts and a number of career posts (approximately equivalent to current non-consultant career grade posts) that will provide flexibility in numbers of specialists. The shrinkage in number of years of training (and hence of training posts) alongside the run-through training programme has meant that there is little flexibility to incorporate International Medical Graduates. The changes in immigration regulations pre-empt the shrinkage in job opportunities arising from this new modality of training.

Finally, these changes must be seen in consonance with wider changes in the NHS including the increasing commercialisation of various aspects of health delivery (Mackintosh and Koivusalo 2005, Timmins 2005). Whilst health provision is still free at the point of delivery, the arrangement is increasingly being organised through public–private partnerships that take the form of independent sector treatment centres (21 operational in February 2006, of which several are owned by Swedish, Canadian and South African firms). Overseas, contracting teams, too, have been recruited to attend to waiting list hotspots so that the nature of involvement of outside providers has been altered. So far, the Overseas Contracting Team has contracted work from France, Germany, Belgium, South Africa, Spain and Scandinavia. The number of professionals circulating through these means is admittedly much smaller than those involved in the NHS. However, the government is expecting to create an Extended Choice Network of Independent Sector providers with investment of approximately £3 billion expected to go into elective provision in the next 5 years (Department of Health 2006; see also BMA, 2005; House of Commons Health Committee 2006; Lethbridge 2002). These new forms of provisioning within the NHS are creating novel labour relationships with a range of Scandinavian, South African and North American health providers as transnational health firms become the new merchants of labour (Connell and Stillwell 2006). New forms of medical migration are being opened up through these channels although there is little research on this thus far.


## CONCLUSIONS

This chapter has briefly traced the recent history of IMGs in the United Kingdom in order to highlight the issues facing the reserve army of medical labour that these migrant doctors represent. In doing so, it is useful to remember that medical migration is shaped by a range of political, socio-economic (particularly educational and occupational) issues both in sending and receiving countries). Historically, migrant doctors have been an explicit part of calculations on how medical care should be delivered in the United Kingdom. However, most recently the United Kingdom has decided to shake off its dependence on migrant doctors (particularly those from outside the European Economic Area) and to write a new script for medical provision in the United Kingdom. This was achieved through the selective disavowal of long-established forms of interdependence between institutions and practices scattered across many places and spaces.

The tendency to adopt nationalistic frameworks in thinking about health service provision is somewhat short-sighted and elides a number of interdependencies and transnational linkages that shape medical migration. Firstly, conjuring up the rhetoric of national labour markets omits the fact that the U.K.'s medical labour market has for many years been a European labour market. As part of the European political and economic space, the circulation of medical professionals has been enabled through the transfer of accreditation across the countries of the Union. More recently, the United Kingdom's decision to allow free circulation to members of the EEA has expanded this labour market even further. This marks a significant shift from a dependence on Commonwealth countries, but for the most part it does only that. It does not (and cannot within the context of European agendas) mark out the boundaries for a national labour market that only locally graduated doctors can enter. Secondly, it ignores the interdependence between training and working that was a central pillar of medical careers. Working in the United Kingdom counted as training for examinations that IMGs took and provided one route for doctors to obtain skills that were marketable both at home and in other countries. Thirdly, the immediacy of the push for independence involves a disavowal of the temporal qualities of the interdependent relationships that have been established over centuries of co-production of health across different parts of the Empire.

The push for autonomy by U.K. government have created new spaces of activism and produced new forms of lobbying. BAPIO has been at the forefront of much of this activism, challenging the regulations in court and involving high-level politicians, including the Indian Prime Minister, in their cause. For the first time in the long history of Indian medical migration, the Indian government has become involved in the injustices meted out to its citizen medical professionals. It has pressed the case of Indian doctors with the U.K. government. At the same time, the Indian government has also recognised the transnationalism of its medical practitioners. It has facilitated their return to India by announcing in January 2007 that public sector medical posts will now be opened up to those who have taken up permanent residence in other countries. The Indian government thus firmly placed Indian medical provision within a transnational Indian diasporic labour market. In doing so, they recognised and validated the contributions made by such diasporic Indians to private sector health provision in India, itself a generator of income for the country through the medical tourism that it has speeded up (Sahoo 2003). Just as the United Kingdom is withdrawing from its transnational allegiances to countries outside the EU, India is recognising its healthworker diaspora and engaging in state-led transnationalism (Margheritis 2007). The Indian government, it appears, is recognising the multiple affiliations that migrants may have and the fluidity of the movements that individuals may have over their life-time, and is urging the British government too to recognise the multiple spatialities and affiliations within which migrants are embedded.

These political interventions point to the tensions between nationalistic frameworks of analysis that often accompany social welfare provision and the transnational social fields within which the service is actually embedded. These tensions are heightened in the case of the National Health Service as this institution is considered to be emblematic of the success of the welfare state principle and a matter of national pride while at the same time enveloping in its folds a range of migrant workers whose labour is then devalued. Analytically, locating medical labour markets in transnational spaces shows the interlocking nature of medical labour markets across different places and spaces, including the new forms of transnational arrangements that commercialisation of health service provision is introducing in the United Kingdom, highlights the extent of interdependence that marks health provision and points out the limits of a nationalistic framework of analysis for understanding medical migration.

## REFERENCES

Attili, S (2006) New UK policy on overseas doctors: International medical graduates invest 7500 pounds sterling in getting first job, *British Medical Journal*, 332(7548), 1033.
Bailey, A (2001) Turning transnational: Notes on the theorisation of international migration, *International Journal of Population Geography*, 7, 413–428.
Beaverstock, J (1994) Rethinking skilled international labor migration: World cities and banking organizations, *Geoforum*, 25, 323–338.
BMA (2005) *Impact of treatment centres on the local health economy in England report*, London: Health Policy and Economic Research Unit.
Bornat, J (2004) 'Chance as narrative theme or pragmatic function? Geriatricians recall their careers'. Paper to Fifth European Social Science History Conference, 24–27 March, Berlin
Brown, G (2006) Keynote speech, Fabian Future of Britishness Conference, 14 January 2006, available at: http://www.fabiansociety.org.uk/press_office/news_latest_all.asp?pressid=520, accessed 10 February 2006.
Buchan, J and Dovlo, D (2004) *International recruitment of health workers to the UK*, London: Department for International Development.
Clarke, J (2005) Welfare states as nation states: Some conceptual reflections, *Social Policy and Society*, 4, 407–415.

Commander, S, Kangasniemi, M and Winters, L A (2004) The brain drain: Curse or boon? A survey of the literature, in R Baldwin and L Winters (Eds), *International Trade and Challenges to Globalization: Analyzing the economics*, Chicago: Chicago University Press, pp. 235–272.

Connell, J and Stilwell, B (2006) Merchants of medical care: Recruiting agencies in the global health care chain, in C Kuptsch (Ed), *Merchants of labour*, Geneva: International Labour Organization, pp. 239–253.

Decker, K (2001) Overseas doctors: Past and present, in N Coker (Ed), *Racism in medicine: An agenda for change*, London: King's Fund, London, pp. 25–57.

Department of Health (2000) *The NHS Plan: a plan for investment, a plan for reform*. Department of Health: London

Department of Health (2001) *Code of practice for NHS employers involved in the international recruitment of healthcare professionals*, London: Department of Health.

Department of Health (2002) *Growing capacity: Independent sector diagnosis and treatment centres*, London: Department of Health.

Department of Health (2005) *Medical and dental workforce census*, Leeds: Department of Health.

Department of Health (2006), *Extra investment and increase in home-grown medical recruits eases UK reliance on overseas doctors*, available at http://www.dh.gov.uk/PublicationsAndStatistics/PressReleases/PressReleasesNotices/fs/en?CONTENT_ID=4131255&chk=TadpQg, accessed 12 August 2006.

Fisher, M H (2004) *Counterflows to colonialism: Indian travellers and settlers in Britain, 1600–1857*, New Delhi: Permanent Black.

Forbes, G (2005) *Women in colonial India: Essays on politics, medicine, and historiography*, New Delhi: Chronicle Books.

HMSO (2006) A points-based system: Making migration work for Britain—CM 6741 available at: http://www.official-documents.co.uk/document/cm67/6741/6741.pdf, accessed 10 March 2006.

Hondagneu-Sotelo, P and Avila, E (1997) "I'm here, but I'm there": The meanings of Latina transnational motherhood, *Gender and Society* 11, 548–71.

House of Commons Health Committee (2006) *Independent sector treatment centres fourth report of session 2005–06, volume 1*, 25 July, available at: http://www.publications.parliament.uk/pa/cm200506/cmselect/cmhealth/934/934i.pdf, accessed 29 August 2006.

Hyndman, J and Walton-Roberts, M (2000) Interrogating borders: A transnational approach to refugee research in Vancouver, *The Canadian Geographer*, 44, 244–258.

Kyriakides, C and Virdee, S (2003) Migrant labour, racism and the British National Health Service, *Ethnicity and Health*, 8, 283–305.

Lethbridge, J (2002) *Forces and reactions in healthcare: A report on worldwide trends for The PSI health services taskforce*, London, December.

Levitt, P (2001) Transnational migration: Taking stock and future directions, *Global Networks*, 1, 195–216.

Levitt, P, De Wind, J and Vertovec, S (2003) International perspectives on transnational migration: An introduction, *International Migration Review*, 37, 561–72.

Lowell, L B, Findlay, A and Stewart, E (2004) *Brain strain: Optimising highly skilled migration from developing countries*, London: Institute for Public Policy Research.

Mackintosh, M and Koivusalo, M (Eds), (2005) *Commercialization of health care: Global and local dynamics and policy initiatives*, Basingstoke: Palgrave.

Margheritis, A (2007) State-led transnationalism and migration: Reaching out to the Argentine community in Spain, *Global Networks*, 7, 87–106.

Martineau, T and Willetts, A (2006) The health workforce: Managing the crisis ethical international recruitment of health professionals: Will codes of practice protect developing country health systems?, *Health Policy*, 75, 358–367.

McNeil-Walsh, C (2004) Widening the discourse: A case for the use of postcolonial theory in the analysis of South African nurse migration to Britain, *Feminist Review*, 77, 120–124.

Medical Workforce Standing Advisory Committee (1997) *Planning the Medical Workforce: Medical Workforce Standing Advisory Committee—Third Report*, London.

Mejía, A (1978) Migration of physicians and nurses, *International Journal of Epidemiology*, 7, 207–215.

Mullan, F (2005) The metrics of the physician brain drain, *New England Journal of Medicine*, 353, 1810–1818.

Mullan, F (2006) Doctors for the world: Indian physician emigration, *Health Affairs*, 25, 380–393.

Narayan, K (2006) Non-European doctors and change in UK policy: What about highly skilled migrant doctors?, *British Medical Journal*, 332(7546), 914.

Pati, B and Harrison, M (2001) *Health medicine and empire: New perspectives on colonial India*, New Delhi: Sangam.

Raghuram, P and Kofman, E (2002) The State, labour markets and immigration: The case of skilled emigrants in UK's medical labour market, *Environment and Planning A*, 34, 2071–2089.

Ray, K M, Lowell, B L and Spencer, S (2006) International health worker mobility: Causes, consequences, and best practices, *International Migration*, 44, 181–203.

Rivett, G (1998) *From cradle to grave*, London: King's Fund.

Robinson, V and Carey, M (2000) Peopling skilled international migration: Indian doctors in the U.K. *International Migration*, 38, 89–108.

Sahoo, S (2003) Healthcare and Indian diaspora: The case of corporate hospitals in Hyderabad, in R Gopakumar (Ed), *Giving patterns of Indians in USA*, New Delhi: Charity Aid Foundation (CAF), pp.129–162.

Saxenian, A (2000) *Silicon Valley's new immigrant entrepreneurs*, CCIS working Paper No. 15, University of California, San Diego.

Tee, J L (2006) New UK policy on overseas doctors: Also affects international medical graduates graduating from UK institutions, *British Medical Journal*, 332, 1033.

Thomson, G A, Foster, M, Sheriff, R, et al. (2005) International educational partnerships for doctors in training: A collaborative framework with the RCP, *Clinical Medicine*, 5(2), 133–136.

Timmins, N (2005) The NHS revolution: Health care in the market place: Use of private health care in the NHS, *British Medical Journal*, 331, 1141–1142.

Vertovec, S (2004) Migrant transnationalism and modes of transformation, *International Migration Review*, 38, 970–1001.

Yeoh, B, Graham, E and Boyle, P (2002) Migration and family relations in the Asia Pacific, *Asia and Pacific Migration Journal*, 11, 1–11.

# 13 The Recruiting of South African Health Care Professionals

*Christian M. Rogerson and Jonathan Crush*

In the early twenty-first century the international migration of highly skilled personnel has increased significantly as a consequence of globalization (Crush 2002, Iredale 2002). Health workers are one of the categories of skilled professionals that have been most affected. In recent years, there have been 'very significant changes in the scale and consequences of professional health worker mobility' (Bach 2006:22). Some have styled this as 'a global conveyor belt' of health personnel or a 'medical carousel,' which channels skilled professionals from poor to rich countries (Schrecker and Labonte 2004; Eastwood et al. 2005). The conveyor belt of medical personnel has seen the recruitment of Canadian doctors for the United States, of British doctors to North America, and of health professionals from developing countries into the United Kingdom, Ireland, the European Union, the United States and Canada (Bundred and Levitt 2000). A major consequence is a serious depletion of the health workforce of the Caribbean, the South Pacific and sub-Saharan Africa. The medical 'brain drain' has catalysed research and energized new policy debates that place a high priority on managing migration (WHO 2003, Adams and Stilwell 2004, Brown and Connell 2004).

As Bach argues: 'The higher profile attached to human resource issues within the health sector and the specific challenges of addressing staff shortages whilst not exacerbating problems of brain drain has ensured that the issue of health worker migration has rapidly climbed the health policy agenda' (2006:22). Accordingly, over the past decade, a substantial body of research has emerged which tracks patterns of international migration of health personnel and its causes and consequences and debates policy responses at global and national scales (Bach 2003, Buchan et al. 2003). A swathe of opinions and debates have been generated by the popularly styled 'great brain robbery' and resultant crisis in health services across much of the developing world (Patel 2003). Health worker migration, as Bach stresses, 'is an inescapable feature of the health sector' (2006:22). Issues relating to the international migration of health professionals need to be positioned as part of the wider dynamics of globalization and the development of an international marketplace for 'talent.' 'Competing for talent' is now recognized as an essential element of international competitiveness in the current world economy. In this regard, a central role is played by private and public sector recruitment agencies in shaping the international mobility of talented or skilled individuals.

Within this emerging body of research and debates on the recruitment of skilled health personnel the case of South Africa is attracting growing interest. For almost 15 years, South Africa has been the target of the 'global raiding' of the country's talent pool of skilled professionals (Rogerson and Rogerson 2000, Crush 2002). The exodus of South African health personnel in the post-apartheid period has been highlighted in several studies (Bhorat et al. 2002, Grant 2003, Padarath et al. 2003, Dumont and Meyer 2004). Dealing with the consequences of this bleeding of health professionals has recently become a core policy issue for national government. The aim of this chapter is to provide new insights on the recruitment patterns of skilled health personnel from South Africa and to examine policy debates and issues concerning the recruitment of skilled health professionals from the country. More specifically, the objective is to provide an audit of the organization and patterns of recruitment of skilled professionals from South Africa in the health sector. This task draws upon a detailed analysis of recruitment advertising appearing in the *South African Medical Journal* (SAMJ) and of a series of interviews conducted with private recruiting enterprises.

## CAUSES OF HEALTH PROFESSIONAL MIGRATION

At one level, 'the reason for the "conveyor belt" is breathtaking in its simplicity. Richer countries and health systems pay better salaries' (Schrecker and Labonte 2004:411). The significance of wage differentials in accounting for the South–North movement of health care professionals cannot be overemphasized. Nevertheless, complex forces shape the international mobility of health professionals. A range of different factors have been aired in international research, much of which analyses flows in terms of 'push' and 'pull' forces. Push factors focus on issues of pay, working conditions, and broad management and governance factors that galvanize health professionals to exit their own health systems and migrate from their country. By contrast, pull factors that tend to catalyse movement relate to shortages and active recruitment from high-income countries. In the case of Africa, Dovlo and Martineau (2004) view the migration decision as linked to the emergence between source and destination of six sets of factors or gradients.

1. Income or remuneration gradient: the differential in salaries and living conditions between home and the destination country.
2. Job satisfaction gradient: perceptions of good working conditions or environment and utilization of one's skills to the best technical and professional ability.

3. Organizational environment/career opportunity gradient: differences in opportunities for career advancement and specialization and a well-managed health system.
4. Governance gradient: differences in administrative bureaucracy, efficiency and fairness with which broader governmental services are managed.
5. Protection and risk gradient: differences in the perception of risk (especially from HIV/AIDS in Africa and the lack of protective equipment) compared to that in recipient countries.
6. Social security and benefits gradient: health professionals are concerned about their security after retirement.

The significance of social networks as an influence upon migration flows also cannot be overlooked. These networks are drawn upon by newly-arrived migrants in destination countries and reduce the costs and risks associated with migration. Thus, 'once migration pathways are established this will stimulate further migration' of skilled health professionals (Bach 2006:14; see Kelly and D'Addorio, this book).

With the recent growth in significance of demand-led migration, the dominant dynamic has been the 'pull' of targeted international recruitment, a factor that some researchers describe more strongly as 'predatory' or 'grab factors' (Muula 2005). Richards goes so far as to argue that the problem of medical migration 'is not so much a drain as a positive suction on the part of many developed countries' (Richards 2002). The WHO differentiates four models of recruitment agency involvement in relation to the international movement of nurses:

1. An agency-provided recruitment model in which the agency actively recruits nurses on their own behalf for placement in other countries.
2. An agency-led recruitment model in which the employer appoints an agency to identify a source country and in which the agency takes the lead on recruitment, selection and placement with some input from the employer.
3. An agency-facilitated recruitment model in which the employer works in active partnership with the agency to identify a source country and the employer is directly involved in selection processes facilitated by the agency.
4. An employer-led recruitment model in which the employer uses its own resources to identify a source country, select, recruit and place health personnel as well as deal with registration or permit issues (Buchan et al. 2003).

In general, 'the opportunity for health professionals to be more mobile has been facilitated by the growth of more formalized channels of recruitment, with increased awareness of the role of commercial recruitment agencies and an increasingly important role for the internet' (Bach 2006:22). The importance of the Internet in facilitating recruitment also cannot be under-estimated. Schrecker and Labonte (2004:412) point to 'the simple aware-ness of opportunities that comes from routine interaction with professional colleagues, in a world where information is often just a mouse-click away.'

## THE RECRUITMENT OF SOUTH AFRICAN HEALTH PROFESSIONALS

The migration of skilled health professionals from South Africa is emerging as a matter of particular policy concern. Research on the international migra-tion of skilled health professionals continues to highlight South Africa as a leading source country for medical personnel for the United States, Canada, the United Kingdom, Australia and New Zealand (Scott et al. 2004; Labonte et al. 2007). Nevertheless, accurate information on the extent of migration is officially admitted to be 'hard to come by and invariably controversial' (DOH 2006). The editor of the *SAMJ* has stated that on the question of the numbers of doctors that leave South Africa 'no one knows exactly how many do so' (Ncayiyana 2005).

Table 13.1 shows that the largest proportion of the 7,363 South Afri-can-born physicians in OECD countries are in the United Kingdom (48%), followed by the United States, Canada and Australia (Clemens 2006). The United Kingdom is also the most popular destination for nurses, followed by Australia, the United States and Canada (Table 13.2). Contrary to some perceptions that South Africa is acting as a magnet for health care pro-fessionals from other Southern African Development Community (SADC) states, there were only 1,557 non-South African physicians and 439 non-South African nurses from other SADC countries in the country in 2001. Of these, by far the greatest proportion (41% of physicians and 41% of nurses) were from Zimbabwe. In part, this is a result of South Africa's stated policy not to 'poach' health professionals from neighbouring countries. Western countries have not been so considerate. In many SADC countries, over 50% of locally-born physicians are resident in OECD countries (Table 13.1). Botswana, Lesotho, Malawi, Mauritius, the Seychelles, Swaziland, Tanza-nia, Zambia and Zimbabwe all have more physicians in the United King-dom than in South Africa. There are also more Angolan and Mozambican physicians in Portugal than at home.

The South African government has observed that the figures for South African health professionals abroad are 'very considerable and worrying, all the more since indications are that the trend is escalating' (DOH 2006:48), so that the exodus is likely to continue (McDonald and Crush 2002). In a survey of the health profession as a whole in 2005, some 8% said it was 'likely' they would leave within 6 months. The proportion increased

Table 13.1  Geographical Distribution of SADC-Born Physicians

| Country of Origin | Home | Abroad | UK | USA | France | Canada | Australia | Portugal | Spain | Belgium | South Africa | Percent Abroad |
|---|---|---|---|---|---|---|---|---|---|---|---|---|
| Angola | 881 | 2,102 | 16 | 0 | 5 | 25 | 0 | 2,006 | 14 | 5 | 31 | 70% |
| Botswana | 530 | 68 | 28 | 10 | 0 | 0 | 3 | 0 | 0 | 1 | 26 | 11% |
| DRC | 5,647 | 552 | 37 | 90 | 139 | 35 | 0 | 42 | 4 | 107 | 98 | 9% |
| Lesotho | 114 | 57 | 8 | 0 | 0 | 0 | 0 | 0 | 0 | 0 | 49 | 33% |
| Malawi | 200 | 293 | 191 | 40 | 0 | 0 | 10 | 2 | 1 | 1 | 48 | 59% |
| Mauritius | 960 | 822 | 294 | 35 | 307 | 110 | 36 | 1 | 0 | 20 | 19 | 46% |
| Mozambique | 435 | 1,334 | 16 | 20 | 0 | 10 | 3 | 1,218 | 4 | 2 | 61 | 75% |
| Namibia | 466 | 382 | 37 | 15 | 0 | 30 | 9 | 0 | 0 | 0 | 291 | 45% |
| Seychelles | 120 | 50 | 29 | 0 | 4 | 10 | 3 | 0 | 0 | 0 | 4 | 29% |
| South Africa | 27,551 | 7,363 | 3,509 | 1,950 | 16 | 1,545 | 1,111 | 61 | 5 | 0 | 0 | 21% |
| Swaziland | 133 | 53 | 4 | 4 | 0 | 0 | 0 | 1 | 0 | 0 | 44 | 28% |
| Tanzania | 1,264 | 1,356 | 743 | 270 | 4 | 240 | 54 | 1 | 1 | 3 | 40 | 52% |
| Zambia | 670 | 883 | 465 | 130 | 0 | 40 | 39 | 3 | 0 | 3 | 203 | 57% |
| Zimbabwe | 1,530 | 1,602 | 553 | 235 | 0 | 55 | 97 | 12 | 1 | 6 | 643 | 51% |
| Total | 40,501 | 16,917 | 5,930 | 2,799 | 475 | 2,100 | 1,365 | 3,347 | 30 | 148 | 1,557 | 0 |

Source: Clemens (2006)

Table 13.2 Geographical Distribution of SADC-Born Nurses

| Sending Country | Home | Abroad | UK | USA | France | Canada | Australia | Portugal | Spain | Belgium | South Africa | Percent Abroad |
|---|---|---|---|---|---|---|---|---|---|---|---|---|
| Angola | 13,135 | 1,841 | 22 | 135 | 12 | 10 | 4 | 1,639 | 8 | 11 | 0 | 12% |
| Botswana | 3,556 | 80 | 47 | 28 | 0 | 0 | 0 | 0 | 0 | 0 | 5 | 2% |
| DRC | 16,969 | 2,288 | 44 | 207 | 206 | 50 | 0 | 9 | 4 | 1,761 | 7 | 12% |
| Lesotho | 1,266 | 36 | 5 | 6 | 0 | 0 | 0 | 0 | 0 | 0 | 25 | 3% |
| Malawi | 1,871 | 377 | 171 | 171 | 0 | 10 | 14 | 0 | 0 | 0 | 11 | 17% |
| Mauritius | 2,629 | 4,531 | 4,042 | 107 | 86 | 75 | 195 | 1 | 0 | 22 | 3 | 63% |
| Mozambique | 3,664 | 853 | 12 | 64 | 0 | 10 | 0 | 748 | 2 | 6 | 11 | 19% |
| Namibia | 2,654 | 152 | 18 | 6 | 0 | 0 | 4 | 1 | 0 | 6 | 118 | 5% |
| Seychelles | 422 | 175 | 80 | 28 | 8 | 30 | 29 | 0 | 0 | 0 | 0 | 29% |
| South Africa | 90,986 | 4,844 | 2,884 | 877 | 20 | 275 | 955 | 58 | 3 | 33 | 0 | 5% |
| Swaziland | 3,345 | 96 | 21 | 36 | 0 | 10 | 4 | 0 | 0 | 0 | 25 | 3% |
| Tanzania | 26,023 | 953 | 446 | 228 | 0 | 240 | 32 | 2 | 1 | 0 | 4 | 4% |
| Zambia | 10,987 | 1,110 | 664 | 299 | 0 | 25 | 68 | 2 | 0 | 0 | 52 | 9% |
| Zimbabwe | 11,640 | 3,723 | 2,834 | 440 | 0 | 35 | 219 | 14 | 3 | 0 | 178 | 24% |
| Total | 189,147 | 21,059 | 11,290 | 2,632 | 332 | 770 | 1,524 | 2,474 | 21 | 1,839 | 439 | |

Source: Clemens (2006)

dramatically as the timeframe was lengthened: 26% said it was likely they would leave within the next 2 years and 52% that they would leave within the next 5 years (Pendleton and Crush 2007).

In addition to the permanent migration of health personnel, there is mounting evidence of temporary losses as South African health personnel are recruited for work overseas on fixed contracts. As Stern (2005:680) argues, 'conditions in the South African private sector support exports of health services.' In respect of the export of health services and the temporary loss of health professionals, South African hospital groups have recently won major tenders to provide staff and services to the U.K. National Health Service (NHS). In particular, the Netcare Group, South Africa's largest hospital group listed on the Johannesburg Stock Exchange, aspires to become 'a global integrated healthcare organization' (Netcare Group 2007). Since 2003, this company has been involved as a preferred bidder in a number of partnerships with the U.K. Department of Health. This partnership has involved a 5-year contract to perform 44,500 cataract operations for the NHS via mobile services and the opening in Manchester in May 2005 of a 45-bed, three theatre facility for performing 44,800 orthopaedic and general surgical procedures. Other contracts have been secured with the Southport and Ormskirk NHS Trust for performing 300 hip and knee replacement operations and with the Portsmouth Hospital NHS Trust for 1,000 surgical procedures on hands, shoulders, hips, knees and feet. As Stern emphasizes, 'In terms of these contracts Netcare sends teams of medical personnel from South Africa for fixed and short-term periods in the United Kingdom' and in terms of retaining skilled staff in South Africa 'these personnel are then prohibited from employment with the NHS for a period of two years' (Stern 2005:680).

In accounting for the permanent exodus of health personnel, the South African Department of Health (2006:49) focuses upon the 'push' and 'pull' factors that affect brain drain. Pull factors that are highlighted include 'better wages, easier working conditions and opportunities for professional advancement in foreign countries.' Push factors, seen as driving personnel out of the country, encompass 'lack of management and support, work overload, poor working conditions, lack of appropriate skills and emotional burnout.' In addition, the report mentions 'high crime rates and uncertainties about the future.' What has been ignored in official analyses of the causes of the migration of skilled health professionals from the country is the role played by organized recruiters as part of wider international recruitment operations that 'target the skill base of developing countries like South Africa' (Crush 2002:148). Nevertheless, the new global marketplace for talent 'facilitates aggressive transnational recruiting by both governments and the private sector' (Crush 2002:149). To investigate this neglected aspect of the loss of skilled health professionals, research was conducted during 2005–2006 on the activities of recruitment agencies involved in encouraging or facilitating local health professionals to step on the 'global conveyor belt.'

Research on recruitment of South African health personnel involved two major components. The first, and largest, component of the investigation involved a 5-year audit, covering 2000–2004, of all advertisements in the *South African Medical Journal* for the international recruitment of medical practitioners (excluding the recruitment of nurses). The *SAMJ* is published on a monthly basis and the study analysed 60 issues over the 5-year period, covering the recruitment agency, positions advertised, where available, contact details and the nature of the advertising. The 5-year coverage allowed an analysis of the changing temporal patterns in international recruiting initiatives. The second component of the research involved a set of focused key informant interviews concerning the organization of medical recruitment, with recruitment agencies with active operations in South Africa. Many recruiters of medical personnel were reluctant to speak openly of their activities and refused to be interviewed. Nevertheless, focused interviews on recruitment were secured with representatives of five different recruiters. Finally, two additional in-depth interviews were conducted with the editor of the *SAMJ* and the Deputy Director General for Human Resources in South Africa's Department of Health. Issues of the impact and policy response to recruitment activities formed the focus of these interviews.

## RECRUITING SOUTH AFRICAN MEDICAL PERSONNEL

Over the period 2000–2004, *SAMJ* yielded a total of 2,522 recruitment advertisements for South African medical personnel. The number of advertisements appearing each year was relatively consistent (Table 13.3). Many advertisements were repeated for a period of several months and, in the case of the global recruiters, appeared almost every month.

The recruitment advertisements targeted (a) applicants for specific positions available in particular countries; (b) general recruitment of personnel

*Table 13.3* Recruitment Advertisements by Year, 2000–2004

|       | *Number of Advertisements* | *Percent of Total* | *Monthly Average* |
|-------|---------------------------|--------------------|-------------------|
| 2000  | 465                       | 18.2               | 39                |
| 2001  | 461                       | 18.3               | 38                |
| 2002  | 646                       | 25.6               | 54                |
| 2003  | 492                       | 19.5               | 41                |
| 2004  | 458                       | 18.2               | 42                |
| Total | 2522                      | 100.0              | 42                |

by international agencies for placement in designated countries; and (c) general recruitment agencies listing for placements across a range of international destinations. The vast majority of advertisements were for specified individual country destinations; a small share of advertising (3%) was for multi-destinations or geographical regions, such as the Gulf or Europe. Recruitment spanned the entire spectrum of medical personnel from general doctors to specialists. For example, in 2004, recruiters were seeking South African personnel for positions including general practitioners, ward doctors, consultants, radiologists, plastic surgeons, anaesthetists, geriatric specialists, rehabilitation specialists, pathologists, dermatologists, cardiologists, oncologists, orthopaedic consultants, trauma specialists, hip specialists, anatomical pathologists, neurosurgeons and urologists. The largest number of individual advertisements was for general practitioners, RMOs (Resident Medical Officer) or 'doctors of all grades.' The majority of advertisements are less than a half-page insert in size, but from 2002, there was a trend toward larger recruitment advertisements of half-page or full-page size (Table 13.4).

The most critical findings relate to the advertised international destinations for South African medical personnel. The overall geographical pattern of recruitment (Figure 13.1) shows that the greatest volume of recruiting was clearly for the United Kingdom, which had 36% of all advertising. The second and third most important recruitment destinations were New Zealand (22%) and Australia (16%). Canada occupied fourth position with a 12% share. As a whole, therefore, these four countries—the United Kingdom, New Zealand, Australia and Canada—accounted for 86% of all recruitment advertising for South African medical personnel. In terms of the existing places of practice of South African-born medical personnel (Table 13.1), what is missing is any significant element of direct recruitment from the fifth member of the 'big five,' namely the United States. Indeed, the United States, with a total of only 15 advertisements, ranked tenth on the listing

*Table 13.4* Numbers of Recruitment Advertisements by Size and Year

|  | *Full Page* | *Half Page* | *Small Insert* |
|---|---|---|---|
| 2000 | 21 (4.5%) | 77 (16.6%) | 367 (78.9%) |
| 2001 | 28 (6.0%) | 91 (19.7%) | 342 (74.2%) |
| 2002 | 80 (12.3%) | 130 (20.1%) | 436 (67.5%) |
| 2003 | 76 (15.4%) | 67 (13.6%) | 349 (70.9%) |
| 2004 | 75 (16.4%) | 70 (15.3%) | 313 (68.3%) |
| Total | 280 (11.1%) | 435 (17.2%) | 1807 (71.6%) |

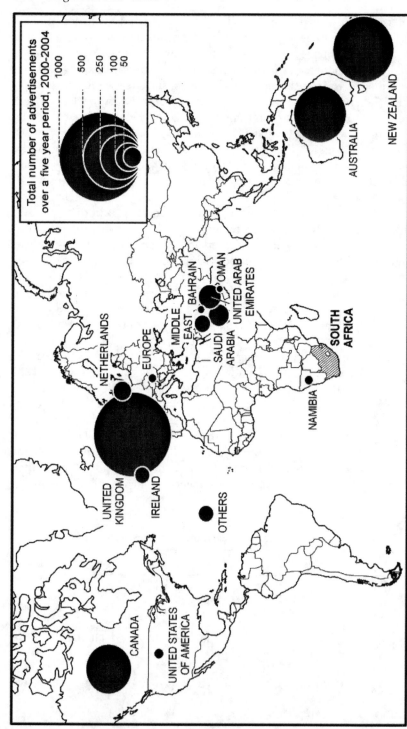

*Figure 13.1* The geography of recruiter advertising, 2000–2004.

of individual countries (see Figures 13.2 and 13.3). The reasons for this are not altogether clear since the United States is one of the major destinations for South African physicians and specialists. Clearly, South African health professionals learn about job opportunities in the United States through other channels. Personal contacts with health professionals already in the United States are likely to play a significant role. Web advertising may also

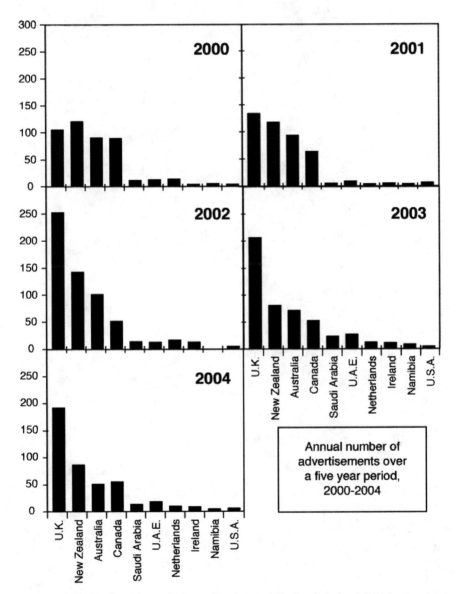

*Figure 13.2* Number of recruitment advertisements by leading destination countries, 2000–2004.

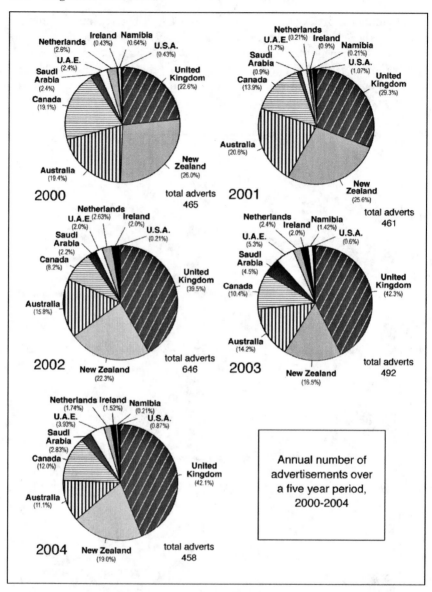

*Figure 13.3* Share of countries in recruitment advertising, 2000–2004.

be important. Many African-trained physicians also enter the United States through residency programmes (Hagopian et al. 2004). Information about residency opportunities in the United States is obtained from other sources. More significant than the United States are Middle East destinations, in particular Saudi Arabia and the United Arab Emirates, plus the Netherlands and Ireland in Europe, and Namibia, the only African destination of any note. Minor recruiting destinations included Bahrain, Qatar, Oman, Belgium and Nigeria. Finally, isolated advertisements appeared for work in the following destinations: Bermuda, Botswana, China, India, Kuwait, Lesotho, Mozambique, Russia, Swaziland, Vietnam and Zambia.

The changing share of countries in the total volume of recruitment advertising is significant (Table 13.5). In 2000, New Zealand was the leading source for recruitment advertising with 26% of the total, followed by the United Kingdom, Australia and Canada, but from 2001 the United Kingdom was the most important destination for recruitment. By 2000, more than 40% of advertisements were for the United Kingdom, and by 2004 the number of advertisements for South African medical personnel to work in the United Kingdom matched the combined total from Australia, Canada and New Zealand. Canada became the third most significant source for recruitment advertising in 2004, in large part due to a marked cutback in advertising for Australia.

Of all the full-page advertisements during the period 2000–2004, some 80% were for work in the United Kingdom (Table 13.6). This analysis underscores, once again, the overwhelming dominance of recruitment initiatives for South African skilled health professionals to work in the United Kingdom.

## THE RECRUITMENT BUSINESS

The business of recruitment is dominated by U.K.-based enterprises such as Global Medics, Medacs Healthcare Services, Corinth Health Care and NES Healthcare United Kingdom. Significant non-U.K. players recruiting in South Africa include Auckland Medical Bureau for New Zealand, AMAQ Services for Australia and Northern Medical Services in Canada. Many of the large United Kingdom recruitment agencies are long-established and have been in operation for 25 years or more. Some agencies deal only in placements in the United Kingdom but others, such as Medacs or Corinth,

*Table 13.5* Share of Recruitment Advertisements by Leading Country and Year

|                | 2000 | 2001 | 2002 | 2003 | 2004 |
|----------------|------|------|------|------|------|
| United Kingdom | 22.6 | 29.3 | 39.5 | 42.3 | 42.1 |
| New Zealand    | 26.0 | 25.6 | 22.3 | 16.5 | 19.0 |
| Australia      | 19.4 | 20.6 | 15.8 | 14.2 | 11.1 |
| Canada         | 19.1 | 13.9 | 8.2  | 10.4 | 12.0 |
| Rest of World  | 12.9 | 11.6 | 14.2 | 16.6 | 15.8 |

*Table 13.6* Full Page Recruitment Advertising by Country/Region and Year

|                | 2000 | 2001 | 2002 | 2003 | 2004 | Total |
|----------------|------|------|------|------|------|-------|
| United Kingdom | 6    | 23   | 64   | 62   | 70   | 225   |
| New Zealand    | 9    | 4    | 8    | 2    | 2    | 25    |
| Australia      | 3    | 0    | 7    | 0    | 0    | 10    |
| Canada         | 0    | 0    | 0    | 5    | 1    | 6     |
| Ireland        | 1    | 1    | 1    | 0    | 1    | 4     |
| Europe         | 0    | 0    | 0    | 3    | 0    | 3     |
| Namibia        | 2    | 0    | 0    | 0    | 0    | 2     |
| Netherlands    | 0    | 0    | 0    | 2    | 0    | 2     |
| Saudi Arabia   | 0    | 0    | 0    | 1    | 1    | 2     |
| Middle East    | 0    | 0    | 0    | 1    | 0    | 1     |

also advertise placements or opportunities in other parts of the world. Most offer placements in both the private sector and the National Health Service of the United Kingdom.

The advertising targeted at South African medical professionals typically offers 'fantastic opportunities,' 'better lifestyles' and 'great rates' of remuneration as well as, in one case, an assurance that 'we will not mess you about, we have genuine positions.' Assistance and advice are offered to recruited personnel about work placement; welcome and greeting on arrival; opening a bank account; mobile phones and answers to such questions as 'What do I do regarding meals, washing and ironing?' The advertising mantra for one international recruiter conveys the message 'With you every step of the way' (Global Medics 2007). One of the most striking themes of recruitment advertising is place promotion and imaging. Australian advertising emphasizes the lure of 'the Tropical lifestyle in Queensland.' In New Zealand, South Africans are drawn by 'great fishing, great fun' or attracted by 'a breath of fresh air . . . sea . . . country . . . or both. You'll find it in New Zealand.' One opportunity in the Bay of Plenty was advertised as 'Looking for a great lifestyle at the beach?. . . . And a working challenge? Then come to New Zealand.' Another New Zealand placement stated: 'Kia Ora! Sail the Bay of Islands, hike the Milford Track or ski a volcano.' An opportunity in rural British Columbia, Canada was 'located on beautiful Stuart Lake with excellent outdoor amenities, including ski hill and golf course.' Other Canadian advertisements sought to assure potential applicants that 'Saskatchewan is a wonderful place to live, raise a family and enjoy life!!'

Likewise, Peace Country, Grande Prairie, Alberta was 'a great place to raise a family and practice general medicine.' In the United Kingdom applicants for positions in Poole were assured simply that it 'is a beautiful place.' Conscious of the global market for medical personnel, recruiters seek to offer comparative benchmarks for potential recruitment: 'Forget the hassle with the GMC for registration—hop on a plane to Ozz where your South African qualifications and experience will be appreciated. Forget the rain and fog of the United Kingdom—go in leaps and bounds to the sunshine.'

The contact details on recruitment advertisements indicate that the largest share of advertising is placed by overseas recruiters. In 2004, for example, only 15% of advertisements included any local contact details, either in terms of an individual, a local telephone, fax or e-mail contact. For the remainder, communication was through e-mail or web contacts outside South Africa and overseas telephone/fax communication. This is of considerable policy relevance for it points to the weak position and limited room to manoeuvre of the South African government in dealing with the activities of the international recruitment industry.

## SOUTH AFRICAN PERSPECTIVES

Looked at from an international industry perspective, the operations of the cluster of recruitment agencies within South Africa are minor. Enterprises are small in size, often branch operations of U.K.-based operations, or represent independent niche operators. Some of the most prominent locally-based recruiting agencies are Elite Locums, The Locum Agency, RS Locums, Global Medics, Thornhill Recruiting, and Workforce Worldwide. Global Medics, the branch of the U.K.-based enterprises, is a more significant player as it operates offices in a number of South African cities. Examples of small niche operators include the Singapore-based Global Medical Services, which focuses on remote emergency assistance in Africa, Medical Place, a home-based agency in Sandton, and Canada Calls, which, as the name suggests, is dedicated to recruiting South African medical personnel for work in Canada. Many of the locally-based group of recruitment enterprises were established in the post-apartheid era. For example, RS Locums, based in Cape Town, was founded in 1996 and seeks to assist health care professionals 'to achieve their dreams of working in the UK' (RS Locums 2004). Some enterprises, such as Elite Locums, deal with both local as well as international placements of medical personnel. Most agencies, however, specialize in the overseas placement of South African health professionals. In certain instances, the entrepreneur who established the recruitment agency was a qualified doctor.

Interviews undertaken with these recruitment agencies are not representative of the views of the entire South African medical recruitment industry, yet they offer powerful statements, perspectives and 'insider' insights into an industry about which little is known. Issues raised in the interviews focused around several central themes: doing business as a recruiter, recent trends and causes of migration, and addressing the policy challenge of the migration of health professionals from South Africa. The next section provides a selection of statements made by recruiters and allows them to 'speak' from a practitioner perspective to the key issues concerning the migration of health professionals from South Africa, covering the business development, rationale for migration and policy issues.

## On Doing Business as a Recruiter

It is a small business that I run from home. It really consists only of me. It is a South African based company that finds placements for South African doctors overseas. It is a unique service that I place specialist doctors in the UK. I match specialist doctors with hospitals that are looking for a specialist. I usually get contacted by people after they see our advert in the *SAMJ* or in *The Star*. Many people hear about the company through word of mouth. I approach some specialists directly and ask if they would like to work in the UK. I find very few problems from this side. There are no laws and regulations.

Global Medics is a U.K.-based company, which has offices in South Africa. There are over 140 companies recruiting doctors worldwide in the UK at the moment. Many of them have South African doctors on their books. We source the positions in the UK and then go through our database to match the job with the right person. The company specializes in transferring health care skills to the UK. The appointments are on a short to medium term basis.

The company that I run with a colleague is based in Canada and has been running for the past 10 years. Both partners are originally from South Africa and we specialize in placing South African health professionals in Canada. We advertise certain positions but usually we ask people to submit their CV and we try to fit with them specifically. We advertise in the *SAMJ* and call for people to submit their CVs. These are screened and we source a position for that person, as an agent for them. We access the positions in Canada either directly or through an overseas recruitment company.

The company based abroad specializes in recruiting all kinds of professionals. A large proportion of the recruitments are doctors. We advertise globally. There are always adverts in the *SAMJ* from places like Australia and New Zealand looking for South African graduates. We advertise in South Africa for doctors because they are highly regarded. We have a data base of doctors on our system. We then offer a doctor a contract if they fit the profile and if the job is suitable. They are not always suited.

There are so many people that are looking to leave. There are other companies that we compete with but there is enough work so there is not much competition.

## Trends and Causes of Migration

Most of the doctors that are leaving are younger doctors, looking overseas for experience. They are looking to make some money overseas and most of them return to South Africa, especially those that go to the UK. There are others that I send to New Zealand, but they tend to be more permanent and a bit older.

When they go overseas it is almost entirely in the public sector. They make money and open a private practice when they return. The ratio is strongly in favour of recent graduates but they often return after a short stay. Some do repeat the locum but this is uncommon. From my experience the market is definitely quieting down. There are many people who want to do temporary locums to make money, but there are not so many people leaving permanently. The permanent placements are less popular. People are looking to make some money and return. The biggest problem that I have is that there are not enough specialists that want to go overseas.

The positions in Canada are usually long-term or permanent but we have started finding placements in the UK and Ireland which are often not so long term. We send many younger doctors to the UK to work for a short period, to make money to bring back to South Africa. It is older people who go to Canada usually. Since 2000 there has been a steady stream that includes younger professionals leaving the country to live in Canada or the UK. It is not always a case of simply money, although some are keen to go for a short period and make a lot of money. For those that emigrate there are considerations of their families, their schooling and their future prospects. Some doctors think that Canada holds a better future for them. About 50% of the doctors that leave are black doctors. Many of them also do not want to come back. So it is not a question of race. The Canadian health system is so good that there is ample opportunity to practice as a doctor.

There is a shortage of doctors in the UK but they are reluctant to poach from poor countries. At the moment the South African companies that are recruiting South Africans to the UK are only allowed to do so for temporary jobs and locums. But people will go to earn money. The exchange rate is a big factor. Nowadays there is more money to be made in other places. The other day I sent a doctor to Mali on behalf of Anglo-Gold. These jobs pay in dollars.

Why do people want to leave the country and work abroad? Recently qualified doctors go to the UK end up working as RMOs [Resident Medical Officer] for 6 months or more. It's not very stimulating work for them. But it is an opportunity to earn some money. Most of them bring that money back to pay their study loans and maybe start a practice.

There was a noticeable exodus of medical professionals in the late 1990s. After 2003 it became more difficult to get into the UK. South African graduates now have to write some exams in the UK and this has stemmed the flow to some degree. Many older doctors won't go back to school. But there are some other places where doctors can go to such as the Republic of Ireland. The Middle East is now open.

Doctors in the UK are paid poorly by British standards but the money is still so good for local doctors that they can go there and make some money. It's almost more affordable to do locum work in the UK than be a junior doctor in South Africa. It's almost more affordable to go and do bar work in the UK! Probably most that are abroad do not want to be there but they are there because they can make money. I know that many of the doctors there do not like being there. It's not a great place to live. But there are few possibilities here.

Locum work is a lifeline for many doctors in private practice. They can earn some extra money, and can then buy new equipment for their practice. Much of this stuff is paid for by British pounds. Health care in this country is in a crisis. There is very little buy in. Many young guys are going abroad. Once they think there is no future here then they will consider staying abroad. We can catch them before they leave but once they have a wife and kids in the UK they are there forever. It's only the climate that pulls people back to South Africa. There is not much else.

The major problem that is facing doctors in South Africa is Manto Tshabalala (the South African Minister of Health). The situation of doctors in South Africa is stimulated by what is happening here at home. Dr Garlic has made a mess of the whole industry. That woman is a bigger threat to South Africa than Robert Mugabe. To stand in a world forum and proclaim that HIV patients must take garlic is an embarrassment. She is, quite frankly, an idiot.

## Addressing Recruitment Policy Challenges

In the 1990s there was a lot of pressure from the South African government to stop recruiting South African doctors for emigration to Canada. In 1997 the company had a call from the office of President Nelson Mandela to ask us to stop sending doctors away. But there is no chance. If people want to leave they will leave.

We have lots of South Africans on the data base but it doesn't necessarily mean that they will all be going out of the country. After their locum most of them will return. It's the money that people are after. In order for people to stay in South Africa they must be paid properly. Not all doctors want to leave the country. If people are paid properly they will work hard.

The crux of the issue is that when you deal with doctors you can't bullshit them. They are educated people. They can think out of the box and see the bigger picture. They will always find other places to carve out a future if they are not happy. It's the same as all professional people. They can objectively look at the situation and decide what the best option is. I have been in the company for 4 years. I know all the complaints and opinions. I want the doctors to stay in South Africa. I know all the doctors on the data base and I have heard from them what they think. There are organizations trying to encourage graduates to return to South Africa. But they are punting the climate and the friendly people. It's airy-fairy bull-shit! They are not addressing the problems as to why people are there in the first place.

Many companies have approached the Health Minister. Netcare wanted to bring doctors to South Africa from India. We could bring people who are willing to work here from the Philippines, India and China tomorrow if we were allowed to.

It is a big mistake to prevent people from moving to places they want to go to. In South Africa we have a constitution that guarantees freedom of movement. The thing is people are leaving for other reasons. Unless the health care system changes then people will leave for good. In my mind the health department should facilitate locums and sort working holidays abroad. After all, the people are bringing money back into the country. People don't all want to leave for good—most want to come back. It's the money that they are after. After working for a short period in the UK they can make enough money to sustain a private practice, or repay a student loan. The government needs to see the potential. It needs a policy turnaround.

Several key conclusions and policy implications are raised by these interviews and the advertising itself. South Africa currently lacks adequate knowledge and data on the numbers of medical personnel that are leaving the country. The core of the recruitment industry is based outside South Africa and local enterprises emerge as only minor players in the global context. Recruiters are responding to a demand that is being fuelled by shortcomings in the existing wage and working conditions in the South African health care system. As the editor of the *SAMJ* noted in a September 2005 interview: 'It is not the advertisements that are making people leave the country and go abroad. These adverts are taking advantage of a number of other issues.' At least two different recruitment channels may be differentiated. The largest is that of young South African medical graduates seeking short-term appointments as locums or RMOs in the U.K. health system. The majority of such recruits now return to South Africa after the close of their temporary contract appointments. A subsidiary channel is the permanent movement of older and more experienced medical personnel to appointments in New Zealand, Canada or Australia. In recent years, the trend toward the recruitment of South African medical personnel for permanent appointments abroad has slowed and been replaced by temporary appointments, the major catalyst for which is the 'wage gradient,' which is attracting medical personnel to the United Kingdom, the Gulf and other destinations (including recently Iraq and Iran). For permanent migrants, issues of long-term working prospects and family considerations are of importance. In contrast to emigration, South African recruiters have identified potential sources of medical skills in several Asian countries but have not yet been permitted to tap these pools of medical talent. Africa offers another potential space for replacement recruitment. As the editor of the *SAMJ* noted: 'We need to recognize that there are doctors in other parts of Africa who would be willing to come and work in the rural areas of South Africa. During apartheid all the hospitals in the Bantustans were staffed from people overseas. Ironically, with the change in the political dispensation there has been a shift of policy and these people have been kept out.'

## WHITHER SOUTH AFRICAN RECRUITMENT POLICY?

South Africa faces an increasingly competitive and aggressive global marketplace for the recruitment of skilled professionals, including health workers. The uncertainties of the country's new democracy made South Africa vulnerable to the growing number of 'skills-raiding' initiatives that were mounted in the late 1990s, most famously by the two Canadian provinces of Alberta and Saskatchewan (Grant 2003, Labonte et al. 2007). Since the 1990s, South Africa has moved from *ad hoc* reactions to a more organized set of strategic responses to the challenges posed by the international migration of health personnel, and after 2002 a shift occurred from a focus on 'control' toward a more active agenda of 'managed migration' of health professionals, where a 'central component of any such agenda is an enhanced recognition of the importance of improved working conditions and more effective human resources planning to encourage retention of health workers' (Bach 2006:22).

South Africa's initial response was to protest to the Canadian government in 2001 against this 'organized poaching' of the country's medical skills base. Essentially the provincial governments of Canada were responding pro-actively to the dynamics of the international marketplace for skilled talent and more particularly the 'global conveyor belt.' Indeed, they were competing in the international marketplace through 'replacement recruiting,' made necessary by the continued poaching of Canadian-trained health professionals by the United States. By contrast, South Africa's own recruitment policy has been based upon an ethical stance wherein the country refused to undertake 'replacement recruiting' in other parts of Africa and thus be complicit in the draining of precious skills from poorer neighbours (Padarath et al., 2003). Rather than recruit medical personnel from Zimbabwe, Nigeria or the Congo, South Africa entered into a bilateral agreement with Cuba to supply doctors and other medical personnel on short-term contract assignments. This 'principled stand . . . benefited neither South Africa, Zimbabwe nor the region' (Crush 2002:160).

During 2002, South Africa's Department of Health issued an official policy statement and guidelines on the recruitment of foreign health professionals, which 'expressly describes such initiatives as designed to recruit personnel to work in underserved areas in the country' (DOH 2002). Alongside this rural focus for recruitment was the critical stance that the Department of Health would not support the recruitment of individual applicants for permanent work in South Africa from any developing country, while 2003 guidelines recommended that employers should refrain from recruiting in developing countries, especially from the SADC. This policy 'emanated from the Ministers of Health in the SADC region' and aimed to ensure that South Africa did not participate in the 'brain drain taking place in fellow developing countries' (DOH 2006:28). The 2002 policy encouraged the setting up of bilateral government agreements with the purpose of 'better control' of movement of health professionals (DOH 2002).

Endorsement of bilateral agreements as the most appropriate policy response to the recruitment of health workers from developing countries was announced by South Africa's Minister of Health at a meeting with Commonwealth Ministers of Health in May 2002. In 2003, a Memorandum of Understanding (MOU) was signed between South Africa and the United Kingdom on the reciprocal exchange of health care personnel. This agreement committed both parties to formulating an agreed plan 'whereby South African healthcare personnel can spend education and practice period for a limited time in organisations providing NHS services.' The South African government argued that 'this strategy will go a long way to reducing the brain drain from South Africa while at the same time ensuring that South African health professionals have an opportunity to get international exposure.' Among the provisions of the MOU was that health personnel from the United Kingdom could be engaged in strategic placements and would be enabled 'to work alongside health personnel in South Africa with particular emphasis on rural areas' (Tshabalala-Msimang 2003).

## MIGRATION AS PART OF HUMAN RESOURCE PLANNING

By 2005, the South African policy discourse on recruitment had shifted to 'human resource planning' as a whole. In a statement issued in May 2005, the Minister of Health proclaimed that 'We need to ensure that international migration and recruitment of health personnel does not undercut our national plan to improve human resource supply and distribution' (MOH 2005). She also argued that:

> Addressing international migration and recruitment of health personnel is one of several interventions that the Department of Health is making to address the challenges of human resource supply and distribution in South Africa. Other interventions involve improving working conditions for health workers and providing scarce skills and rural allowances to attract and retain health workers in the public health sector in general and rural or underserved areas in particular.

An important milestone was the release in August 2005 of the Draft Framework for the Human Resources for Health Plan. The release of the draft framework was followed by a period of input and discussion with stakeholders that culminated in the revision and release in 2006 of the final document titled *A National Human Resources Plan for Health to Provide Skilled Human Resources for Healthcare Adequate to Take Care of All South Africans* (MOH 2006). This document represents the most comprehensive and strategic response yet to issues regarding the recruitment and retention of health professionals in South Africa's public health sector. The plan is seen as a watershed as the first human resources plan for South Africa's health sector as a whole. A key underlying premise of this strategy, according to the Deputy Director General: Human Resources of the Department of Health, is that 'migration is not something that can or should be stopped.' Another fundamental starting point is that, as it is not realistically possible to stop private sector recruitment, 'the question then is how best to manage the problem.'

In relation to recruitment of South African health professionals to work outside the country and to the replacement recruitment of foreign health professionals for work in South Africa, the 2006 framework elucidates two critical guiding principles. Principle 7 asserts that 'South Africa's role in international health issues contributing to leadership, scientific advances and global health professionals is critical' (DOH 2006:62). Activities aligned with this guiding principle are the design of MOU agreements in line with the strategic focus of the South African health system and the undertaking of a review with the objective of developing clear policies on recruitment and employment of foreign health professionals. Guiding Principle 8 states that 'South Africa's contribution in the short and medium term to the global health market must be managed in such a way that it contributes to the skills development of health professionals' (DOH 2006:79). Activities under this umbrella include the "optimization of the bilateral agreements that South Africa enters into with various countries" involving the placement of South Africans in institutions that would allow them to acquire new skills (DOH 2006:80).

Although the 2006 strategic plan provides a foundation for the 'managed migration' of South African health professionals, an unresolved issue is that of foreign health professionals seeking work in South Africa. The plan states that the national Department of Health will review the policy in this regard. The key issues under review are that:

1. International recruitment shall preferably be done in terms of government-to government agreements
2. No active recruitment for permanent employment in South Africa will be directed at other developing countries in the African region.
3. Foreign health professionals who do not enjoy permanent resident status shall not be permitted to enter private practice.
4. The position of the group of African health professionals, who have been working outside their country of origin for periods of between 5–10 years and 'do not feel that employment in South Africa will be robbing their own countries of the skills they dearly need' (DOH 2006:49).

## CONCLUSION

South Africa's re-integration into the global economy in 1994 exposed the new democracy to the full forces of international competition for talent. The state's initial policy responses were weak and failed entirely to comprehend the organizational dynamics and structures that shaped the new global movements of professionals. The country hemorrhaged an important segment of its most experienced medical personnel. Without the enactment of countervailing replacement strategies, and a national strategy for managing the country's human health resources, South Africa remains vulnerable to the ongoing activities of 'global raiders' (Crush, 2002) evident in extensive recruitment activities. Only limited impact can be expected on health staffing in South Africa despite the widely supported ethical recruitment guidelines of developed countries. However, in terms of South African health professionals there has been an important and welcome policy shift by national government away from the early reactive *ad hoc* policy responses to the development by 2006 of a more comprehensive strategic response for managing the mobility of health professionals.

A number of important conclusions concerning the activities of recruiters, and changing policy responses to their activities, indicates recommendations on how to deal with recruiters. First, the existing lack of knowledge and data to monitor flows of health professionals into and out of South Africa demands immediate attention. Recruitment agencies operating in South Africa can be an important source of information and reporting for such a data base, but improved monitoring systems are required to track flows of South African health professionals overseas and foreign health professionals entering South Africa.

Second, the majority of initiatives for the recruitment of the country's health personnel are undertaken by agencies based outside rather than inside South Africa. The few local recruitment agencies are only minor actors in overall international recruitment. For South Africa, the heart of this global recruitment industry are operations anchored in the United Kingdom and to a much lesser extent, in New Zealand, Australia and Canada. This necessitates the strengthening of existing bilateral and multilateral inter-governmental agreements that affect the flow of South African professionals to the United Kingdom and other Commonwealth countries. One element to strengthen inter-governmental agreements, especially with the United Kingdom, would be reliable and regular information on the recruitment of South African professionals for locum work there.

Third, local recruitment agencies cannot be blamed for the creation of a desire to migrate among South African health professionals. The core reasons for migration do not relate to the operations of these agencies, though these agencies facilitate response. Instead, they link to the wider set of 'gradients' of wages and working conditions that impel talented South Africans to make a decision to step on the global conveyor belt of health. Support for the comprehensive implementation of the strategies set forth in the 2006 framework, including those concerning a review of wage conditions, will be an important basis for managing the future migration of South Africa's health workers.

Finally, local recruitment agencies have been constrained in their activities in terms of South Africa's ethical stance on recruitment of health workers from other developing countries, whereas there is substantial potential for recruitment of health workers from developed countries and health professional exporting countries such as India, the Philippines, Sri Lanka and even China. Monitoring the potential recruitment of foreign health professionals needs to be extended to incorporate these potential recruitment sources of medical talent in Asia and to move away from a focus on inter-governmental agreements as the sole focus of policy on skills import. Ultimately recruitment agencies could become part of the solution rather than an extension of the problem.

## ACKNOWLEDGMENTS

The authors wish to thank the UK-DFID for its support of the Southern African Migration Project (SAMP), which funded this research; Wanjiku Kiambo and Alex Wafer for research assistance; and Wendy Job for the cartography.

## REFERENCES

Adams, O and Stilwell, B (2004) Health professionals and migration, *Bulletin of the World Health Organization*, 82, 560.
Bach, S (2003) *International migration of health workers: Labour and social issues*, Geneva: ILO Working Paper No. 209.
Bach, S (2006) *International mobility of health professionals: Brain drain or brain exchange?* Research Report 2006/82, United Nations University-WIDER, Helsinki.
Bhorat, H, Meyer, J and Mlatsheni, C (2002) *Skilled labour migration from developing countries: Study on South and Southern Africa*, Geneva: ILO International Migration Paper No. 52.
Brown, R P and Connell, J (2004) The migration of doctors and nurses from South Pacific Island Nations, *Social Science and Medicine*, 58, 2193–2210.
Buchan, J, Parkin, T and Sochalski, J (2003) *International nurse mobility: Trends and policy implications*, Geneva: IUCN.
Bundred, P and Levitt, C (2000) Medical migration: Who are the real losers? *The Lancet*, 356, 245–46.
Clemens, M (2006) *Medical leave: A new database of health professional emigration from Africa*, Washington: Centre for Global Development, Working Paper No. 95.
Crush, J (2002) The global raiders: Nationalism, globalization and the South African brain drain, *Journal of International Affairs*, 56, 147–172.
Department of Health (2002) *Policy on recruitment, employment and support of foreign health professionals in the Republic of South Africa*, Pretoria: Department of Health.
Department of Health (2006) *A national human resources plan for health to provide skilled human resources for healthcare adequate to take care of all South Africans*, Pretoria: Department of Health.
Dovlo, D and Martineau, T (2004) *A review of the migration of Africa's health professionals*, Cambridge, Mass., Joint Learning Initiative, Working Paper 4-4.
Dumont, J and Meyer, J (2004) The international mobility of health professionals: An evaluation and analysis based on the case of South Africa, in OECD (Ed), *Trends in international migration*, Paris: OECD, pp. 150–205.
Eastwood, J, Conroy, R, Naicker, S, West, P, Tutt, R and Plange-Rhule, J (2005) Loss of health professionals from sub-Saharan Africa: The pivotal role of the UK, *The Lancet*, 365, 1893–1900.
Global Medics (2007) *With you every step of the way*, Retrieved 14 April, 2007 from www.globalmedics.com

Grant, H (2003) From the Transvaal to the Prairies: The migration of South African physicians to Canada, in Cohen, R (Ed), *Migration and health in Southern Africa*, Cape Town: Van Schaik, pp. 185–96.

Hagopian, A, Thompson, A, Fordyce, M, Johnson, K and Hart, L (2004) The migration of physicians from sub-Saharan Africa to the United States of America *Human Resources for Health*, 2(17), 2–17.

Iredale, R (2002) The migration of professionals: Theories and typologies, *International Migration*, 39, 7–26.

Labonte, R, Packer, C, Klassen, N, Kazanjian, A et al. (2007) *The brain drain of health professionals from sub-Saharan Africa to Canada, Cape Town*: South African Migration and Development Series No. 2.

McDonald, D and Crush, J (Eds) (2002) *Destinations unknown: Perspectives on the brain drain in Southern Africa*, Pretoria: Africa Institute.

Ministry of Health South Africa (2005) *Africa unites against brain-drain in health*, Retrieved 19 May, 2006 from www.doh.gov.za

Muula, A (2005) Is there any solution to the "brain drain" of health professionals and knowledge from Africa? *Croatian Medical Journal*, 46(1), 21–29.

Ncayiyana, D J (2005) *Migration and the crisis of human resources for health in South Africa*, Presentation at Walter Sisulu University, Mthatha, 7 September.

Netcare Group (2007) *About us*, Retrieved 14 April, 2007 from www.netcare.co.za

Padarath, A, Chamberlain, C, McCoy, D, Ntuli, A, Rowson, M and Loewenson, R (2003) *Health personnel in Southern Africa: Confronting maldistribution and brain drain*, EQUINET Discussion Paper No. 3.

Patel, V (2003) Recruiting doctors from poor countries: The great brain robbery, *British Medical Journal*, 327, 926–928.

Pendleton, W and Crush, J (2007) *The retention of health professionals in South Africa, Cape Town*: SAMP Migration Policy Series No. 47.

Richards, J (2002) Rapid response: Suction rather than drainage, *British Medical Journal*, 326, 4 March, 112–113.

Rogerson, C and Rogerson, J (2000) Dealing with scarce skills: Employer responses to the brain drain in South Africa, *Africa Insight*, 30(2), 31–40.

RS Locums (2004) "Turn your dreams into reality," Retrieved 14 April, 2007 from www.rslocums.co.za

Schrecker, T and Labonte, R (2004) Taming the brain drain: A challenge for public health systems in Southern Africa, *International Journal of Occupational and Environmental Health*, 10, 409–415.

Scott, M, Whelan, A, Dewdney, J and Zwi, A, (2004) "Brain drain" or ethical recruitment? Solving health workforce shortages with professionals from developing countries, *Medical Journal of Australia*, 180, 174–176.

Stern, M (2005) Botox and bridges: South African exports of health and construction services, *Development Southern Africa*, 22, 680.

Tshabalala-Msimang, M (2003) *Speech, signing of the memorandum of understanding between South Africa and the UK*, Retrieved 24 October 2006 from www.doh.gov.za/docs

WHO (2003) *International migration, health and human rights*, Geneva: WHO.

# Index